Yale French Studies

NUMBER 68

Sartre after Sartre

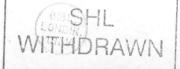

Yale French Studies

Fredric Jameson, *Special editor for this issue*
Liliane Greene, *Managing editor*
Editorial board: Peter Brooks (Chairman), Alan Astro,
    Ellen Burt, Paul de Man, Shoshana Felman,
    Richard Goodkin, Karen McPherson, Elissa
    Marder, Charles Porter
Staff: Elise Hsieh, Peggy McCracken
Editorial office: 315 William L. Harkness Hall.
Mailing address: 2504A Yale Station, New Haven,
    Connecticut 06520.
Sales and subscription office:
    Yale University Press, 92A Yale Station
    New Haven, Connecticut 06520.
Published twice annually by Yale University Press.
Copyright © 1985 by Yale University
Designed by James J. Johnson and set in Trump
    Medieval Roman by The Composing Room of
    Michigan, Inc.
Printed in the United States of America by The Vail-
    Ballou Press, Binghamton, N.Y.
ISSN 0044-0078
ISBN for this issue 0–300–03365–6

90 041

FREDRIC JAMESON

Introduction

What still interests me today is . . . [the relationship] of Sartre to the
University. It is said that he resisted or eluded it altogether. Yet it
seems to me that the norms of the academic determined his work in
the most fundamental inner fashion, as they so often do in the case of
writers who deny or ignore this reality. An analysis of his
philosophical rhetoric, his literary criticism, and even his plays or
novels, would have much to gain from attention to the role (for good
and ill) of the models and the history of grade school, lycée, "khagne,"
Ecole normale and agrégation [in Sartre's work].

—Jacques Derrida*

Consider for instance an older generation, that of the fifties organized
around Sartre (himself no longer a member of it) and around the Temps
modernes: it is hard to imagine a greater accumulation of errors (both
in analysis and prediction), more catastrophic ignorance of the true
oppressed bougés of history, more slackness and laziness in
intellectual attention and writing. But these are after all happy folk: in
any case it would seem that they can still see and talk to each other,
that their thought can withstand the light, that without sinking in
their own self-esteem, they can still more or less function. Even if time
has divided or set them against each other, some reference still
continues to subsist which creates no opacity when they evoke the
past and quite the contrary, tends to heal subsequent wounds.
But today, it is in the very place of the signifiers, successively
assembled in the form of proper names and nouns that dispersion has
set in.

—Jean-Claude Milner†

The long silence which it had become obligatory to respect in relationship to Sartre's works was lifted when Roland Barthes dedicated his
last book (La Chambre claire) to the most important of Sartre's early
ones, L'Imaginaire. The notoriety of the philosopher as a public figure
and political activist during the 1960s and early 1970s made it that
much easier to dismiss the content of his philosophy, whose tendencies—existential, phenomenological, and finally Marxist and dialectical—were central in the self-definition of the whole structuralist peri-

---

*Jacques Derrida, Interview, Le Nouvel observateur, September 9, 1983, vol. 64.
†Jean-Claude Milner, Les Noms indistincts (Paris: Seuil, Connexions du champ freu-
dien, 1983), 147–48.

od, which initially claimed its own identity by their negation and inversion.

Other reasons were, however, frequently given for the increasingly offhand dismissal of Sartre's life work. Derrida's remarks (above) are for example largely characteristic of an ironic commonplace whereby the theoretician of commitment (who never held a university position) is unmasked, via the well-known mannerisms of the graduates of the Ecole normale, as the most pedantic of academic philosophers. If one feels some distant hint of *ressentiment* in this assessment of an older generation by a younger one, its source is perhaps identified in our second quotation, a reflexion by one of the most brilliant Lacanian linguists of that whole next period. One presumes indeed that the crudeness here designated of the existential generation was principally betrayed by their relationship to linguistics and to psychoanalysis. Sartre's critical practice (as we can see from the unpublished pages of *The Family Idiot* translated in this special issue) was not wholly innocent of any interest in language or linguistics; but it was a practice more closely related to the stylistics of a Spitzer rather than to the figural analysis of a Jakobson. As for Freud, yes, it must be admitted that the existentialists maintained a fairly "vulgar" version of his writings, which they certainly did not, however, ignore. What is most fascinating in Milner's evaluation is his sense of the generational nature of Sartre's group practice: it is rather ironic, indeed, that the theoretician of small group dynamics (in the *Critique of Dialectical Reason*) should have been associated with collective relationships more closely affiliated with the confraternity of the fellow-traveller than the guerrilla discipline of the sectarian party.

Certainly a very different conception of the intellectual (and of the political intellectual) was at work in these two historic moments of recent French history, the first of them dominated by free-lance journalism, the second by increasing academic specialization of a type more familiar to American intellectuals. Now that, regrettably but inevitably, "Sartre" will have become the name for an archival specialization in its own right (owing to the mountains of unfinished and unpublished manuscripts he left behind), we tend to forget that in the heyday of classical existentialism he was one of the most popular writers in French cultural history. For reasons that will become apparent below, one is tempted to think of him as a philosophical Victor Hugo.

Nonetheless, the "Sartrean" of the classical period was a species in its own right, one which has as yet received insufficient zoological attention. The species is still with us, even though it seems to have bifurcated somewhere along the evolutionary path, in the general area of the Gaullist coup d'état: thus we have the existential Sartrean of the Fourth Republic, identifiable in a general family likeness which includes fidelity to themes like "freedom and "anxiety"; and then the "late Sartreans," an ensemble of subspecies each marked (or deformed) by the characteristics of that particular late text to which (as to some labyrinthine eco-system) he or she remains attached: the *Critique*, the *Flaubert*, or even that miniature emploded black hole, *Les Mots*. And there are also "former Sartreans" (I tend to feel that there are very few "ex-Sartreans" in the sense in which one thinks of ex- and anticommunists): what they have become it would be very interesting indeed to investigate, but I suspect many of them to have discovered a general vocation for semiotics which I have not yet adequately explained to myself.

Still, the "conversion" to "Sartreanism" was itself always rather different from more conventional modernist conversions of either the aesthetic or the philosophical type. As far as this last is concerned, doctrine, for the Sartrean, was never so crucial as it seems to have been for the Spinozan or the Kantian, the Heideggerian or the Derridean; and was more a matter of a general problematic than of agreement with Sartre's own positions, about which one was always at liberty violently to disagree, as I remember hearing one of the most eminent of classical Sartreans (and an early editor of the present journal) frequently say: I'm referring to Kenneth Douglas, whose tragic and premature death is still regretted.

Meanwhile, although many of us had initially been electrified by the force of the aesthetic works (oddly enough, this was most frequently *L'Age de raison*), we were rather more defensive about Sartre as *Dichter* than we were in our other (sometimes simultaneous) conversions to Faulkner, Gide, Pound or Thomas Mann; Sartre's world seemed less binding on the reader than the obsessive geographies of the other great moderns, or perhaps it was not even a "world" in that sense at all. It was obvious that the overlap between the philosophical and the aesthetic, in Sartre, left some leeway for the Sartrean's self-definition that gave this position a certain historical and structural originality in contrast to the other kinds of conversions I've mentioned (which I take to be the last faint afterimages of older religious commitments, contaminated by the emergent logic of the brand-names of a then nascent consumer society).

I must now feel, however, that the aesthetic and the philosophical distances which seemed to be inherent in "Sartreanism" can be understood in function of Sartre's profound voluntarism, a trait the first

Sartreans could scarcely have been aware of—given the powerful and damaging denunciations of the Will and of will power in *Being and Nothingness*—but which *Les Mots* first gave news of, and the late interviews and unpublished journals (see Kirsner, below) have now made central to any reevaluation of this writer. This was not an "organic" work (hence the difficulty of converting to it); rather, it seems to have emerged from an empty will to produce writing at any and all costs, from a fiat that made language work in the absence of any particular need for it (save the empty need of that will itself). But if this was so, then the Sartrean enigma must present itself to our historical moment in the following appearance: how, out of a drive of this kind, empty of all "content" in the Hegelian sense, could anything but the most vacuous and aestheticizing autoreferentiality have come? (Or, as in the distantly analogous case of Orson Welles, a kind of equally autoreferential and narcissistic self-denunciation?)

Indeed, it seems possible that the problem of his voluntarism may someday make a new history of his intellectual trajectory possible, furnishing the elements of that initial situation—the will itself—from which he had to escape before he could become "Sartre." Indeed, we have seen above that one of the most powerful vocations of *Being and Nothingness* can be to denounce the conceptuality associated with the very force that brought it into being (as is well known, the peculiar and idiosyncratic thing Sartre calls freedom is very different indeed, one is tempted to say the inverse, of what is normally thought of as "free will," let alone of will power).

Still, the starting point for any voluntarism would seem to be a radical disjunction between the world or the "scene" (or Being itself) and human action: something registered in the extraordinary Sartrean evocations of contingency on the one hand, most notable in *La Nausée*, and, more peculiarly, in the whole notion of reification of the Other and the Look, which stands as the initial phenomenology of human relationships (but not really of human action) on the other. This, which is far and away the most original theme in Sartre's philosophy (there is nothing like it in Heidegger, and even the Hegelian Master/Slave dialectic is a very faint precursor indeed), and which marked virtually the first appearance of other people—let alone of their sexuality—on any philosophical stage, has never found the historical analysis and evaluation it merits. In it, Sartre found a remarkable opportunity to electrify his public-to-be by formulating aloud what everyone knew but no one had ever thought of mentioning before. I believe that eventually the thematics of alienation-by-the-other will take its place in some more general field theory of alienation, as this topic ranges from the narrow analysis of commodity fetishism in Marx himself, across Lukács's idiosyncratic and Weberian version, all the way to some more ontological conception of the repression of history and the validity of the dialectic, of which it might offer the social foundation. Not only did Sartre never write the novel of that kind of alienation, however—it was given to his great contemporary Witold Gombrowicz to do so, in a classic novel, *Ferdydurke* (1938), which has been called the Polish *Nausea,* and in which the concept of "immaturity" (*niedorjrzaność*) dramatically, but in a very different way from the Sartrean Look, conveys our sense of inner formlessness as we confront those Adults, other people; nor did Sartre ever work through the connections between this interpersonal description of alienation and the grounding of the dialectic aspired to by the *Critique.*

Instead, the early reflexions on action—his most urgent yet difficult problem, given the empty and gratuitous nature of the Sartrean *experience* of the will—took an essentially passive or negative form, in that remarkable theory of the Imaginary to which Barthes very properly paid tribute. Alongside this theory of the imaginary an empty place was reserved for a theory of praxis which could not, at this time, come into being. Sartre vainly attempted to give it content by a misguided detour through the classical traditions of ethical philosophy. But the collective and the political cannot be adequately theorized in terms of the individualistic categories of ethics—something the great Hegelian opposition between *Moralität* and *Sittlichkeit,* between moralizing ethics and collective values, had already long since demonstrated, by way of a fundamental critique of the Kantian project. Sartre himself finally reached this point in his own definitive statement on the subject, not a philosophical text, however, but the play, *Le Diable et le bon Dieu,* which concludes with a repudiation of ethics as such and a dialectical leap onto the plane of History.

The result of Sartre's personal "leap" was, of course, the *Critique of Dialectical Reason,* about which one may feel that it overleaps the matter of individual praxis too radically to be altogether sucessful; but more on all this in the present issue. The *Flaubert,* however, seems to pick up, once again, the much earlier thread of the Imaginary, now amplifying it and giving it all the extraordinary resonance of social history itself. Now it becomes clear that the passive drive, the passion for the Imaginary, constitutes something like the secret libido and vice of the bourgeoisie itself as a social class; while its binary opposite, the drive towards action and production—called praxis—had already in the momentous final pages of *What is Literature?* been identified with the working class and socialist construction. Reread in this way, perhaps *The Family Idiot* corresponds a little more faithfully than they thought to that "proletarian novel" Sartre's Maoist friends urged him in vain to write during the later years.

But all this is to outrun our own materials, which begin, as is appropriate, with a still classical existential Sartre, albeit viewed in some unexpected lights. In particular George Bauer brings out a whole libidinal dimension of Sartre's work—via the oral—which is normally dismissed as a kind of Sartrean puritanism: amateurs of the viscous indeed have tended often to read the Sartrean account of this in terms of a more generalized—and Jansenist—horror of matter and the flesh. Bauer suggests a rather different reading, in which the Sartrean libido is not an anti-Proust but rather a kind of "alternate" Proust.

Meanwhile, Philip Wood spiritedly insists on a reconnection of the problematic of the *Critique* with that of *Being and Nothingness*. Wood makes the most sweeping case for the relevance of the Sartrean approach to contemporary criticism generally, not merely as some additional method in the pantheon of pluralism, but rather as that reflexion best suited to resolve a whole range of problems raised in late and poststructuralism. His rebuke to me is perfectly proper, and underscores the evident fact that even the Marxists have begun to forget the lessons they learned from Sartre and to sell his work short in inadmissible ways. Wood's proposals go well beyond the studies of *Les Mots*, the *Critique* and *The Family Idiot* which follow; they do not merely affirm the interest of these works, but assert that more general primacy of Sartrean method which it was the burden of the late works to demonstrate.

The two essays we include here on *Les Mots* will both, in their very different ways, radically modify our approach to that short but significant work. Davies expands its subtext into a symbolic commentary on Freudian and structuralist anthropology which can be taken as a fresh and complex philosophical statement in its own right. Brombert, meanwhile, amplifies the otherwise seemingly merely autobiographical or "private" references to Victor Hugo in that text into a relationship to the great precursor, which in genuine Sartrean fashion is more than the merely "psychoanalytic" and implies a whole new relationship of Sartre to literary history and to previous models of political commitment.

As for the *Critique*, in the continuing absence of its second volume, Ronald Aronson furnishes a useful preliminary account, which cannot but whet our appetite. And against a somewhat different Aronson (and the ultimate judgements he makes in his recent book), Simont reasserts the validity of this enormously ambitious Sartrean project. Even though the *Critique*, and in particular its theories of small group dynamics,— virtually alone among Sartre's works—continued to be referred to during the sixties and seventies (see the footnotes of the *Anti-Oedipus* of Deleuze and Guattari)—its formal aim—the philosophical grounding and justification of historical and dialectical thought—had long since ceased to interest a structuralist and poststructuralist generation (including that generation's Marxists). One hesitates, in the virtually universal crisis of Marxism today, to assert that the Sartrean problematic— the problematic of History—has recovered its original urgency. But it does not take much daring to assert that it will, and soon.

The great Flaubert psychobiography, although longer even incomplete than the completed *Critique*, may seem somewhat less universally significant alongside the latter; in fact, the deeper interrelationships between the two projects remain to be worked out, and the task has not unfortunately been started here. But in a different and equally revealing way Pierre Verstraeten positions the analysis of *The Family Idiot* within the Hegelian tradition, in relationship to the spiritual form Hegel called the "belle âme": a positioning which suggests a whole new way of rethinking Sartre's work within a still Hegelian historiography (previous attempts to do this, have tended, even in Herbert Marcuse's subtle appreciation of the Sartrean sexual Other, towards the reductive and the denunciatory). David Gross, meanwhile, suggests that on at least one score Sartre's analysis of Flaubert is itself significantly reductive and unsartrean; reinforcing the obvious authorial positions of *Sentimental Education* with unpublished notes by Flaubert himself, written at the time of the February revolution, he suggests that what is often (and by Sartre himself) too easily described as Flaubert's reactionary political attitudes can much better be understood as the discouragement and cynicism which logically followed upon the failure of a revolutionary hope and spirit in which Flaubert himself participated for a time. This kind of ideological deconversion is very different from the persuasion and convictions of what we might call "organic" conservatives and reactionaries; but it is even more widespread, as the host of right-wing converts from our own 1960s testifies. Gross's criticism does not cancel the analytic riches of *The Family Idiot*, but it does suggest that Sartre himself may have had too simple (one hesitates to say, too vulgar) a conception of the nature and sources of political commitment—a conception itself subject to historical discouragements of the type of the notorious and much debated "final testament" (which may be said to have had its own prefiguration in the specifically French tradition in the end of Martin du Gard's novel *Jean Barois*).

The final essays once again approach Sartre's work from a somewhat longer perspective: McCarthy's important piece on the relations with Nizan, indeed, very powerfully suggests that more long and painful reflexion is due on the nature of Sartre's political commitments; while Kirsner's essay, drawing on a wide range of contemporary therapies, just as provocatively asks us to consider the possibility that this life's work, far from being an implacable negation of the "objective spirit" or "objective neurosis" of our own age, may well have been the latter's faithful reflection and symptom. That is finally perhaps not so damaging a position as one might at first think, and not merely returns us to the implacable self-criticisms with which we began (and which Sartre expressed most openly in *Les Mots*), but also foreshadows the ambiguities and ambivalences of a significant new approach to Sartre, that of Denis Hollier in *Politique de la prose*, of which we have felt it appropriate to conclude with a brief account by Alexandre Leupin.

Save perhaps for this last, none of our presentations constitute the kind of radical reevaluation and reinterpretation of Sartre's work which one might have hoped for, but which it is perhaps too soon to expect. Something new, however, will certainly emerge from the publication of hitherto unknown manuscripts, of which the notes to the unwritten fourth volume of the *Flaubert* are the last in time and the most enigmatic and tantalizing. We are most pleased to present an extract of these notes here, for the first time, in the original and in translation: pages which will have a particular fascination for readers with a postcontemporary taste for the aphorism and the fragment, and which are of course extremely uneven—some of the notes being mere mnemonic jottings of the obvious thoughts an author needs to remember to put in, others having that suggestivity of creative neologisms, of the new names for absent and original concepts we find a certain pleasure in supplying ourselves, and are just as pleased to confront in this now definitively unelaborated state.

The notes clearly mark a return to one of the richest of Sartre's early sidelines, that talent for stylistic analysis to which allusion has already been made and which can best be observed in the critical essays collected in *Situations 1* (but also in various chapters of *Saint Genet*). The younger Sartre—like much of the school of Spitzer's stylistic analysis in general—restricted a keen sense of the comparative analysis of sentence structure and tense predilection to a still relatively simple and idealistic interpretation in terms of philosophical world view. In the analysis of Genet, the resonance of such interpretation begins to expand—the writer's categories are compared to the agricultural forms of medieval culture, for example, owing to his own upbringing among peasants (as an orphan) and his isolation from industrial praxis and productive activity (as a marginal). Yet for precisely such reasons of class and marginality, the analysis of Genet does not yet present the full challenge that a reading of Flaubert will demand, that of a writer of unique private stylistic capacities who nonetheless very centrally expresses the ethos of a ruling social class and its ideological categories. The fourth volume of *The Family Idiot* might then have been expected to involve linguistic investigations of the type of *Situations 1*, infused now with all the historical and social content developed in the preceding volume of the psychobiography (volume 3 in the French edition). We must therefore try to imagine the notes on tenses in the light of the whole ensemble of bourgeois categories of time, while the even more tantalizing fragments on the "sentence-image," referring back to the Imaginary, also anticipate the reifications of consumer society today. It is an exercise that can be expected to send us back to the texts of Flaubert fully as much as to those of Sartre.

My own experience suggests that all of the recent issues of *Yale French Studies* owe very much indeed to the intelligence, energy and determination of Liliane Greene. How much more is this not the case with the present one, inherited from an earlier project, and intermittently pursued under the most complicated circumstances? I must also express a particular debt to Peggy McCracken and Philip Wood for their very special contributions to this issue.

Part I

GEORGE H. BAUER

Just Desserts

Give them according to their deeds, and according to the wickedness of
their endeavors; give them after the work of their hands; render to
them their desert.

—*Psalms* 28, 4.

Proust, not Sartre, has come to represent for readers of the contemporary
French novel the master of things culinary. No seminar on *A la Recherche du temps perdu* can resist savoring the deliciousness of the
madeleine both in the text and in the inevitable appearance in class of
the little cakes and cups of *tilleul* suddenly produced by a young student
whose *Larousse Gastronomique* and Pléiade Proust lie side by side on
the bed table. But the crumbs of the shell-shaped madeleine and sips of
involuntary memory should not obscure Jean Paul Sartre's own fascination with pink cakes and chocolate cookies. Just how the cookie crumbles becomes a serious part of his philosophy. In *L'Etre et le néant* Sartre
calls for the unravelling of the existential meaning of food, of eating, of
digestion in terms of the eater's original project. "This chocolate
cookie, at first, resists my bite, then suddenly gives way and crumbles,
its resistance, then its crumbling *is* chocolate."[1] This experience gives
rise to reflection on the temporal dimensions of taste and the visual
appearance of the dessert seen, then eaten. "Certain tastes reveal themselves in a flash, others are delayed action bombs, others give themselves up step by step, some fade slowly until they disappear, and others
vanish just at the moment when you think you possess them. If I eat a
pink cake, the taste of it is pink; the light sugary perfume and the
oiliness of the butter cream *are* the pink. Hence I eat pink just as I see
sugary. Because of this it is understood that flavor derives a complex
architecture and a differentiated matter; it is this structured matter . . .
that we can assimilate or reject with fits of nausea, according to our
original project" (*L'Etre et le néant*, 707). There are no irreducible preferences or tastes. Sartre gives us the task of comparing them, classifying
them. They are our emetic, our purge. *Ad nauseam.*[2]

1. Jean Paul Sartre, *L'Etre et le néant* (Paris: Gallimard, 1943). Hereafter cited in text
as *L'Etre et le néant*. The translations are mine.
2. This article is part of a larger study on the alimentary, the culinary, in Sartre's
work, both literary and philosophical. The original version was given at a seminar on the

3

Unsatisfied with his short story, "Dépaysement," a "tourist" piece on Naples, Sartre withdrew it from his collection of short stories published in 1939. He did rework the heart of it as a short piece and gave it the title "Nourritures" ("Food" in the English version) when he published it in *Verve*.[3] It is a gem, a tightly written essay that condenses the food-sex elements of his "Dépaysement" *raté*. The importance of the essay, for us and for Sartre, is emphasized by its republication in a small edition illustrated by Sartre's drunken artist friend, Wols, with the experience of eating and nausea joined in the title. (More on that later.) In "Nourritures" Sartre links the elegant inhabitants of Naples's Via Roma and their dazzling displays of comestible fare. Caught up as a tourist in the splendor of the street filled with shops garlanded with lemons, windows laden with delicate slices of ham, blood sausage, and brightly colored pastries, he rubs elbows with "men decked in white linen, gleaming teeth, and sparkling, but weary eyes" ("Nourritures" 2128); however, it is alimentary choice that is the focus of Sartre's gaze. "I stared at them, and to my right, stared at their food, that food that dazzled in the shop windows; I said to myself: There's what they eat! How appropriate: proper food—more than proper: chaste" (2128). Safely installed behind glass, these slices of ham (Parma?) have the appearance of chiffon; the scarlet tongues of sumptuous velvet are the richly deserved food of these Neapolitans who hide their bodies beneath garments of the same material, white linen, bloody velvet, and pink chiffon: "they secret their bodies beneath garments of the same dazzle and feed on stuff and wall paper (*papiers peints*)" (2128). The culmination of their taste is their desserts. The pastry shops are jewelers' windows filled with sparkling gems and porcelain.

Temporarily stunned by the array of glistening bibelots of the elegant Patisserie Caflish, he muses on desserts in general. "On the whole desserts are human, they resemble faces. Spanish cakes are ascetic—with a certain swagger; they crumble to dust when bitten into; Greek desserts are unctuous, small oil lamps, when pressed they ooze; Ger-

---

Culinary Aspects of Fiction at the 1977 MLA. Related material may be found in "Sartre's and the 'Sugars' of History," *L'Esprit Créateur*, vol. 15, no. 3 (Fall 1975), 377–86; "Sartre's Homo/Textuality: Eating/the Other," in *Homosexualities and French Literature: Cultural Contexts/Critical Texts*, ed. Stambolian and Marks (Ithaca: Cornell University Press, 1979), 312–29; and in "Visages et Nourritures" in *Les Actes du Colloque Sartre à Cerisy* (Paris: Etudes Sartriennes, 2–3, forthcoming).

3. *Verve*, no. 4, 1938, 115–16. Both "Dépaysement" and "Nourritures" are now published in Sartre's *Les Oeuvres romanesques*, (Paris: Gallimard, editions de la Pléiade 1982). I focus here on "Nourritures." For a fuller study of "Dépaysement" see "Visages et Nourritures."

man desserts are redolent with the fragrance of shaving cream, they are concocted for fat, soft men to eat with abandon, without really savoring them, simply to fill their mouths with sweetness" (2128). These tough little Neapolitans are something else and become a key to the men and women of Naples. *See Naples and die*. They are not made to be eaten, but display instead a kind of cruel perfection: "small, sharply etched— hardly bigger than petit fours, they are rutilant. Their tough, shrill colors remove all desire to consume them, on the contrary you think only of displaying them on consoles—painted porcelain" (2128). Half-baked, twice-cooked, these "biscuits" join the ceramics of Bouville's museum and *La Nausée*. Men of Mudville, Naples, and Bouville, are cooked and baked fakely to appear in masks painted for man in the disgust (*dégoût*) of existence. The paintings of the Bouville museum, another pastry shop, terrify the flesh and deceive, but only for a moment, the Sartrean tourist and the excluded bachelor. The surface of the *style léché*, Titian-inspired *objets d'art* like the *vitrine* and the glassy eyes of Neapolitans hide and bar human contact of eating and sexuality.

In another issue of *Verve*, Sartre published together two essays (both unsigned), one on the official portrait, the other on faces. These were subsequently republished, and signed, in a single volume with the playfully telling title *Visages précédé de Portraits officiels*.[4] The official portrait is the painted porcelain, the pastry, the rich stuff of fabric that precedes and masks the human face and its fleshly existence—and one that Sartre, and Roquentin like him, refuses to eat. The 1948 edition is illustrated by his drunken painter friend (who lives and dies by the bottle as Sartre underscores in his essay "Fingers and Non-fingers")[5] and the drypoints of Wols (his art) acidly strip away the chiffon and velvet, the linen and lace, by revealing the biological man in his full nakedness—the King stripped bare. Wols also illustrates Sartre's essay-tale on Neapolitan "Nourritures" when it is published in limited edition: *Nourritures suivi des extraits de La Nausée*.[6] The title eventually evokes a smirk of complicity, but provides the hungry reader with a key to which Sartre has constructed his *Hunger*. "Nourritures" begins abruptly: "J'ai découvert à Naples la parenté immonde de l'amour et de la Nourriture" ["I uncovered the dirty link between love and Food in Naples"] (2127). The *pâté*, the *petit pâté*, the *gros pâté*, and the *pâtisserie* are at the center. The truth and horror of food are hidden by the

4. (Paris: Seghers, 1948).

5. This essay was published first in Wols's *En Personne* (Paris: Delpire, 1963) and reprinted in *Situations 4* (Paris: Gallimard, 1964), 408–34.

6. (Paris: Jacques Damase, 1949).

shame the citizens, those privileged frequenters of the *Via Roma,* feel in their existence incarnate. Their icing on their cakes, their costumes *à la mode* will melt before the tourist's eyes. The underlying nakedness of the flesh of the king and the aristocrat is covered by Titian. The man is replaced by the false embodiment of Absolute Monarchy. The tourist, Sartre, like the bachelor, Roquentin, is momentarily frightened, tricked by effects worthy of Le Musée Grévin, and shuffles his postcards, regrets his travel poster dream and abandons, once, but not for all, the *style léché* conjury of oil and encaustic and the wax works of Neapolitan palaces, villas, and casinos: "I was incapable of seeing, beneath the pomades, the suspect wounds of their flanks" (2128). His distress comes upon him as he is seated on the terrace of the Café Gambrinus staring at one of those famous Neapolitan ices—"une granite qu'[il] regardai[t] mélancoliquement fondre dans sa coupe d'émail" (2127). His experience has been bits of multicolored facts, mere confetti. He has no grip on Naples. He wonders if it exists at all or whether it is like Milan, a fake city that, like other cities "*crumble* (my emphasis) when entered." Here Naples is not a cookie bitten into but a frozen desert refused. The ice of Naples, this dessert, echoes the melting away of the varnish from the surface of the painted canvases of the Mud-City Museum. From hard to soft, from icy solid to a disagreeable warm creaminess, the artistic creations of confectioners and painters disappear before the gaze of the melancholy artist-tourist; the hardness of sugar confections (*les sucreries de l'histoire*) with the brightly colored sprinkles displayed with confettilike brilliance simply melt away. The glass of the pastry shop window, the glaze of the iced cakes, the varnish of the surface begin to slip.

Not twenty meters from the Patisserie Caflish, a beckoning wound draws him away from the painted elegance of the tourist city distracting him from *la panse* (paunch) and *la pensée penchée* of artistic melancholia to *pansement sommaire* (first aid). Rodin's melancholy thinker in his Cartesian alimentary philosophical position (*Je pense 'donc je suis*) begins to walk about and to discover existentially a new way, "Je panse donc je suis" ["I tend to wounds therefore I follow"]. The wound that attracts him is in one of the myriad tiny streets opening in darkness off the broad boulevards and their cafés and pastry shops. At its center is "un aliment—ou plutôt une mangeaille" ["food—or rather—grub"] (2128). The bloodred wound, covered with mud and flies drips silently in the rays of the setting sun, is situated in brute reality unprotected by *vitrines.* This slice of bright bloody watermelon seen as rotting meat contrasts sharply with the watermelons of Rome (and la Via Roma) that "appeared to be simply pistacchio and raspberry ice dotted with coffee beans" (2128). One is dessert and remains safely uneaten like the *granite* and cakes of the Via Roma; the other is taken quite naturally by a ragged (ragtime) urchin of the street and bitten into. Drawn into this gaping hole, Sartre discovers existence in its raw state: "they were also surrounded by their food, living refuse, shells, cores, obscene meat, open dirty fruit, they reveled in their organic life with a sensual indolence" (2128). From the melancholy of the tourist unable to eat his dessert to this revelation of eating and digestion, Sartre makes his way and feels himself a part of the organic, digestive process. "I felt that I was in turn being digested: it began with the need to vomit, but quite gentle and sweet and then it spread throughout my whole body like a strange tickling" (2128).

Before all this flesh, in the midst of all this flesh, something must be done. But what? "Manger? Caresser? Vomir?" (2128). Everything has become flesh to be touched, sucked, fondled in the rich smell of sweat, of urine, of milk. A father takes his child, lifts her dress and bites into her gray cheeks as if they were bread while yards away on the Via Roma men dressed in white linen buy their "bibelots vernis." Just Des(s)erts.

To dismiss the culinary in Sartre as just desserts, as lightweight post-Proustian play with echoes of the famous Brillat-Savarin's "You are what you eat" would be easy to do. Sartre's essay on—"Nourritures," a salvaged, modified fragment from his previously unpublished "Dépaysement," is one of Sartre's earliest writings and admirably demonstrates the seriousness of this alimentary enterprise. Just des(s)erts are and are not just desserts. In his *Baudelaire*, Sartre asks "Whether, if *idées reçues* to the contrary, men ever have anything except the life that they deserve?"[7] The existential choices in food, in politics or sexuality are there to be read. "J'ai découvert à Naples la parenté immonde de l'amour et de la Nourriture. Ce n'est pas venu tout de suite" ["In Naples, I discovered the ignoble kinship between love and Food. It didn't happen all at once."] (2127). "It is not a matter of indifference whether we like oysters or clams, snails or shrimp, if only we know how to unravel the existential signification of these foods. Generally speaking there is no irreducible taste or inclination. They all represent a certain appropriate choice of being" (*L'Etre et le néant*, 707). The search for profound *traditional* philosophical meanings have prevented even the most qualified of writers on Sartre from taking him at his word concerning the culinary aspect of his work. It is not to be dismissed.

7. Sartre, *Baudelaire* (Paris: Gallimard, 1947), 18.

La Nausée, Melancolia in its origins, relies on eating, digestion, smoking, and drinking for a great deal of its success. *Les Mouches* couples the tourist and the culinary and enlarges the buzzing flies of the Neapolitan watermelon to enormous proportions. His *Saint Genet, comédien ou martyr* continues his flirtation and discovery of the relationship between sexuality and eating. Here is not the place to catalogue Sartre's obsession with "Nourritures" in his work. I choose but one other example and sketch in some detail the way in which the concept of "just des(s)erts" is worked out in the second half of *La Mort dans l'âme* and the incomplete, open-ended "La Dernière Chance."

Three characters, four if we count the resurrected Mathieu, play major roles in the drama of capture and imprisonment of *Les Chemins de la liberté:* Brunet, Schneider/Vicarios, Moûlu, and Mathieu. Their fates are inextricably linked and the culinary plays an essential role. Brunet, bronzed and robust, is the natural leader of men in the comradeship of the Party. Sartrean onomastics grounds Brunet in his relationship with his strange and disturbing double. Schneider, by the position he has taken towards the Germano-Soviet pact is cut from the Party and both hides and reveals his expulsion in his name. He is, as well, the vicar, a pope played to Brunet's Jesus Christ, interpreter and prelate in relation to the heretical activities of Brunet-St. Pierre in the absence of party directives in prison camp life. Vicarious sharing and substitutions characterize his symbiotic existence with Brunet. Moûlu, with his curious circumflex, is marked from the beginning. *Mou,* "soft," easily gives into pressure; easily molded he carries his mark as if it were a fly, a *mouche,* slipping quite naturally to *mouchard* buzzing busily around carrion and shit. Sycophantic spy and betrayer, his rhyming name produces *goulu/goulue* as he voraciously eats and shifts from male to female, a little housekeeper anally protecting the larder and tending the fire: a glutton, a woman, a fag, quite simply a mouth.

Brunet stands head and shoulders above his fellow captives, now a formless mass. Moûlu, a big man, introduces himself to Brunet "My name is Moûlu, I'm from Bar-le-Duc,"[8] as thousands of men, no longer soldiers but not yet prisoners, shuffle to their destiny. Hunger hangs heavy in the summer heat. Defeat brings rumblings in the stomach, loss of discipline and self-respect, and inevitably filth and lice as habits of personal hygiene are abandoned. The conqueror's clean-shaven cheeks and well-fed bellies, their buttoned uniforms and shiny equipment con-

---

8. All references to *Les Chemins de la liberté*, including the previously unpublished *La Dernière Chance* are to his *Oeuvres romanesques* (Paris: Gallimard, éditions de la Pléiade, 1982) and will be cited in the text. The translations are mine.

trast sharply with the unkempt French. Moûlu is the first to cave in to his need to be comfortable. "Moûlu trots and sweats, pants, takes off his jacket, throws it over his arm, unbuttons his shirt, and says with a smile: 'Now jackets can be taken off: we are free' " (1351). A fountain is spotted, a number of the men break into a run to slake their thirst. "Moûlu y court, il se penche maladroitement, goulûment. . . . Moûlu court comme une femme, en tournant les genoux, ils se bousculent, ils rient, ils crient, scandaleux et provocants comme des tapettes; leurs bouches se fendent en plaies hilaires au-dessous de leurs yeux de chiens battus. Moûlu s'essuie les lèvres, il dit: 'C'était bon.' Il regarde Brunet avec étonnement: 'Tu n'as pas bu toi? Tu n'as pas soif?" [Moûlu runs to it, leans down awkwardly, gluttonously. . . . Moûlu runs like a woman, knock-kneed. They jostle one another, they laugh, they shout, scandalous and provocative as fags; their mouths agape as hilarious wounds beneath the eyes of beaten dogs. Moûlu wipes his lips. 'That was good.' He looks at Brunet with astonishment: '*You* didn't drink? Aren't you thirsty?' "] (1352). Brunet simply shrugs his shoulders and watches the handsome, bronzed males, clean-shaven, rested, and thinks "Ils s'enfoncent dans la France" ["They are sticking themselves into France" (1354).

Brunet, having shaved before capture, stands above these hungry women-men who are having it stuck to them by the rugged invaders and feels alone for the first time in ten years. He is hungry and thirsty but ashamed of it. Moûlu can only think of his stomach. He turns to Brunet and declares " 'They are going to give us something to eat.' " (1355). Brunet is disgusted by this false feminine hope (I am reminded of Electre of *The Flies* who in her wait for her white knight brother does the dirty dishes, not understanding that "human life begins on the other side of despair") and reflects, knowing that this hunger is healthy if not satisfied: "They'll not give them anything to eat. They have to slobber, they'll never slobber enough" (1355). The march continues throughout the day until night falls and these tired, hungry men become a pack of stray dogs who rush willingly into a courtyard and the door of defeat and imprisonment closes behind them. The warmth of physical proximity momentarily makes them forget their hunger: "The warmth must have tricked their stomachs" (1558) Down and out, but inside. "Il y en a une chiée qui n'a pas pu rentrer: faudra qu'ils couchent dehors" ["There's a shitpot full of them who couldn't get in; they'll have to sleep outside."] Once again Brunet stands alone above the grey sleepy mass. But there in the dusk appears another who stands and defiantly smokes a cigarette. These two alone are coupled by mutual attitudes: Brunet and Schneider/Vicarios. "Brunet notes sympathetically that he is shaved. . . he has large heavy eyes with rings beneath; except for his broken nose he would almost be handsome" (1359). "Standing and almost clean, shaven" thus begins this "drôle d'amitié." They stand apart from the group and finally share a blanket. Their stance toward food and smoking are carefully interwoven by Sartre to underline their similarities and differences. Neither are sleepy, but Schneider, unlike Brunet, indulges in a cigarette that promptly goes out. Stretched-out finally on their common blanket, Brunet feels uneasy in the presence of Schneider's warmth as the latter slips into sleep. Again Brunet is alone, awake, among these sleeping, defeated men.

Day brings a predictable comment from Moûlu: "Another day without grub." Talk of food is everywhere. Brunet perceives it as the ideal *modus operandi,* "an excellent point of departure, food (*la bouffe*); it's simple, it's concrete, it's real: a guy who is hungry, *ça travaille en pleine pâte.* They only talk of food" (1373). If defeat and war are without importance, if food is the thing, then it will be Brunet's key to the formation of a group. Moûlu refuses to join the band until he eats; others go off only to return with a pile of empty plates, hoping that they will magically cause food, now become an obsession, to appear. It does, but the shame of hunger and its satisfaction is heightened in a dramatic scene as Sartre mingles questions of sexuality and eats. Bread slices are thrown from the back of a truck by a handsome German—echoing an earlier scene in the trilogy in which the homosexual, Daniel, stoops to pick up a pack of cigarettes thrown at his feet by one of the bare-armed German men who have just penetrated Paris—and humiliated by their bodies' needs the French scramble to pick up these crumbs offered by their conquerors. "A Heinie at the back of the truck, naked to the waist, indolently watches them. Tanned skin, blond hair, long, fine muscles, *un homme de luxe,* he looked like one of those handsome young men who skied bare-chested at Saint-Moritz" (1377). Toying with them he cuts slices of bread and throws them out of the truck. The game continues as the bread falls to the ground. Brunet melodramatically crushes the slice that falls at his feet in a gesture of superiority and defiance. Schneider and Brunet have words over the latter's act of contempt for the men fighting for something to eat. "You don't like us very much. *We* were hungry. Why us? Didn't you pick up any?" (1379). Schneider lies, saying that he did, effecting solidarity with the others and rages at Brunet: "Oui, nous sommes gourmands! Oui, nous sommes lâches et serviles. Est-ce que c'est notre faute? On nous a tout enlevé: nos métiers, nos familles, nos responsabilités. Pour être courageux, il faut avoir quelque chose à faire; autrement tu rêves. Nous n'avons plus *rien* à faire, pas même à gagner notre bouffe, nous ne comptons plus. Nous rêvons; si nous sommes lâches, c'est en rêve. Donne-nous du travail et tu verras comme nous nous réveillerons" ["Yes, we are ravenous! Yes, we are cowardly and servile. Is it our fault? Is that our fault? Everything has been taken away from us: our jobs, our families, our responsibilities. To be courageous, you have to have something to do, otherwise you are just dreaming. We no longer have *anything* to do, not even to earn our bread, we don't count anymore. We are dreaming; if we are cowards, it's in a dream. Give us some work and you'll see how quick we wake up"] (1379–80).

And so the work begins, but not before Brunet is himself confronted with a splendid culinary dream brought on by hunger pains. Before he is brought down by his body's needs he observes the others from his superior point of view. He will not indulge his flesh. He overhears a conversation of some of the men who are provoked to laughter because they no longer shit. Normal. What would you shit with? But Moûlu is quick to add "Il y en a pourtant qui chient. J'ai vu" (1382). They are the ones who have secreted their rations, their *boîtes de singe*, their tins of "monkey meat." Moûlu receives an accusing stare when the trucks he so ardently wishes for do not appear, filled with food for his gluttonous mouth; his body response is the gurgling of his stomach. Schneider awakes from a *dream* of croissants and café au lait—and of a touch of vin rouge, a buddy adds. A search for cigarettes, an effort to trick the hunger pains, begins. Schneider shares his. Brunet intervenes, refusing to permit the men to have recourse to personal, individual generosity and indulgence. He forces them to pool their resources and establishes a ration for the group. Schneider loses the most—a full pack—but the work begins. The cigarettes become the property of the group—*un groupe en fusion?* A group within the group is formed—the Comrades. They light up. "Ça trompe la faim." Hunger is tricked, momentarily. *Des bouffés, pas la bouffe.* [Puffs, not foodstuffs.]

But Brunet's struggle with the hunger angel follows immediately. He thinks to himself that he hasn't been hungry all day. "Il s'endort, il rêve qu'il a faim, il se réveille, il n'a pas faim, plutôt une légère nausée et un cercle de feu autour du crâne" ["He falls asleep, he dreams he is hungry, wakes up, he isn't hungry, just a slight feeling of nausea and a ring of fire around his skull"] (1384). He tries to wash up, to shave. He is too weak. He's a big guy. He should eat, but refuses the temptation. In his weakened state he slips into sleep and dreams of monkeys in a cage (*boîtes de singe*), of the taste of fresh pineapple on his tongue and of his love for his comrades. "Un soir, je vous dirai de douces choses, un soir je vous dirai que je vous aime" (1389). He is half-awakened from his dream by Moûlu, by the sound of trucks bringing food. I love them. I love them, give them cigarettes. Desire. Desire. Manger? Caresser? Vomir?/ Manger? Caresser? Dormir. Dreams of Westphalian ham. He returns to consciousness with Schneider spoon-feeding him *la soupe d'orge* (barley soup, a sty in his eye!) that the handsome Germans have brought. He now shares the food and a certain complicity with Moûlu. "Cet immense désir coupable, ce n'était que la faim" ["That immense guilty desire was only hunger"] (1390). Nourishment begins to break the bond the group has established. Now it is German food and German language in their mouths, their bodies. "Il a suffi d'une bouche de pain" ["One crust, one mouthful was all it took"] (1391). Now they are learning a foreign tongue.

And with the food comes the inevitable. They shit and piss once again. All is back to normal. Loaded into a train they continue their journey into captivity. Sartre fills the pages with the problematics of food, of drink and tobacco. Gifts of bread and cigarettes are sprinkled as German guards secretly provide the prisoners with rations; one hand holding the prick, the other offering food; piss falls on the wheels of the railroad cars. Hope abounds, but at each fork in the tracks it becomes more evident that Germany is their destination. In warm dark proximity of transit, their nourishment is digested by their bodies. The *boîtes de singe*—their new monkey cages—now pass from hand to hand filled with liquid yellow warmth, and spill upon the rails of steel, and on France, disappearing behind them. Brunet feels himself inside a huge garbage can where everything is stagnant.

Just as Sartre never published "Dépaysement," he never published *La Dernière Chance*, the fourth volume of *Les Chemins de la liberté*. He abandoned the work leaving only fragments, several long episodes of prison life. These are now published in his *Oeuvres romanesques* in the Pléiade edition and permit us to pursue "Just Desserts" in that volume, continuing the question asked in his work of the thirties: "Manger? Caresser? Vomir?" Here are conjoined a resurrected Mathieu, Brunet, Schneider/Vicarios, and Moûlu. The latter's obsession with food continues. Their existence is characterized by one of their fellow prisoners: "Si on ne se fait pas d'idées, on pourrait avoir une bonne petite vie: graisse de baleine, quatre cents grammes de pain par jour, on n'a pas faim; on couche sur des planches mais on dort assez, un travail pas trop fatiguant, les coups sont rares et on est payé: trente marks par jour. Une bonne petite vie, seulement elle est invivable. Nous sommes des femmes, des esclaves et des morts. Nourris, logés, entretenus" ["If you don't get any ideas, you have a good little life: blubber, four hundred grams of bread a day, you're not hungry, you sleep on planks but you get enough sleep, the work is not too tough, not too many knocks and you get paid: thirty marks a day. A good little life, only it is unlivable. We are women, slaves, dead men. Fed, housed, kept" (1613).] Installed in a barracks with Brunet and those Party members they have uncovered, Moûlu assumes the role of the little woman of the house, scrounging coal, making chocolate, fixing bouillon; *gourmand par excellence* he jealously guards the larder. Schneider cuts himself from the Communist pals, from the warmth of camaraderie, until Brunet introduces him near the fire, offering him their common fare and assigning him the job of being his interpreter—to Moûlu's great distress. News from the outside (they are also hungry for news) brought by the newly arrived Chalais (*Chais, Chaud, Châlet*) reveals Brunet's tactics and discipline to be heretical activity that does not conform to the new Party line. Moscow and Berlin have reached an accommodation. The Russians now supply food, commodities and fuel to the Fascists. Schneider is revealed by Chalais to be the famous Vicarios, who like Sartre's great and good friend, Paul Nizan, had been expelled from the Party. He is now expelled from the Communist band. Brunet's new friendship and his errors move him to join Vicarios in an escape. His friend, his vicar, dies in his arms for, even though they carry on their person the bread of others and filched civilian clothes, they are betrayed. Somewhere *behind* their failure is a *donneuse*, a *moucharde*. Brunet is placed in solitary confinement. Alone again.

Once freed, Brunet begins his search for the rat. In his blindness, he can only believe that the guilty party is Chalais. Moûlu greets him on his release and informs him that their Comrades have been shipped out. Brunet's obsessive desire for revenge motivates a second escape attempt. He must find Chalais at any cost. Moûlu insists that he will go with him. There is an escape committee. Brunet is still unable to read Moûlu's name (his interpreter now dead), to see the inevitable link between his gourmandise, his taste for gilt-tipped cigarettes and his betrayal. Only a resurrected Mathieu, now a member of the escape committee, can interpret for him the too obvious signs of the feminine, the voracious, the gatherer of foreign butts. Moûlu has had intercourse with handsome, well-fed Heinies. He is the *moucharde*, the *donneuse*. Mathieu forces Brunet to see the truth and to see himself. Brunet has lost his clean-shaven look. With the death of his new friend comes a loss of faith in the Party. He is now one of the conquered. Mathieu offers him a mirror and a razor—and escape—on condition that he be the fall guy, responsible for the death of Moûlu. His revenge, out of rage, would be sweet, but it is not to be his. Moûlu is strangled by the group without Brunet. He lived by his mouth, his throat, his avidity. "Les types viennent de me dire qu'ils se sont fendus la pipe tout du long" ["The guys just told me that they choked him all the while"] (1650). Now he dies by it. Brunet accepts the deal, but asks out of curiosity what will be done with the body. *Aux chiottes.* [To the shit house.] Just Deserts.

"C'est sa faute," Brunet is reminded by Mathieu, and adds "On a l'assassinat qu'on mérite" ["you always get the death you deserve"] (1650), echoing Sartre in his essay on Baudelaire: "Men never have anything except the life they deserve." The comic overtones of this *opera bouffe* are deadly serious. Eating is bad. The "alimentary philosophies" criticized by Sartre in his essay on Husserl's intentionality[9] suck, feed on, assimilate, unify and identify; criticism of the idea "connaître, c'est manger" has its parallel in Sartre's fiction and drama. His work continues the negative stance of Flaubert toward eating. Emma does not eat. It is Charles Bovary who slurps his soup. Emma is tempted by the ices offered her and eats, only to die by ingestion of arsenic. The Sartrean tourist refuses those desserts. He is drawn to real food, food in all of its disgusting (*dégoûtant*) aspects. The men in Sartre become men who can neither eat nor vomit. They simply hold the *indigeste* in their mouths unable to swallow or spit, unwilling to add to their fleshly incarnation. Held within the body, within the organic experience of life, the culinary object is not assimilated, digested and excreted but held in suspense (phenomenologically bracketed?) as the individual ponders his alimentary choice. The barriers of shop windows behind which lie the icy seductive pastries are gone; gone are the temptations of the artist-termite, Proust and Wols, who eat their way through the world and leave behind them their droppings—the beautiful termitarium that is their eaten work to be seen and eaten. What remains is the question asked years before: Manger? Caresser? Vomir? *Food followed by extracts of Nausea* is a first step on the *Roads to Freedom.* If art is culinary, *nous sommes à cul* (we're in a pickle). Sartre is the anti-Proust in search of a vicar and a *bande à part.*

9. *Situations 1* (Paris: Gallimard, 1947), 31.

PHILIP WOOD

Sartre, Anglo-American Marxism, and the Place of the Subject in History

I

Sartre's most important contribution to historical materialism was to address himself, on the basis of a deliberately uncompromising and literal reading, to the apparent paradox in Marx's celebrated dictum which opened *The Eighteenth Brumaire of Louis Bonaparte:*

> Men make their own history, but they do not make it just as they please; they do not make it under circumstances chosen by themselves, but under circumstances directly encountered, given and transmitted from the past.[1]

The *Critique of Dialectical Reason* was Sartre's attempt to create a theoretical language capable of doing justice to precisely this paradoxical dialectical unity between freedom and necessity in history: the fact that we are the victims of the historical dialectic insofar as it produces us, and that we produce the dialectic in the very moment in which we are its products. Beginning with individual *praxis* and moving out through series and groups, the work culminated, in the uncompleted and as yet unpublished second volume, in a singular moment of the historical totalization[2] itself, in the form of a dialectical account of Soviet society after the revolution up to the death of Stalin.

1. Karl Marx, *The Eighteenth Brumaire of Louis Bonaparte* (Moscow: Progress Publishers, 1977), 10.
2. This term, *totalization*, which is often bandied about rather loosely, should be defined carefully: Jean-Paul Sartre, *Critique de la raison dialectique* (Paris: Gallimard), 1960, 138–39. "If there does indeed exist something which appears as the synthetic unity of the diverse, it must be an ongoing unification, that is to say, an act. The synthetic unification of a habitat is not merely the labor which has produced it, but also the activity of inhabiting it: reduced to itself, it reverts to the multiplicity of inertia. Thus totalization has the same status as the totality: through the multiplicities, it continues that work of

In his attempt to provide a coherent logic of explanation of the respective roles of agency and necessity in the historical process—of how "the different practices which can be found and located at a given moment of the historical temporalization finally appear as partially totalizing and as connected and merged in their very oppositions and diversities by an intelligible totalisation from which there is no appeal," or how "a plurality of epicentres of action have a single intelligibility"[3]—the second volume of the *Critique*, if we are to believe Perry Anderson's account of the unpublished manuscript, foundered on the location of the ultimate intelligibility of Soviet society in the totalizing figure of the despot Stalin. A conclusion running counter to Sartre's original intention (to describe a totalization *without* a totalizer) and in flagrant contradiction with the Marxist principle that it is the mode of production which provides the ultimate intelligibility of a historical process. Hence, according to Anderson, Sartre's dissatisfaction with the book as a whole and the failure to publish it.

Very well.

It is not generally recognised that Sartre's last major work, *The Family Idiot*, his massive three thousand page biography of Gustave Flaubert—in its attempt to answer the question of how an author produces a work which is simultaneously unique, a contestation, a (dé-

---

synthesis which makes each part a manifestation of the whole and which relates the whole to itself through the mediation of its parts. But it is an *ongoing* activity, which cannot cease without the multiplicity reverting to its original status. This act delineates a practical field which, as the undifferentiated correlative of *praxis*, is the formal unity of the ensembles which are to be integrated; within this practical field, the activity attempts to effect the most rigorous synthesis of the most differentiated multiplicity: thus, by a double movement, multiplicity is multiplied to infinity, each part is opposed to all the others and to the whole which is in the process of being formed, while the totalizing activity tightens all the links, making each differentiated element both its immediate expression and its mediation in relation to the other elements." Translations of French texts, unless otherwise indicated, are my own, and the page references are to the original edition.

This process of totalization applies not only to the most straightforward of acts—picking up a pen, for example, in the course of which I have to organize my body's motor-sensorial capacities in terms of the prevailing conditions of lighting, gravity, time and space, etc., in a process which synthesizes all these elements around the aim itself—but also to the historical process itself. In the latter, of course, it is not a question of an *act* totalizing the diverse historical phenomena (there is no *totalizer*) but, in the last instance, the economic mode of production which organizes the ensemble of social relations and group or individual actions within a total context which assigns them their ultimate significance and meaning.

3. Jean-Paul Sartre, quoted in Perry Anderson, *Arguments within English Marxism* (London: Verso, 1980), 52.

passement)[4] or transcendence of universal History and yet conditioned thoroughly by History itself in its minutest details—addresses itself to essentially the same broad problem. (Which is perhaps some explanation as to why Sartre was prepared to devote the best part of seventeen years to the project, instead of writing the proletarian novels which his Maoist friends of the later years felt would be more befitting.)

The central theoretical notion underpinning the entirety of the latter work is the *universal singular:*

> No man is ever an individual; it would be better to call him a *universal singular:* totalized and, thereby, universalized by his epoch, he retotalizes his epoch in the course of reproducing himself in his epoch as a singularity. Universal by the singular universality of human history, singular by the universalizing singularity of his projects, he requires being studied simultaneously from both ends.[5]

The problem to which this notion is addressed, the precise nature of the relation between freedom and historical necessity or conditioning, featured preeminently in probably the most important controversy in English Marxism in recent years: E. P. Thompson's now celebrated assault on Althusser's version of Marxism and Perry Anderson's assessment of the differences between the two writers. These arguments took place without a single reference to Sartre's notion or, with the minor exception of Anderson's brief discussion of the second volume, to the theoretical machinery of the *Critique of Dialectical Reason.* An omission which testifies to the enduring failure of "Western Marxists" to come to grips with the most powerful and rigorous articulations of this question yet developed.

I shall be concerned, here, in the course of an application of the notion to a specific concrete example, Joseph Conrad, primarily with what I hold to be the crucial importance of the universal singular, as developed in *The Family Idiot.* Certainly, this work, in its preoccupation with a nineteenth-century French novelist, and despite its wide-ranging and brilliant meditations on the history of France, perhaps has the superficial appearance of being a far cry from the gigantic sweep and sheer sociohistorical dimensions of, say, *The Making of the English Working Class* or the second volume of Sartre's *Critique,* both of which

4. The English equivalents—as Sartre uses the word—of *dépasser* (to go beyond or transcend) having unfortunate connotations, I have preferred generally to keep the French original.

5. Jean-Paul Sartre, *L'Idiot de la famille* (Paris: Gallimard, 1971), 7–8.

might seem more properly to come within the purview of a Marxist examination of the issue in question. If we are to find the means of annealing the opposition between what, broadly speaking, we can call the Althusserian and Thompsonian positions on the place of freedom and necessity in history, then the universal singular does present us with the opportunity of obtaining some intelligibility on this question—even if the application of the notion is restricted to the limited sector of one man's life and his artistic production.

The Family Idiot however, like so much of Sartre's production, is incomplete. To draw out the full implications of the universal singular for the case of Gustave Flaubert would require one to complete the fourth volume of Sartre's study. Besides which, from a purely practical point of view, the choice of another novelist has seemed to me to be necessary: the readership of *The Family Idiot* must surely be a fairly limited one; particularly in the absence, for the meantime, of a complete English translation. The choice of Joseph Conrad will require my readers to be familiar with no more than a couple of short stories; in addition to which, a discussion of this novelist will enable us to engage with the most important recent statement in Marxist aesthetics: Fredric Jameson's *The Political Unconscious.*

II

We shall turn to Conrad in due course. First, it is necessary to draw attention to the serious neglect and misrepresentation which Sartre's work has suffered.[6] Certainly, there has been no lack of *commentaries,* of a more or less respectful tenor, of Sartre's work as a whole; but what is striking is the minimal impact which his work has had on people working *creatively,* out there in the field. Hardly anybody *uses* Sartre. One has only to think of the relative influence of other contemporary French writers—the tremendous proliferation of work done under the influence of any one or several of the following: Althussser, Derrida, Lacan, Foucault[7]—to be made forcibly aware of this fact. The Frankfurt School, the Italian Marxists, or even Lukács, have fared much better.

6. It will already be clear that I do not accept the now dominant view that Sartre has been largely superseded by poststructuralism. Indeed, much of what follows here will necessarily enter into direct conflict with the broad premises of a poststructuralist position. The exigencies of space have prevented me from undertaking here the kind of head-on confrontation between Sartre and poststructuralism which I shall attempt elsewhere.

7. It is highly desirable that a comprehensive analysis of the rise of structuralism and poststructuralism as historically specific ideological formations should be attempted some day, in the course of which, among other things, the supposed supercession of Sartre

The omission on the part of Thompson is, despite the sometimes striking similarities between his writing and Sartre's—the shared emphasis on and commitment to human freedom and the intensely *moral* tenor of the two men's work—perhaps not so surprising after all. So that, along with a gesture of recognition in the direction of the superiority of Sartre's "understanding of history and relationship to political reality" (compared with Althusser's) Thompson tells us, with the characteristic tartness of his defiantly English idiom when the question of French philosophers arises, that he cannot "as a good Englishman" always follow Sartre's thought in its "subtlety," nor always assent to it.[8] Still, one marvels at how close Thompson repeatedly comes to a Sartrean "problematic" without ever evincing any awareness of the conceptual difficulties which such a problematic has at least *given rise to* in the work of Sartre. One thinks, for example, of Thompson's favorite notion of "experience," the conceptual aporias of which Anderson convincingly exposes,[9] and which bears such a close resemblance (at the very least at the level of the difficulties it should be wrestling with) to Sartre's notion of the individual or group "project," as it simultaneously interiorizes, transcends, and is alienated within, its historical situation.[10]

Rather more difficult to account for is the identical omission on the part of the otherwise dauntingly cosmopolitan Perry Anderson. Concluding a lucid account of the differences separating Thompson and Althusser on the issue of "agency," and correctly identifying the identically erroneous and unbalanced extremism of their opposing versions of history—"process without a subject" and "unmastered human practice"—he is left lamely lamenting the lost "classical equipoise of the founders of historical materialism," Marx and Engels:

> Althusser's unilateral and remorseless stress on the overpowering weight of structural necessity in history corresponds more faithfully to

would assume its rightful place in a generalized ideological assault on Marxism in France in the last two decades of which these broad movements are undoubtedly a part. Something of greater philosophical rigor and historical ambition than the useful but ultimately merely suggestive material in the standard texts in the area such as Henri Lefebvre, *L'Ideologie structuraliste* (Paris: éditions anthropos, 1975), Ernest Mandel, *Late Capitalism*, trans. Joris de Bres (London: NLB, 1975), chapter 16, Terry Eagleton, *Walter Benjamin or Towards a Revolutionary Criticism* (London: Verso, 1981), 131 ff.

8. E. P. Thompson, *The Poverty of Theory* (London: Merlin Press, 1978), 301.

9. *Arguments within English Marxism*, 25–31 and 79–83.

10. At the same time, it should be recognized that Thompson's highly idiosyncratic and very formidable achievements have almost certainly required for their very realization an aggressive assumption—at least at certain key points—of typical British insularity.

the central tenets of historical materialism, and to the actual lessons of scientific study of the past—but at the price of obscuring the novelty of the modern labour movement and attenuating the vocation of revolutionary socialism. Thompson's passionate sense of the potential of human agency to shape collective conditions of life, on the other hand, is much closer to the political temper of Marx and Engels themselves in their own time—but tends to be projected backwards as a uniform weft of the past, in defiance of the millennial negations of self-determination in the kingdom of necessity. Strangely, of two unbalanced sets of generalizations, Althusser's inclines better towards history, Thompson's towards politics. The classical equipoise of the founders of historical materialism is some distance from both.[11]

One would not want to argue with any of this; but one wonders at the omission, on the part of a writer whose characteristic strength is to be able to refer us (always most usefully) to the *locus classicus* of any particular issue, of any extended discussion, if one excepts the brief treatment of the second volume of the *Critique*, of Sartre who, over some four thousand pages if one puts together the two albeit rather different treatments of the same problem, in the *Critique of Dialectical Reason* and *The Family Idiot*, concerned himself with exactly this problem; namely, that we are simultaneously our own products and the products of history. For it is precisely the contribution of Sartre to have afforded us the possibility of uniting, within a single theoretical discourse, these two moments, obverse and reverse of the human condition—freedom and determination—the disjunction of which results in the extremist binary oppositions and dislocations of a fragmented and contradictory experience of the world which is none other than the experience of alienation[12] under capitalism itself, and which it was the original aim of Marxism to overcome.

No less puzzling is the omission of any reference to the universal singular in Anderson's *Considerations on Western Marxism*. Under the

11. *Arguments within English Marxism*, 58.
12. Alienation—although it takes many other forms—is originally that condition which arises from the fact that the worker's own productive labor (in commodity production) comes to stand over and against him as a hostile, alien force insofar as the commodity which he produces does not belong to him. Because, under capitalism, the rate of productivity is sufficiently high for the worker to produce more value (commodities) than the cost of his own wages (and machinery, raw materials etc.), this *surplus-value* will be recuperated by the capitalist in the form of a new mass of capital which will perpetuate his own hold over the means of production and the worker's necessity to sell his labor for wages. In addition to which *all* commodities on the market being the products of this process, it follows that each consumer (the bulk of whom are workers and not capitalists), when he spends his wages in order to survive, is the means whereby the capitalist realizes the surplus-value which has accrued to the capitalist's product as a result of the labor of his

heading "Thematic Innovations," Anderson gives pride of place to Sartre's notion of *scarcity*—in itself hardly the most interesting novelty developed in the *Critique of Dialectical Reason*. There is perhaps not much point in speculating at any length about Perry Anderson's choice of priorities in his deliberately brief and broad survey of an enormous field, but the absence of any mention of either *The Family Idiot* or the universal singular may perhaps serve to explain the silence in the more recent *Arguments within English Marxism*. I suspect that Anderson shares widespread disapprobatory assumptions about the incorporation of *existentialism* into Sartre's later Marxist writings. One finds this view cropping up all over the place, and a few examples here will serve to illustrate what is very rapidly, and alarmingly, becoming an unquestioned commonplace in the literature.

In a recent, and excellent, history of critical theory, the French writers Gérard Delfau and Anne Roche have this to say:

> (Sartre) proposes to enable Marxist analysis to benefit from acquisitions in the social sciences: psychoanalysis, linguistics, sociology, history, criticism, etc. In short, he wants to include in his operation *the whole of man*, and *each individual* in his intimate existential history. Which is what he attempts in the case of Flaubert, outlining of course what will become the three volumes of *The Family Idiot*. There is something exemplary in this willingness to assume the contradiction, *even if we do not necessarily accept the existentialist premises.* Sartre seems to us to have posed the problem of our times: how to theorize within Marxism the specificity of the individual, as well as the various domains of the ideological instance . . .[13]

More recently, we have had Göran Therborn speaking of Sartre's *Critique* as "a subjectivist theory of history."[14] Or Janet Wolff, in a book published only last year:

_____

own workers. In this sense, then, the worker is constrained to be the "free" agent of the perpetuation of his own subordination to the mode of economic production which assigns him his position as owner of the means of production. Thus, we say he is alienated.

We use this term, broadly, to designate all activity which, because of the inescapable historical structural processes in which it is imbricated, has the undesired result of producing effects running counter to those originally hoped for (e.g. competition among capitalists/workers for markets/jobs leads to lowering of prices/wages).

I have described this phenomenon at some length because—as we shall see—it has a crucial role to play in the interpretations texts suffer and the historical significance which texts acquire.

13. Gérard Delfau and Anne Roche, *Histoire, littérature: histoire et interprétation du fait littéraire* (Paris: Editions du Seuil, 1977), 307. Emphases mine.

14. Göran Therborn, *The Ideology of Power and the Power of Ideology* (London: Verso, 1980), 133.

Sartre's critique of "lazy Marxism," while often quite justified in attacking a Marxism which disallows subjects altogether, also resorts to an existential theory of the subject, which fails to recognise that subject's constitution in social and ideological practices.[15]

Fredric Jameson—surely the leading contemporary Marxist aesthetician—in *The Political Unconscious*, a book which explicitly addresses itself to the broader antagonism in which the above remarks find their context—namely the ongoing conflict between Hegelian and structuralist Marxisms—is characteristically more subtle. Jameson puts forward the suggestion—surely heretical—that even Sartre's earlier purely existentialist work, *Being and Nothingness*, may not be ideological.[16] This kind of adventurous flirtation with unorthodox possibilities is what we have come to expect from Jameson; he is rightly famous for his omnivorousness, for his exceptional ability in retrieving, reprocessing and exploiting even the most ideologically resistant material in new and exciting dialectical ways. In this respect he is following in the best tradition of Marx who often insisted that all ideology contains its elements of truth. Nevertheless, even Jameson's cast-iron dialectical digestion seems to baulk at certain aspects of Sartre's work, although this takes the form of significant omissions rather than explicit rejections.

The easiest and most obvious starting-point for the discussion of these omissions would be to compare the methodological blueprint of the "three concentric frameworks"[17] which Jameson holds to be the "ultimate *semantic* precondition for the intelligibility of literary and

15. Janet Wolff, *The Social Production of Art* (London: Macmillan, 1981), 131.

16. Fredric Jameson, *The Political Unconscious* (London: Methuen, 1981), 259.

17. "Thus, within the narrower limits of our first, narrowly political or historical, horizon, the 'text' . . . is still more or less construed as coinciding with the individual literary work . . . [but] grasped essentially as a *symbolic act.*"

"When we pass into the second phase . . . [the text] has been reconstituted in the form of the great collective or class discourses of which a text is little more than an individual *parole* or utterance . . . our object of study will prove to be the *idéologème*, that is, the smallest intelligible unit of the essentially antagonistic collective discourses of social classes."

"When finally, even the passions and values of a particular social formation find themselves placed in a new and seemingly relativized perspective by the ultimate horizon of human history as a whole, and by their respective positions in the whole complex sequence of the modes of production, both the individual text and its ideologemes know a final transformation, and must be read in terms of what I will call the *ideology of form*, that is the symbolic messages transmitted to us by the coexistence of various sign systems which are themselves traces or anticipations of modes of production." (*The Political Unconscious*, 75–76). The full description of these three frameworks covers pp. 75–102 of Jameson's book.

cultural texts," and Sartre's *hierarchy of significations*[18] of which they so irresistibly remind us. (Indeed, it will be precisely this similarity between Jameson and Sartre, and the significant differences separating them, which I shall exploit here, the better to distinguish what is peculiar to Sartre's achievement). Methodological proposals being necessarily abstract, however, I have preferred to postpone discussion of them until we have looked at some of Jameson's specific analyses. For example, his account of the following description of the approaching storm in Conrad's *Typhoon:*

> At its setting the sun had a diminished diameter and an expiring brown, rayless glow, as if millions of centuries elapsing since the morning had brought it near its end. A dense bank of cloud became visible to the northward; it had a sinister dark olive tint, and lay low and motionless upon the sea, resembling a solid obstacle in the path of the ship. She went floundering towards it like an exhausted creature driven to its death. . . . The far-off blackness ahead of the ship was like another night seen through the starry night of the earth—the starless night of the immensities beyond the created universe, revealed in its appalling stillness through a low fissure in the glittering sphere of which the earth is the kernel.[19]

Jameson chooses this passage in order to demonstrate what he calls "the Utopian vocation of Conrad's style"—a vocation which depends on an inversion of the *fin de siècle* stereotypical and ideological semes of cosmic entropy and the ship of civilisation heading for apocalypse in the construction of its radically new sensorial productions of an unearthly and unprecedented beauty. Jameson accounts simultaneously for the historical emergence and the beauty of this kind of writing in terms of "the libidinal transformation of an increasingly dessicated and repressive reality."[20] Conrad's style, and impressionism in general "are to be understood in terms of the concrete situation to which they are both responses: that of rationalisation[21] and reification[22] in late nineteenth-

---

18. Jean-Paul Sartre, *Questions de méthode,* in *Critique de la raison dialectique* (Paris: Gallimard, 1960), 89–95, but especially 92–93.

19. Joseph Conrad, quoted in Jameson, op. cit., 230.

20. *The Political Unconscious,* 237.

21. ". . . that characteristic reorganizational process of capitalism which Weber described under the term *rationalization.* The older, inherited ways of doing things are broken into their component parts and reorganized with a view to greater efficiency according to the instrumental dialectic of means and ends, a process that amounts to a virtual bracketing or suspension of the ends themselves and thus opens up the unlimited perspective of complete instrumentalization of the world: cultural institutions could scarcely hope to resist this universal process, which sunders subject from object and

century capitalism". And it is this "response," this "libidinal transformation" at the heart of Conrad's impressionism "which alone makes it a complex and interesting historical act, and ensures it a vitality outside the cultural museum."[23]

I am condensing Jameson's argument considerably, but it would seem to run something like this: impressionist painting, through its emphasis on the act of perception and its constitution of objects through the reorganization of sense data, rather than on the object itself—perception as an end in itself—is a form of libidinal compensation for the sensuous aridity of life under nineteenth-century capitalism. I suspect—the issue is outside my area of competence—that all kinds of questions could be raised here; and, certainly, I am not entirely convinced that the connection Jameson makes between Conrad and Impressionism is not itself problematical; but what is far more crucially at stake here is the status of Jameson's theoretical discourse, in which a 'symptomatic' reading reveals significant lacunae. What, for example, "responds" to rationalization in late nineteenth-century capitalism? Who or what is at the origins of that "libidinal transformation" of a reified reality? And to what logic of explanation might one be compelled

---

structurally colonizes each separately, producing hierarchies of functions according to their technical use (thus, the quantifying, 'rational' parts of the psyche are to be developed, indeed, overdeveloped, while the more archaic are allowed to vegetate in a kind of psychic backwater)." (*The Political Unconscious*, 220)

22. Jameson seems to use *reification*, citing Lukács as his authority, interchangeably with *rationalization*. The terms are ultimately identical—simply ways of emphasizing different aspects of the same process; but for my own part, here, I have preferred to retain Marx's original sense: Karl Marx, *Capital* (London: Dent, 1974), vol. 1, 45. "Thus the mystery of the commodity form is simply this, that it mirrors for men the social character of their own labour, mirrors it as an objective character attaching to the labour products themselves, mirrors it as a social natural property of these things. Consequently the social relation of the producers to the sum total of their own labour, presents itself to them as a social relation, not between themselves but between the products of their labour. Thanks to this transference of qualities, the labour products become commodities, transcendental or social things which are at the same time perceptible by our senses. . . . We are concerned only with a definite social relation between human beings, which, in their eyes, has here assumed the semblance of a relation between things."

Another form of reification occurs in a more obvious and readily comprehensible manner in the labor process itself; referring to the division and specialization of labor in manufacture, Marx writes: "What is narrowness, and even imperfection, in the detail worker, becomes perfection when he is regarded as no more than a limb of the collective worker. The habit of doing only one thing transforms him into an unfailing instrument, while his connexion with the integral mechanism compels him to work with the regularity of a part of a *machine*." (*Capital*, 1, 368). Emphases mine.

We shall be emphasizing the importance of a phenomenological description of reification *as it is lived*.

23. *The Political Unconscious*, 225.

to have recourse in order to account for transformations in general, and libidinal transformations in particular? These various terms imply a whole multitude of assumptions about agency and structural determination which are either being taken for granted or deliberately avoided. The very term *reification* itself is highly problematical, and has already been sneered out of court by an Althusser, along with the rest of that cluster of "ideological" terminology which tacitly subscribes to the "humanistic" opposition of human/inhuman.[24] While I would not myself wish for a moment to go along with the dismissal of Jameson's critical vocabulary entailed by the adoption of a strict Althusserian position (or indeed the presuppositions of Althusser's position as a whole), one is nonetheless obliged to concede that until we have the "concepts," as Althusser would say, of "reification,"[25] "dehumanization," "response," "transformation," or "the negative," these terms remain "theoretically empty,"[26] dangerously attractive vacuums to the surrounding pressures of ideology.

Now, it must already be obvious that I believe that a theoretical discourse adequate to the articulation of these notions within Marxism is to be found in the work of Sartre (specifically in the notion of the universal singular); and that in such a way as to enable us to avoid any commitment to the disabling notions of the "individual" or "Man" or human "essences" which some of these terms can be interpreted as implying. Of course, there is nothing new in this—Sartre's attempt to integrate existentialism within Marxism is at least notorious, even if any survey of the current literature suggests that, with a few notable exceptions, this attempt has still to be accorded genuine scrutiny. What is important is to point out the consequences of the omission of any theorization of these notions for the concrete results of Jameson's analyses. This omission is all the more strange because, as already mentioned, Jameson concedes at one point that even in the early work of Sartre, *Being and Nothingness*—that massive description of the lived experience of reification "from the inside," and a considerably more dubious source of inspiration in the present climate, one would have thought, than the universal singular or *The Family Idiot*—there exists "a whole anatomy of lived time, action, choice, emotion . . . (which) is not necessarily in itself ideological."[27]

But let us come back to Jameson's quotation from *Typhoon*. It

24. Ibid., 237.
25. Louis Althusser, *Pour Marx* (Paris: Maspero, 1965), 236 n. and 243 ff.
26. Louis Althusser, *Lire le Capital* (Paris: Maspero, 1968), 2, 57; 1, 187.
27. *The Political Unconscious*, 259.

should immediately be conceded that Jameson is talking at the level of his third framework (mode of production) and that the libidinal transformation in question is one which is itself dependent upon a sufficiently advanced degree of industrialization having been attained in order to give rise to that "autonomization"[28] of the senses which Jameson identifies as a simultaneous product of and response to rationalization. To this extent, the detour I shall make presently through what the early Sartre called the singular author's "recuperation of the totality of being"[29] may seem out of place. In other words, it is obvious that Conrad's being in a position to perform this libidinal transformation does not depend on him alone, but on the extent to which certain sensorial productions are genuine historical and personal possibilities and thereby able to be created by him. That is to say, in Sartre's terms, that Conrad can only produce an original singular response to, or retotalization of, a reified reality if he has already been totalized—that is to say universalized—by his epoch. (The exact coordinates of the meeting-point between Joseph Conrad and History are of course a matter of the utmost complexity, the components of which would be susceptible to detection and analysis only in terms of the gigantic critical apparatus of something like *The Family Idiot* which analyses its object simultaneously within the perspective of an existential psychoanalysis, and within the total history of nineteenth-century France, in an endless shuttling back and forth between these two perspectives which finally converges on the emergence of Flaubert as France's greatest novelist of the second half of the nineteenth century. Although one might speculate that the conflict which Conrad interiorizes—between the prudent, rationalist, eighteenth-century imperatives of his mother's family, the Brobowskis, and the conversely Romantic affirmation of the imagination and the negative of his father, Apollo Korzeniowski—is one which eminently prepares him for his novelistic function of problematizer of reification.)

We can now proceed to our Sartrean alternative account of the *Typhoon* passage. We recall that Jameson explains the beauty of this passage in terms of a response to reification. So can Sartre. First, howev-

---

28. Ibid., 228 ff.

29. Jean-Paul Sartre, *Situations* 2 (Paris: Gallimard, 1948), 106–07. I say "early" Sartre; although it will be clear that I draw constantly on the entirety of his work, deliberately juxtaposing the earlier notions with the later ones, and even using them interchangeably. I do this in order to vindicate Jameson's suggestion that the categories of the earlier existentialist work are not necessarily ideological; but more important is the necessity of showing thereby the way in which existentialism, historicized, is consistent with and *indispensable* to Marxism.

er, we must bear in mind that Sartre shares with many aestheticians the now suspect conception of the work of art as a *totality*:[30] that is to say, an entity which is greater than the sum of its parts to the extent that it exists only insofar as all its diverse parts can be grasped in reciprocal relations of differential, dispersed significance—with each other individually and with the overall ensemble, such that the totality is found within each one of its parts in some *relational* form or another, as present-absences, (but *not* as some ubiquitous Hegelian *essence* which would give rise to what Althusser correctly condemns as "expressive causality," but which he incorrectly ascribes to Sartre).[31] (It goes without saying that Sartre is talking at the level of the existential acts of reading and writing where totalization—as Sartre describes it (see note 2)—necessarily takes place; of course, this process of totalization can only be effected on the basis of *différance* which far outstrips the totalizing capacity of the reader and writer; this much said, *différance* too can itself only "exist" (be effective) if totalizations are constantly taking place: these two notions, frequently held to be incompatible, are in fact indispensable to each other. I shall demonstrate this in another publication).

In passing I should also like to point out that we find, in the twin notions of *totality* and *totalization*, satisfactory, to my mind, responses to the following perennial aporia which Terry Eagleton reiterates in his latest book—unnecessarily, if people would only give Sartre the attention he merits:

> Benjamin's "non-metaphysical metaphysics" thus represent an ingenious response to the problem which, as we have seen, obsessed Adorno too, and to which we have as little satisfactory answer today: how are we to think totality and specificity together, steadfastly avoiding a self-indulgent sport of the fragment even as we undo tyranical unities?[32]

Totality being the formulation corresponding to the mechanisms of works of art—or any dimension of the pratico-inert (machinery, for example)—and *totalization* referring both to the singular act (eg. picking up a pen) or longer-term project and the broader movement of history itself. Here is an even better example of Sartre's capacity for the description of the relations between totality and specificity:

30. Jean-Paul sartre, *Critique de la raison dialectique*, 138. I have reworked, slightly, in what follows, Sartre's formulation in what seems to me a more satisfactory version.

31. *Lire le Capital*, 2, 62–63. *Pour Marx*, 208.

32. Terry Eagleton, *Walter Benjamin*, 118.

the whole is entirely present in each part as the part's actual meaning and destiny. In this case, the whole confronts itself in the same way as the part confronts the whole in its *determination* (negation of the whole) and just as the parts are in contradistinction to each other (each part is the negation of the others but each one is the whole determining itself in its totalizing activity and endowing the partial structures with the determinations which the total movement requires) the part, as such, is mediated by the whole in its relations with the other parts: within a totalization, the multiplicities (as liaisons of absolute exteriority: quantities) are not suppressed but interiorise each other. The fact . . . of being *one hundred*, for example, becomes for each one of the hundred a synthetic relation of interiority with the ninety-nine others: each one is modified in its singular reality by its characteristic of being-the-hundredth . . . Thus the whole (as a totalizing act) becomes the relation between the parts. In other words, the totalization is the mediation between the parts (considered under the aspect of their determinations) as a relation of interiority: within a totalization and through this totalization each part is mediated by all the others in its relation to each one and each one is a mediation between all the others; the negation (as determination) becomes the synthetic bond of each part with every other part, with all the others and with the whole. But at the same time the interrelated system of the parts conditioning each other mutually opposes itself to the whole as an act of unification and that in *the very degree* to which this system in movement only exists and can only exist as the very incarnation and the present reality (here, now) of the whole as an ongoing synthesis.[33]

If this is grasped, then Eagleton's accurate demonstration of the antimonies present in Lukács's simultaneous invocation of "contradictions" and "essences" can no longer have that aspect of an insurmountable problem for contemporary Marxism which he grants it:

In his reply to Bloch's defence of Expressionism, Lukács speaks in one sentence of the artefact having a "surface of life sufficiently transparent to allow the underlying essence to shine through," and writes a few lines later of art "grasping hold of the living contradictions of life and society." But it is surely very strange to think at once in terms of essence and contradiction. For one meaning of "contradiction" simply cancels the whole notion of "essence"; it is only the reifying ploys of Hegelian parlance that allow us to conceptualize contradiction as unity. That Lukács, like the rest of us but more than some, remains the prisoner of a metaphysical problematic is perhaps nowhere better demonstrated than in this. The capitalist social formation is a totality of

33. *Critique*, 139–140 n.

contradictions; what therefore determines each contradiction is the unity it forms with others; the truth of contradiction is accordingly unity. It would be hard to think up a more flagrant contradiction. One has only to ponder the nuanced distinction between arguing that "contradiction is essential to capitalism," and that "the essence of capitalism is contradiction," to recognize how extraordinarily difficult it is for any of us to think ourselves outside that crippling essence/phenomenon "model" which is for Lukács the very key to historical truth.[34]

This problem was solved a quarter of a century ago in the *Critique*. Once again one has to lament the neglect of Sartre which condemns us to rehearsing outmoded theoretical dilemmas. Althusser too, uncharacteristically, has an excellent description of the kinds of complexities involved in these relations in his concept of "a structure in dominance." Although the essentially static quality of Althusser's formula, as Thompson points out, makes for the superiority of notions like Sartre's. Totalities and totalizations can only become *efficacious* (they can only *be* these things) to the extent that they are totalized in their turn—whether by individual action or the movement of history.

If one pushes this notion of totality to its logical conclusion, one comes up with some curious results. For example—I deliberately choose the most incongruous one possible—that one of the reasons for the beauty of our *Typhoon* passage is that it is read in the context of the knowledge that Captain MacWhirr is a strangely dignified and admirable half-wit. It is, of course, a contemporary commonplace that any element in a system is an "effect" of total structure. Still, it may seem odd to declare that anything so stolid as that amazing old buffer could possibly have anything to do with the beauty of this luridly sumptuous and otherworldly evocation of approaching cataclysm; and yet we can establish the point quite simply and convincingly by considering what would be the effect of this passage if we stuck it into another of Conrad's novels—say, *The Nigger of the "Narcissus."* I suggest that its power would be considerably diminished; and this for any number of reasons (for example, the fact that the titles of the two works lead the reader to accord differing degrees of centrality to these books' respective storms). But *one* of the reasons—this is a fiendishly complex and multifactorial affair—would be that this passage, in its rightful place in *Typhoon*, is heightened or electrified by *irony* at MacWhirr's expense—an irony which is set in motion with the title of the book. So that this passage is

34. *Walter Benjamin*, 86–87.

all the finer to the extent that we know that MacWhirr is spectacularly blind to the awesomeness of the scene and stubbornly insensitive to the dangers it represents ("There's some dirty weather knocking about"). I shall develop this point in greater detail subsequently. Conversely, one has only to imagine Captain Alistoun of the *Narcissus* on the bridge of the *Nan-Shan* for the very *language,* for the very *style* itself, of this passage—*without the alteration of a single word*—to acquire something of the torrid, overblown verbosity which never quite leaves even the finest passages of *The Nigger of the "Narcissus."* A shrill verbosity which is a part of the pervasive bad faith of that profoundly nasty anti-working-class novel, of which Alistoun, in his stiff-necked hard-arsed and insufferably correct way, is a principal weapon.

Well, what, one might ask, does any of this have to do with rationalization and reification? (The exigencies of space and time have required my deliberately restricting myself, with respect to the universal historical dimension of Sartre's formula, to Jameson's very illuminating invocation of these particular Marxist "codes"). Both books address themselves to that familiar Conradian antinomy of successful action and the demands of the imagination, the negative and, yes, the Utopian. That the aesthetic centrality of this problematic is itself one which arises in a context of rationalization, increasingly intensive division of labor and consequent fragmentation and autonomization of faculties like "action" or "imagination" is a fact which Jameson has established in masterful fashion and should not require detailed argument. What is significant for our account of the *Typhoon* passage is that both these tales present us with imaginary "solutions" to the contemporary *imperative* of reification *as exis.* By which last term I mean the problematical ensemble of daily practices which arise from an individual's (or class's) situation and enterprise, and which give it—prior to any verbal explicitation—a certain image of itself, *lived* rather than articulated.[35] Furthermore, it is the qualitative difference between the two solutions which Conrad proffers—the degree of internal distanciation from ideology, or freedom, mobilized—which makes for the superiority of *Typhoon* over *The Nigger of the "Narcissus"* and, in part, for the beauty of our passage.

This, once established, will enable us to see more clearly what it is that Jameson consistently omits in his analyses and the deleterious consequences which flow from such omissions.

---

35. I quote from memory—the original passage, which I am unable to locate, is somewhere in the third volume of *The Family Idiot.*

III

The solution offered in *The Nigger of the "Narcissus"*—to the problem of how to live that existential imperative of reification generated by one's situation as an inessential cog in the transport system of British imperialism, and the correlative existential *temptation* of the denial of freedom, of the negative, of imagination, of *need*, in an alienation to the exigencies of the Human Thing or commodity—is broadly that of heroic *stoicism*.[36] This is perfectly evident in the didactic opposition of Alistoun/Singleton vs. Wait/Donkin. What is ugly about this book is not only the opposition itself but the fury with which the opposition is rammed home, notably in the caricatural figure of Donkin and the shape of that correspondingly mythicized and preposterous old epic Yeti, Singleton, whose thirty hours at the helm seventy-five degrees from the perpendicular in a northwesterly gale off the Cape of Good Hope belong more properly in the comic strip pages of *The Incredible Hulk*. However—and this is the secret of the success of Conrad's tale *despite* the dross of reactionary class-invective or a negative reaction to that class-invective—it is more complicated than this. For we *admire* Singleton. *Not* just because this response is constructed into the text itself. Although that too is true. But because stoicism, the decision to retrieve the hardships of an irremediable imposed condition—as inessential means to other people's means to further invisible ends *ad infinitum* in the overcycling autoinstrumentalization of capitalism—*as one's own choice*, elevating one's instrumentalization into an *end* in itself, this minimal and ultimately ineffectual recuperation of the situation (except insofar as it enables one to *live* with that situation), in the process of which one merely alienates oneself still further, is an affirmation of freedom which commands spontaneous respect. In short, it is this choice which is at the origin of Singleton's *dignity*. Put differently, the imperative-to-reification-as-exis generated by the situation is freely assumed and *dépassé* by the singular project which denies its own initial and spontaneous negation of the situation in order to master its circum-

36. In what follows I am heavily indebted to the existential analysis of stoicism in André Gorz's *Fondements pour une morale* (Paris: Galilée, 1976), 206–10. Written largely during the early fifties, this book was only published in 1976. "Dated" to the extent that it hales from the high period of Sartrean existentialism, it constitutes a brilliant attempt, quite on a par with anything Sartre ever wrote, to produce the *Grande Morale* promised by Sartre at the end of *Being and Nothingness* and never completed. This book is nevertheless of the utmost importance. Not only for the understanding of *Being and Nothingness* itself, to which it provides a most illuminating counterpart; but also insofar as it is indispensable to any retrieval of Sartre's earlier existentialist work for Marxism.

stances by retrieving the irremediable as its own choice. It goes without saying that, in existentialist terms, this choice of stoicism is accompanied, in Conrad's case, by a will-to-autoreification which takes the form of a flight into the bad faith of attempting to endow that which is free choice (and therefore utterly *unjustifiable*) with the substantiality of a *thing* (what the early Sartre called the inauthentic project of the for-itself-in-itself). (Which project is symbolized in the text by the following passage in which the older passing generation of sailors represented by Singleton are described thus:

> They were the everlasting children of the mysterious sea. Their successors are the grown-up children of a discontented earth. They are less naughty, but less innocent; less profane, but perhaps also less believing; and if they had learned how to speak they have also learned how to whine. But the others were strong and mute; they were effaced, bowed and enduring, *like stone caryatides* that hold up in the night the lighted halls of a resplendent and glorious edifice.[37]

Nevertheless, *if the situation really is irremediable,* stoicism, or the decision to comply completely with the situation to the point of trying to *become* it, commands respect. And it does in Singleton's case to the extent that Conrad makes sure that the former is of an older generation (if such a generation ever existed) to whom the revindications of an aggressive working-class consciousness were not a conceivable historical possibility. In addition to which, Conrad also makes it impossible for the reader to sympathize with the claims of human need by, very impressively, making an absolute stoicism the indispensable means to the survival of the group. (Thus the whole thematic of the subtle corruption spread by Wait's inability to face his impending death, Donkin's egoistic priority given to personal comfort, etc.) Hence the confusion of response which even the most unshakeably left-wing reader understandably feels when reading this work. Unfortunately for Conrad, however, there is Donkin and his contestation of the social status quo (that this contestation can only stem from personal egoism is of course staple Conrad): *other historical possibilities exist;* or, at least, are conceivable; and therefore speedily ridiculed or silenced.[38] Which is why Conrad has

37. Joseph Conrad, *The Nigger of the "Narcissus"* (London: Dent, 1967), 23. Emphases mine.

38. Conrad, *Nigger,* 99. " 'You've been braying in the dark about "See tomorrow morning!" Well, you see me now. What do you want?' He waited, stepping quickly to and fro, giving them searching glances. What did they want? They shifted from foot to foot, they balanced their bodies; some, pushing back their caps, scratched their heads. What did they want? . . . . They wanted great things. And suddenly all the simple words they knew

to create as vile as possible a foil to Singleton, in the shape of Donkin, if only to preserve the integrity of the former; and which is also the source of the maniacal rigidity of Alistoun and the incantatory shrillness of the overall effect itself, as Conrad strives to persuade the reader, and especially *himself*, with classic bad faith, that the *status quo*, if stern and inhuman, is nevertheless all that can legitimately be hoped for.

This very shrillness is a sure sign that we are touching at Conrad's existential freedom itself. I am thinking of Jameson's astute remark that those who most rail against *ressentiment* are themselves *hommes de ressentiment*. That the Polish gentleman had some difficulty in reconciling himself to his humble station as a British merchant seaman is evinced by Conrad's imaginary attempts to distinguish himself somehow from his objective social status: for example, the "Russian Count" *imago* in which he draped himself and was recognised by his shipmates. One thinks especially of the hilarious description of Conrad given by Paul Langlois, his Mauritian charterer, and which speaks volumes:

> Captain Korzeniowski was always dressed like a fop . . . in a dark jacket, usually a lightcoloured waistcoat, and a fancy pair of trousers, all of these well made and of great elegance; he wore a black or grey bowler hat slightly to one side, always had gloves on and carried a goldheaded Malacca cane . . . (His) relations with . . . the other captains were of purely formal politeness . . . he was not very popular among his colleagues who called him, ironically, 'the Russian Count'.[39]

This outfit could only have been maintained, one suspects, with the ever generous help of Uncle Brobowski back in Poland. What, one wonders, would the Donkins, the Captain MacWhirrs, the Jukes, have made of this? Despite his declarations to the contrary, one imagines easily the secret revulsions Conrad must often have experienced in his position; and the constant *tension*, the constant watchfulness of himself and others which these extravagant imaginary solutions and posturings must have involved him in. Hence, in part, the notorious irascibility, touchiness and neurasthenic twitchings. He must have been, on many occasions, simultaneously very formidable and yet constantly verging on the ridiculous. There can be no doubt that a hysterical stoicism must have been a constant temptation to him. What other solution was there? The only alternative—uncompromising contestation of the social order

---

seemed to be lost for ever in the immensity of their vague and burning desire. They knew what they wanted, but they could not find anything worth saying."

39. Quoted in Ian Watt, *Conrad in the Nineteenth Century* (London: Chatto & Windus, 1980), 19. Emphases mine.

which humiliated him—would have required him to put in question the class of his origins *as well* as the class of ignoble bourgeois in whose employ he served. A choice which was especially difficult for him insofar as any socialist conception of history as *progressive* had been foreclosed for him by his early Polish experiences. And, of course, to articulate one complaint, one single dissatisfaction, would be to *acknowledge* his social *déchéance;* which is why the intimately related and by no means paradoxical counterpart to all this is that systematic idealization and elevation into heroic epic of life at sea—an existence generally acknowledged to have been one of endless tedium, drudgery and privation. That stoicism was an unsatisfactory solution is testified to by the shrillness and falseness of *The Nigger of the "Narcissus"* as a whole. Unsatisfactory insofar as each new vertigo of revulsion and resentment would elicit a more violent nose dive into frenetically willed submission; which would in its turn generate fresh fits of loathing, and so on, in an unending *tourniquet,* or vicious circle, of mutually exacerbating reactions.

IV

The difference when we turn to *Typhoon* is striking. (Here, for purposes of exposition, I must split my account of the tale into two sections, dealing with its Utopian dimension—broadly, that which "stirs" us— in an uncritical or naïve fashion—before passing on to the ideological function of this Utopian dimension in the work as a whole. I hope the reader will bear with me for the duration of what may well seem an unreflecting complicity with the text.) Certainly, the same fundamental ideological position is sustained: the lower orders, in this case in the shape of the "coolies," threaten the vital social order of the ship by their base materialism, grovelling and brawling amongst themselves for filthy lucre. Order, civilization, life itself, are ensured only by the disinterested and efficient officers' and crew's necessarily brutal quelling of bestial anarchy from below. Nevertheless, *Typhoon* constitutes a more complex response to reification. The difference is to be found in the person of Captain MacWhirr. Once again, Conrad advances as the only viable solution to this imperative a thoroughgoing heroic assumption of its demands—almost to the point of imbecility—in the figure of MacWhirr. It is his total denial of imagination which brings the *Nan-Shan* through the hurricane. Nothing less than this, and his stubbornly *literal* interpretation of the proper discharge of his functions as ship's captain are what keep his first officer from disintegrating and defeat the storm.

So far this is not markedly different from *The Nigger of the "Narcissus."*
The new element is to be found in the greater complexity of Conrad's
attitude to this choice of autoreification. Most obviously in that complex form of humor at MacWhirr's expense. Complex because, paradoxically, it is always utterly respectful; and yet critical to the extent that it
is a form of recognition of what *has* to be sacrificed in the interests of
successful action. A criticism—or constatation, rather—which is perhaps even suggested in the man's name. It is this wry humor which
lightens *Typhoon* and makes it a far greater work than *The Nigger of the
"Narcissus,"* transcending that shrill and simple-minded endorsement
of reification which is so offensive in the earlier work.

Furthermore—to return to the passage Jameson selects for analysis—this humor is implicated in the beauty of the description of the
approaching storm. Nowhere signified in the passage itself, its ambient
presence imparts an authenticity of menace and awesomeness to the
passage in question which is itself a function of the truer measure which
has been taken of MacWhirr. Which is why, conversely, the storm in
The Nigger of the "Narcissus" never quite floats free from its function
as ideological decor in the vindication of Alistoun and Singleton and the
exposure of Donkin and Wait.

In addition I must take exception to Jameson's use of the term
"libidinal" in this context; in particular, I do not accept the statement
that it is this libidinal transformation "which alone makes [Conrad's
impressionism] a complex and interesting historical act, and ensures it a
vitality outside the cultural museum." For beauty of this order has little
to do with the *libidinal*: true, the sensuous charge of this passage is
intense; and to the extent that it does introduce historically novel per-
ceptual dimensions Jameson is correct in speaking of transformations.
But one has only to recall that one is always libidinal with one's whole
being to recognise the inadequecy of such a description: that is to say,
the sensuous detail of this passage is *dépassé towards something else;*
and it is this something else which, in the last instance, endows the
sensuous details with their undoubted *éclat*, without which they would
collapse back into flaccid ornamentation.

To make this clearer I must cite the use which Sartre makes of the
term *universal singular* when applied to the work of art itself:

> If the work of art has all the characteristics of a universal singular,
> this happens in such a way that it is as if the author had taken the
> paradox of his human condition as a *means* and the objectification *in
> the midst of the world* of this same condition in an object as an *end in
> itself*. Thus beauty, today, is none other than the human condition

presented not as a facticity or contingent given, but as if it were produced by a creative freedom (that of the author). And, to the extent that
this creative freedom aims at communication, it addresses itself to the
creative freedom of the reader and incites him to recompose the work
by reading it (which process is, also, an act of creation), in short, to grasp
freely his own being-in-the-world as if it were the product of his own
freedom; in other words, as if he were responsible for his being-in-the-
world in the very moment of submitting to it or, if one likes, as if he
were the world freely incarnated.[40]

We can take a couple of more manageable examples of beauty, in this
sense, from elsewhere in *Typhoon* before returning to our passage. For
instance:

> He watched her, battered and solitary, labouring heavily in a wild
> scene of mountainous black waters lit by the gleams of distant worlds.
> She moved slowly, breathing into the still core of the hurricane the
> excess of her strength in a white cloud of steam—and the deep-toned
> vibration of the escape was like the defiant trumpeting of a living crea-
> ture of the sea impatient for the renewal of the contest. It ceased sud-
> denly. The still air moaned.[41]

The simple touch of using "distant worlds," rather than the more obvious "stars," utterly transforms the impact of this passage. The knowledge that those miniscule spots of light are gigantic worlds is so familiar
to us today that it almost passes by unnoticed. We forget the excitement
and awe with which this knowledge was seized upon and vulgarized by
Wells, for example; but this deliberate reminder of those vast distances
all at once gigantically expands the significance of and context in which
that defiant release of steam takes place. Singular emblem of the human
project—by virtue of that universalizing series of resonating protometaphorical allusions, *felt* incipiently but never *signified* in the text,
whereby the polysemous ship-facing-a-storm is made dimly to recall
the State, the individual, or existence itself—this release of steam,
"that deep-toned vibration," is *felt*, if not *seen*, by the reader, to defy the
entire Cosmos; and, by the same token—by the same universalizing
means (this use of "distant worlds" is precisely one such device) which
enable the reader, from another singular sociohistorical situation, to
grasp an incident on board a British steamship in the China Sea at the
beginning of the twentieth century as emblematic of *his* being-in-the-

40. Jean-Paul Sartre, *Plaidoyer pour les intellectuels* (Paris: Gallimard, 1972), 104.
Emphases mine.
41. Conrad, *Typhoon*, 190.

world—it defies and surpasses *all* disasters, *le Mal* in general, whether they comprise typhoons, the Bomb, or alienation under capitalism. (That this affirmation of human freedom is one which, in the context of the tale as a whole, is *also* mobilized in the service of a reactionary political ideology is an additional complicating factor with which I shall deal shortly.)

A better example would be that constantly reiterated "voice" of MacWhirr which "shoves aside the hurricane"; or the engine-room telegraph which, at the climax of the tale, the moment after the ship has been swept from end to end and Jukes and Rout, down below, are convinced that all is lost with MacWhirr and the wheelhouse swept overboard—"steering-gear gone, ship like a log. All over directly"—suddenly drops like a flash from STOP to FULL. These words, and MacWhirr's voice, are the epitome of those tiny and yet supremely victorious acts which, in their dwarfing of the deliberately and commensurately dwarfing natural phenomenon, affirm *meaning*, human freedom and possibility over and against a universe which not only resounds with the "appalling silence" of the absence of God but threatens its inhabitants with extinction. These are not merely moments of tremendous excitement, but *profoundly moving*[42] moments to which we can give our unqualified adherence: we need have no ideological reservations at moments like these—at least, not in the instant of our reading them within the restricted local moment in which they appear in the text.

To return to our passage, it is for similar reasons that the magnificent description of the approaching storm *acquires* its magnificence: the fact that there is human intention behind that ship, that there are men on board whom we know to be *in danger*; and that this ship is commanded by a man who, without any of the fuss or flamboyance of self-representation, turns his face to the storm, refusing to change course by so much as a degree; and, especially, that there is a complex humor, a genuine inquiring freedom, involved in the presentation of

---

42. In view of the recent climate—especially in England and France—in which a phrase of this kind has been all but *streng verboten*, it was with great pleasure (and some amusement) that I came across the following passage in Terry Eagleton's latest book: "The practice of the socialist cultural worker, in brief, is projective, polemical and appropriative. Such activity may from time to time include such things as encouraging others to reap pleasure from the beauty of religious imagery, encouraging the production of works with no overt political content whatsoever, and arguing in particular times and places for the 'greatness', 'truth', 'profoundly moving', 'joyful', 'wonderful' qualities of particular works . . . " (*Walter Benjamin*, 113) I do hope that this is one of those "particular times and places" when this phrase may be invoked. . . .

that eminently reified man. How different Conrad's existential choice, here, from the feverishly anxious endorsement of reification which underlies the intensely unattractive theatrical rigidity of Captain Alistoun in *The Nigger of the "Narcissus."*

Without all of this, there is no real beauty. Mere prettiness. Libidinal beauty, in fact.

Cultural museum indeed!

V

To resume the argument thus far: if an account of *beauty* necessarily involves reference to the historical circumstances which are not only the very *conditions* for the work of art being created in the first place, but which also permeate and determine the ideological (and psychoanalytic) structures of the work, then it is no less the case that reference must be made to the freedom of the artist: not only insofar as that freedom may or may not contest or subvert the ideological and historical given, but insofar as that freedom also necessarily has its limits, and in the very moment of contestation may contribute, as we shall see, to the actualization of historical necessity.

I hope to have shown, for example, that the invocation of the author's freedom is not only indispensable to a discrimination of the relative merits of two of Conrad's tales, but is also necessary for any theoretically coherent account of what a singular "response" to a universal historical reality (reification) might be. I would suggest, furthermore, that universal historical phenomena such as reification require, for our complete understanding of them, existential accounts of what it is to *live* them. And that, too, requires one to talk about freedom. In short, if Joseph Conrad, totalized and universalized by his age, is confronted constantly with the imperative of reification as an existential temptation which he often cannot refuse, the singularity which is his literary career (a retotalization of his age which is singular by the universalizing singularity of his projects) nevertheless requires us to mobilize a theoretical language capable of articulating the notion of freedom dialectically *within* the overarching movement of historical necessity.

I believe that the language of *Being and Nothingness*, which I have invoked here—loosely, and in as nontechnical a manner as possible—if suitably imbricated in the historical dialectic of the universal singular, answers this requirement. If so, Jameson's statement to the effect that "the classical period of Sartrean existentialism, according to which it

was possible to read literary styles, the structure of imagery, charac-
terological traits, and ideological values in terms of anxiety and the fear
of freedom"[43] was "short-lived" and, by implication, played-out, is not
only premature, but the work of the early Sartre, suitably dialecticized,
appears indispensable to a materialist historiography.

I should add: there is nothing "subjective"[44] (at least not in the
pejorative sense of the term) or "idealist" about any of this. If we insist
on the place of freedom in history it is because the mobilization of
freedom is a *material event* without which materialist accounts are
impoverished. Nor does such an account of agency commit us to an
ideology of the autonomous bourgeois "centered subject." We shall see
very shortly, in Conrad's case, the extent to which freedom, in the
presocialist societies of our age, is simultaneously irreducible and illusory, eternal and unalienable, and profoundly alienated; but it must
be pointed out before we proceed any further that Sartre's notion of
freedom was never, even in the early work, anything more than a "nothingness": a capacity for negation and *dépassement;* there is no sense in
which Sartrean freedom participates in some extrahistorical *essence* or
the "human nature" of a full subject. This capacity for negation is
perfectly compatible with an "insertion" in to any number of "orders"—symbolic, economic or whatever. In fact, as we shall find out
presently, Sartre's conception of the dialectic between freedom and
necessity provides us not only with a far more chilling awareness of the
extent of our unfreedom—insofar as the order of alienation more often
than not maneuvers us into passing sentence on ourselves, and pulling
the trigger too—than anything that ever happened to the tame little
Trägers of Althusser's world, but, in addition, the realization that freedom, in a particularly infernal twist to the dialectic, is also *necessary* to

43. *The Political Unconscious,* 61.

44. For the correct use of this sadly abused term: "I cannot describe here the real
dialectic of the subjective and the objective. It would be necessary to show the joint
necessity of 'the interiorisation of the exterior' and 'the exteriorization of the interior'.
Praxis, in effect, is a passing from the objective to the objective via interiorisation; the
project as subjective *dépassement* of objectivity towards objectivity, held between the
objective conditions of the *milieu* and the objective structures of the field of what is
possible represents *in itself* the moving unity of subjectivity and objectivity, those car-
dinal determinations of activity. The subjective appears thus as a necessary moment of the
objective process. [One might add: and vice versa. (P.W.)] In order to become real conditions for *praxis,* the material conditions which govern human relations have to be lived in
the particularity of particular situations: a reduction in buying power would never
provoke revindicative actions if the workers did not feel this reduction in their flesh in the
form of a need or a fear based on cruel experience . . . " (*Questions de méthode,* 66)

the functioning of any such order (whatever the decisive rôle of the mode of production, "in the last instance," which we do not deny for a moment).

If one assumes a determinist position—commiting oneself to what is essentially an eighteenth-century, eminently bourgeois, pre-Marxist concept of causality in the social sciences (of course, no one—I mean, on the Left—ever *explicitly* dares to go this far, but the implications of the conceptual middle in which many writers—Althusser is a case in point—get themselves on this point is effectively to commit themselves to such a position)—if one assumes a determinist position, then one lands oneself in distinctly idealist contradictions. A materialist account of agency which does not articulate itself around freedom is contradictory insofar as the notion of necessity itself, as that which alienates us, can only be held to be functional or even meaningful if there exists a freedom to be constrained in the first place. It is the *real* contradiction of the dialectical unity between necessity and freedom which is free of *conceptual* contradictions.

It is to this phenomenon that we must now turn.

VI

Up to now we have concentrated, for purposes of exposition, on one half (one "end," as he puts it) of Sartre's formula: that restricted moment in which the writer retotalizes his age in the form of a "solution" to or *dépassement* of the problematical *exis* with which he finds himself confronted, and which is generated by the totalizing movement of history in which he is situated or "inserted," as they say. Strictly speaking, following *The Family Idiot*, this should have comprised the entirety of Conrad's internalization and reexteriorization of the historico-psychoanalytic circumstances of his unique biography, including his relation to the artistic imperatives generated by the three national literary traditions to which he is the heir. For practical reasons, however, I am constrained to consider, following Jameson, all of the above under the sole aspect of the shorthand notations of reification and alienation. This will suffice for our purposes here. What must be done now is to expand our account—from this limited moment of Conrad's confrontation with the immediate problematical *lived experience* of reification, which he lives obscurely, groping, snatching his instruments where and as he finds them—to a consideration of the respect in which these intensely lived personalised *gestures* are not only supremely singular acts but *also* a highly significant *historical* response to the mode of production which has totalized and universalized him, and which will prescribe for him the very limits to the solutions available to him. In short, following the earlier formula of the *Critique of Dialectical Reason* (which is none other than a more condensed and cryptic precursor of the universal singular itself), we have to demonstrate not only the freedom of necessity but the necessity of freedom.[45] This will inevitably involve close consideration of that tangled connivence, in *Typhoon*, between ideology and subversive Utopian impulses: an account which, it will be seen, draws heavily on Jameson's important heuristic formulation of this relationship,[46] but which also attempts to elaborate and clarify the relationship by mobilizing the powerful machinery of the universal singular.

   To begin with, it is clear that Conrad's portrayal of one individual's defeat of a natural danger by a series of "real acts"—real insofar as they originate in his freedom of choice, and with a deliberate defiance of established "storm strategy,"—represents an implicit protest or revolt against the predominant quality of action in the capitalist world. This is a world in which our actions seem to come to us from elsewhere— already half made-up and requiring no more than inconsequential additional touches—then to be whisked away to some end either unknown or even reprehensible to ourselves . . . In a word, it is clear that *Typhoon* is as "epic," as heroic, as "magnificent" as the world in 1900 is bourgeois, capitalist and alienating. This is a real protest: although it is true that MacWhirr's actions do not put in question the historical given—on the contrary, he risks his life in the interests of precisely those relations of production which assign him his particular function in the creation of surplus value—nonetheless, the exigence of nonalienated action which underlies MacWhirr's acts is authentically subversive to the extent that

45. "If the dialectic exists, we must undergo it as the insurmountable rigor of the totalization which totalizes *us* and grasp it in its free practical spontaneity as the totalizing *praxis* which we are; at each level of our experience, we must find in the intelligible unity of the synthetic movement the contradiction and the indissoluble liaison of necessity and freedom, although, at every moment, this liaison presents itself in different forms. In any event, if my life, in its wider implications, becomes History, it must discover itself at the bedrock of its free development as a rigorous necessity of the historical process in order to find itself once more, at a still deeper level as the freedom of this necessity and finally as the necessity of freedom."*

   * "When I give this form to the ultimate liaison of these realities, I do not terminate the enumeration of these contradictory unities with the consideration of the two terms of the comparison: nothing would prevent us from conceiving *in circular form* other dialectical moments where we would find once again, reversed, the succession of the above-mentioned unities." (*Critique*, 157)

46. Fredric Jameson, "Reification and Utopia in Mass Culture," *Social Text*, 1 (Winter, 1979), 130–49.

the kind of world in which this demand could be fulfilled would require for its existence the kind of transformation of the existing relations of production which could only be realized through revolution.

This is the primary reason for the authentic appeal of *Typhoon*—at least, under capitalism. Clearly the appeal of works of art varies significantly in relation to the movement of history. An interesting example which springs to mind is the difference between the readings of Homer by Hegel and Auerbach.[47] The readings are similar to the extent that both are to be understood in the light of a historically specific urban bourgeois *nostalgia* for the radically different forms of social existence which distinguish the precapitalist age of Homer from their own. (Here we find what lies behind Marx's deceptively simple-minded explanation, in the *Grundrisse*,[48] of our enjoying the works of art of the ancient Greeks because they represent the "childhood of humanity.") But the readings differ significantly insofar as Hegel, writing at the beginning of the nineteenth century, goes no further than regretting the lost independence of action which characterizes the ancient heroes, compared with the increasingly constricted ambit within which the agents of bourgeois civil society move and have their being. (In point of fact, Hegel's account of the heroes, while not strictly inaccurate, is strongly colored by an individualistic conception of that "independence" and should be qualified by the point made by Alasdair MacIntyre (*see note 50*) namely, that the quality of action of the Homeric heroes is *one* with their social roles.) Auerbach, writing in the context of more than a century's industrialization of the planet, draws attention to the *transparency* of the Homeric narrative: newly introduced objects, implements and characters, or Odysseus' scar, whatever the urgency of the immediate action, are always fully accounted for in terms of their *origins*. Auerbach finds this wonderful because this aesthetic possibility is one which is no longer available to us: the quality of this nostalgia is one which is intimately bound up with the *anonymity* of objects in a world in which the direct transformation of material objects has disappeared and the vast majority of objects are commodities—dependent for their very existence on the massively complex historical process of a world economy which includes the extraction of raw materials, transport and communication systems, machines, machines to make those machines,

47. G. W. F. Hegel, *Esthétique*, trans. S. Jankélévitch (Paris: Flammarion, 1979), 239–55. Erich Auerbach, *Mimesis—The Representation of Reality in Western Literature* (Princeton, N.J.: Princeton University Press, 1968), chapter 1.

48. Karl Marx, *Grundrisse*, trans. Martin Nicholaus (London: New Left Review, 1973), 110–11.

marketing techniques and so on *ad infinitum*. The effect of all this, and the corresponding forms of social organization which are an indispensable part of such a mode of production, is to to make our lived experience of the world increasingly meaningless and *mysterious* to us—an experience which achieves its ful' est expression in the work of Kafka, for example. Simultaneously, the instrumentalization which this process entails—in which most action is subordinated to that reorganization of the means and ends distinction, in the course of which ends are ceaselessly transformed into means along the circular continuum of surplus-value becoming production becoming surplus-value etc. etc.— results in a fragmentation and dispersal of the time-dimension such that the experience of the present, having been effectively alienated to the past and the future, is reduced to a mere nothingness, a simple shifting dividing-line between the other two dimensions. (One could study *Being and Nothingness* most fruitfully in this light.) The best-known aesthetic solution to this particular form of alienation is, of course, *A la recherche du temps perdu*—the world only regains its wholeness and integrity when recollected. And it is not for nothing that Proust's favorite rhetorical figure is the *simile*—massively developed and obsessively reiterated—so that the anonymity, fragmentation and meaninglessness of the lived is transformed and redeemed by a structure of *resemblances*.

What is no less evident, however, is the ambivalence of Conrad's attitude to reification.[49] We have already mentioned that the ironic distance established vis-à-vis MacWhirr simultaneously disturbs and endorses the phenomenon. But more insidious, perhaps, are the very historical limitations to the possibilities for the construction of an *epos* at the turn of our century: Conrad is not Homer. This becomes immedi-

---

49. This ambivalence is of course largely class-determined. Conrad's objective class status as a Merchant Naval officer condemns him to an uneasy position: he is caught between the Holroyds (*Nostromo*) or the Belgian Company (*Heart of Darkness*) and the working-class Donkins or the blacks and Chinamen of the Third World. It is precisely the contradictions this lands him in which generate the interesting slippery ambiguous attitude of *Heart of Darkness* towards Western civilization, which Eagleton has drawn attention to, simultaneously condemning and endorsing it. (He is the unwilling instrument of an imperialism which he despises morally, but whose victims he cannot in any practical sense identify or unite with.) However, it is no less true that one has to choose how to live one's class-being: that Conrad had enough room to manoeuver to be able to evolve two different responses to reification in *The Nigger of the "Narcissus"* and "Typhoon, we have already seen. Whether he ever really had the means to go beyond *all* the unreduced enclaves of ruling-class ideology which persist in *Typhoon* or anywhere else in his work seems strongly unlikely. Which means that one can be condemned to *choosing* bad faith. But there is nothing determinist about that; there is a crucial difference between determinism and having no alternatives. That is exactly what alienation is all about.

ately apparent when we ponder the fact that Conrad is only able to achieve his Utopian version of action in the drastically simplified and historically anachronistic context of the confrontation with Nature: as soon as he widens the circle of his preoccupations to include those aims which transcend the narrowly immediate one of the preservation of a ship, we return to the more familiar Conradian world of *Heart of Darkness, The Secret Agent,* or *Nostromo,* in which he uncovers the futility, the delusions, and criminal compromises fatally attendant upon all action once its inescapably *social* imbrication within an alienating world is recognized. In other words, what we find here is a disturbingly ambiguous phenomenon to which it is fiendishly difficult to do full justice: that magnificently subversive, liberating even, exigence of meaningful nonalienated action *can only come into existence* riding on the back of an ideological Trojan Horse: namely, the supremely mystifying illusion of the autonomous bourgeois subject, whose very being always depends on precisely such an evacuation of the social dimension, and who acts in freedom of choice, freely selling his labor power for wages, freely choosing his political representatives and his sexual partners, freely owning or selling commodities. In brief, at this level, *Typhoon* contributes to a bourgeois liberal ideology of individualism and, thereby, the reproduction of a world in which real or nonalienated action does *not* exist.

There is another respect in which this tale reinforces the ideology of the bourgeois subject.[50] When Odysseus slays the suitors, or Achilles Hector, the heroic virtue in the name of which these acts are performed is very much *socially defined:* these heros perform their feats because, to a large extent, they are intrinsic to their very social identity as the ruler of Ithaca and the leader of the Myrmidons; they act in accordance with what is right and proper for men of their caste in an aristocratic society which survives by warfare. MacWhirr's heroism, on the other hand, is sustained by personal choice and the affirmation of individual selfhood alone (despite the Merchant Naval code, which he carries to extremes, and his interpretation of which Jukes considers lunatic). This heroism is amplified by his very ordinariness; and, of course, this is what is sublime about MacWhirr; but this is also what is treacherous about him: his heroism is only possible in the historically anachronistic "non-place"[51] of the sea and the confrontation with Nature: insofar as narrative is always simultaneously exigence *and* re-presentation (as

---

50. Here I must acknowledge my debt to the splendid pages which Alasdair MacIntyre devotes to Homer in his recent *After Virtue* (London: Duckworth, 1981), 114–23.
51. Jameson, *The Political Unconscious,* 213.

Jukes, MacWhirr's First Mate, would himself say, the latter is "a real character"), MacWhirr stands fatally condemned as a mystification of the real historical possibilities open to the vast majority of Conrad's urban, alienated public.

There is a real poignancy in this particularly tormented example of the necessity of freedom in the age in which Conrad lived. Conrad himself is scarcely to blame for this particular element of ideology peddled by *Typhoon:* his authentic Utopian impulse, which can *only* find expression in the anachronistic confrontation with Nature, is *stolen* from him by the historical context of an urban reading public into which it ineluctably falls, delimiting contextual meanings for the text itself in a cruel antidialectic which effectively reinforces those very relations of production from which Conrad, obscurely to be sure, is trying to free himself. In short, the subversive impulse is *alienated* (see note 12).

We now find ourselves in something of a dilemma (although most of the elements for a satisfactory resolution of the problem are already in place): we seem to have arrived at some contradictory account of the text in which mutually exclusive propositions about the worth or "greatness" of the work, on the one hand, and its ideological function in relation to class conflict, on the other, jostle for position in what could only be an impossible "conclusion" as to its final assessment. I suggest that, rather than attempting the latter, our function as critics is, on the contrary, to heat and madden this ambivalence to a point of incandescence in which these contradictions can be annealed in a truly dialectical synthesis.

Perhaps, before proceeding any further, it would be as well to recapitulate and be quite sure of the precise nature of our dilemma. Our argument has been two-pronged: that is, on the one hand, we feel that *Typhoon* is great literature: it is a magnificent affirmation of freedom and heroism which—as Althusser would say—exists in a relation of *internal distance*[52] to the imperative of reification; or, as Jameson might put it, *Typhoon* presents a Utopian exigence of unalienated action. On the other hand, as we have seen, these very aspects of the tale are exactly those which lend it an ideological function in the maintenance and reproduction of those same relations of economic production which give rise to the impulse of Utopian revolt in the first place. Our dilemma is not unlike those well-known diagrams, much exploited in

---

52. Louis Althusser, "Letter to André Daspar," in *Lenin and Philosophy and Other Essays,* trans. Ben Brewster (London: NLB, 1971), 204.

introductory manuals of the psychology of perception, where one sees flights of stairs which go up and out of the picture or down and into it, the perspective shifting frustratingly because the visual cues are indeterminate.

The bewilderment we feel when we reach this point in our accounts of the politico-moral ambivalence of even the finest moments in all great literary works is precisely that phenomenon which, in the absence of adequate theoretical instruments, generates the splitting of the two sides to the question into the artificial oppositions of, for example, the great controversies between Adorno and Lukács, Lukács and Brecht, or Bloch and Lukács. So that one finds oneself debating unnecessary antinomies, and correspondingly extremist conclusions on both sides of the particular controversies, along the lines of: Beckett is representative of the worst petty bourgeois tendencies to a panic-stricken flight into solipsism and nihilism in the face of historical realities (Lukács),[53] or: Beckett gives admirable and disturbing expression, in his portrayal of solipsism and nihilism, to the lived historical realities of atomization and the impossibility of individual action under late capitalism (Adorno).[54]

Our problem here is not so much that of trying to decide *which* of our rival accounts is "correct": it was exactly that historical fixation at the level of analytical Reason, or Aristotle's Law of the Excluded Middle, which plagued the debates of the thirties. Nor can it be a question of neatly evading the conundrum by recourse to the bland invocation of a "dialectical relationship" which—while perfectly correct—merely conjures away our inability to arrive at a satisfactorily rigorous and complete *understanding* of that relationship.

Jameson, in his crucially important article *Reification and Utopia in Mass Culture* (developing leads from the Frankfurt School), has already provided us with some of the elements for such an understanding, developing the hypothesis "that the works of mass culture cannot be ideological without at one and the same time being implicitly or explicitly Utopian as well: they cannot manipulate unless they offer some genuine shred of content as a fantasy bribe to the public about to be so manipulated."[55] There are important differences between the works of mass culture and something like *Typhoon;* but it must be obvious by

53. Georg Lukács, *The Meaning of Contemporary Realism*, trans John and Necke Mander (London: Merlin, 1963), 66.

54. Theodor Adorno, "Reconciliation under Duress," trans. Rodney Livingstone, in *Aesthetics and Politics* (London: NLB, 1977), 166.

55. Op. cit., 144.

now to what extent my own account of this short story is heavily indebted to Jameson's hypothesis and practical examples. Nevertheless it
is in Sartre's work alone, I believe, that we find the instruments truly
adequate to an account of the precise relationship between the ideological and the Utopian dimensions of literature:[56] namely, in the notion of
the "universal singular."

This notion enables us to locate the Utopian impulse in the moment of freedom, or *dépassement*, as a singular response to the problematic situation which is one "individual's" existential adventure. No
one else has demonstrated as masterfully as Sartre, in *The Family Idiot*,
this dimension of the *historical act* which this process involves—
namely, the totalization of a historical epoch in the course of a *unique*
or singular biography which is nevertheless *universal* to the extent that
it is thoroughly conditioned by its imbrication in universal history.
This moment of freedom or the Utopian impulse, however, is immediately totalized by the movement of universal history itself: the Utopian
vision of nonalienated epic action in *Typhoon*, generated by the freedom
of the writer, *becomes* ideological (although it *also* remains subversive)
because of the historical context into which it falls and is swept up. It is
the historically situated *reader* who effects the historical ideological
significance of the work in the ultimate unification of these two otherwise irreducible and distinct moments—singular totalization of the
epoch and universal historical totalization of the artist's *dépassement.*[57] It is the reader living under capitalism who—in the very instant
in which, touched in his deepest yearnings for nonalienated action, he

---

56. Obviously, the following account would have to be modified somewhat for the
cases of oral epic or cinema, for example.

57. Which is not to suggest that there are not elements of ideology which Conrad
connives at: i.e. it is not *just* a question of that nice old Captain Conrad having been taken
for a ride by horrible old History; but up to now we have been talking about Conrad *at his
best*. We have tried to explain how it is that genuine moments of subversion in *Typhoon*
can simultaneously be ideological. This is the more interesting problem.

This is also the moment to deal with a possible objection: one might be tempted—on
the basis of something like Jameson's valuable hypothesis that all class-consciousness
(even that of the ruling classes) contains Utopian elements (*The Political Unconscious*,
289–91)—to suggest that the Utopian heroism of *Typhoon* is merely a product of that
Boy's Own ethos, which was so important an ingredient of the ideology of British imperialism, and whereby the bright-faced young lads were persuaded to shoulder the White
Man's Burden. This is not convincing (for all kinds of reasons, but the following will
suffice): one has only to consider the fact that MacWhirr's heroism is *gratuitous—it serves
no end other than itself*. To descend to vulgar details, the damage incurred by the *Nan-
Shan* during the hurricane represents a greater cost than the "three hundred extra miles to
the distance, and a pretty coal bill to show" (*Typhoon*, 155) which would have been
incurred by the circumnavigation of the bad weather. A six-thousand ton steamer, the

thrills to the splendid heroism of *Typhoon*—*makes* the book into an instrument of the ideology of individualism and the centered subject.

We find a similar state of affairs at the other end of the whole process: in Conrad's relation to worked matter. The ships Conrad sailed in—those movers and carriers of British imperialism—in the very dullness and drudgery of their daily routine, in the very nature of the *praxis* they required for their functioning, dreamed—through their aristocratic and literate Polish crewmember—of heroic tempests to beguile more young Joseph Conrads onto the high seas to serve at their helms.[58] The freedom of the author is that by which he realizes and accomplishes the historical necessity of his age.

VII

If the above serves as some kind of account of the relationship between freedom and historical necessity, or the ideological and the Utopian, in great literature, we might round it off with some remarks about the complexity of our reactions to such works.

One might begin by taking up some of the ideas developed by Jameson in the course of his fruitful extension and development of Lukács's own use of the Weberian notion of *rationalization:*

> . . . (that) dynamic . . . in which the traditional or "natural" . . . unities, social forms, human relations, cultural events, even religious systems, are systematically broken up in order to be reconstructed more efficiently, in the form of new post-natural processes or mechanisms; but in which, at the same time, these now isolated broken bits and pieces of the older unities acquire a certain autonomy of their own, a semi-autonomous coherence which, not merely a reflex of capitalist

China Sea, a hurricane, the commerce of the British Empire itself are brought into being solely in order to defy history.

Yes, *Typhoon* has its origins in the *Boy's Own* ethos, it draws on it, perhaps (it certainly exploits its readership); but solely in order to transcend that ethos towards something incomparably finer.

This is Conrad's freedom. We alienate him still further if we reduce this to class-consciousness or ideology.

58. See Sartre's brilliant analysis of the origins of sexual reverie in the female operators of semi-automatic machinery in the last century, in which he shows that this phenomenon is the product of the particular kind of semi-concentration which the machine requires for its efficient operation (*Critique de la raison dialectique*, 290–91).

One should add that proletarian representations of life at sea—I am indebted here to Ken Worpole's recent article "Expressionism and Working-Class Fiction" (*New Left Review*, 130) on the novels of Garrett, Hanley and Phelan—suggest that these heroic phantasies were available to and entertainable only by the occupants of the bridge, and not the stokehold.

reification and rationalization, also in some measure serves to compensate for the dehumanization of experience reification brings with it, and to rectify the otherwise intolerable effects of the new process.[59]

Jameson immediately goes on to make use of the notion in a brilliant demonstration of the historically novel "autonomization" of the senses which is one manifestation of this process; but perhaps an earthier example will serve our purposes here: at the level of the capitalist processing of raw materials—in particular, food. A familiar example to those living in the "advanced" industrial countries is that wheat is now processed into nutritionally useless and harmful white flour, which dominates the vast bulk of the products of the bakery industries, while a considerable proportion of the nutritious wheat germ is either sold as such in expensive Health Food Shops, or as costly vitamin B medication, which subsidiary industries feed parasitically on the health hazards generated by the rationalization and fragmentation of the original raw material. It is not difficult to see the parallel with cultural production. I should immediately add, it is not a question of drawing *analogies*, of that "adjacentism" which Adorno detected in so much of Benjamin's work. Exactly the *same* process obtains. It is reification and alienation which give rise to those very Utopian phantasies of real action in *Typhoon* which will simultaneously serve ideological ends; this is what is truly infernal about capitalism: that the most profound and healthful of our yearnings, essentially capitalism's wasteproducts, are in turn retrieved by the historical temporalization to become the means of our further enslavement, contributing to the reproduction of the original pathology. This is the measure of our historical condition: that a masterpiece like *Typhoon*—contestatory and Utopian in so many of its demands and longings, splendent with freedom—may actively contribute to our bondage. We seem to be driven to an increasingly internecine experience of simultaneously revering and loathing great art: an experience which is as unmanageable and contradictory as it is itself a product of alienation.

It behooves us to face this experience squarely, and achieve at least the minimal mastery to be had from complete description. A particularly disturbing example in *Typhoon* would be the whole question of the "coolies." It is MacWhirr's insistence that Jukes reestablish order among the rampaging Chinamen in the forward hold which enables Jukes to maintain a grip on himself, and which implicitly has a part in the defeat of the hurricane. The eminently imperialist, racist, ideologi-

59. Jameson, *The Political Unconscious*, 62–63.

cal message generated by these protometaphorical or quasi-allegorical resonances is clear: keep a firm grip on your lower orders (or the Third World) and Nature will be mastered by the men on the bridge; on this condition the industrialization of the planet and triumph of the Human Thing, or commodity production, will be achieved.

On this reading, then, MacWhirr is one of the earliest forebears of that long line of figures which culminates in the likes of John Wayne: valiant cowboy wins the hand of white woman in the course of slaughtering a hundred Indian "attackers"/courageous British seaman becomes existential hero on the backs of two hundred Chinamen.

So much for the beauty of *Typhoon*. So much for our "masterpiece," it would seem. But, no, this is *not* where we should conclude; although all of the above is true. For MacWhirr's achievement remains all that we have described it, earlier, as being. And it is not, either, a question of the real beauty of the tale *redeeming* its racism. Racism is irredeemable. Simply, the Utopian or epic dimension of the story is not only incontestable but the indispensable gilding of the ideological pill; and the gilding *is* fine. But, we enjoy it *guiltily*. Those who *can* enjoy it; and it may well be that one has to be white, middleclass, Anglo-Saxon, and perhaps even male, to do so. Certainly, one cannot insist that a Chinaman be alive to the beauties of *Typhoon*.

But there should be nothing particularly surprising in this. Our finding *Typhoon* beautiful is no more scandalous, in these terms, than our reaction to, say, *King Lear*. While kingship is certainly no longer as politically hot an issue as racism is for us today, is it not true that much of the vastness and grandeur of that play—and hence the tragic pain and the *beauty* of that tragic pain—is dependent upon one's collusion with the fact that Lear is a *king* (notwithstanding the deeply critical investigation by Shakespeare not only of Lear himself but of all forms of institutional power)? One might add that there is a further ironic twist to this phenomenon, insofar as the Elizabethans' reaction to Lear's tragedy—no doubt as contradictory and ambivalent as Shakespeare's—would nonetheless have involved an element of quasi-religious horror at the sacrilege of *lèse-majesté*; while our own reaction is fatally compounded by the nostalgia of a bourgeois age for the earlier social formation or *gemeinshaft* (mythological or otherwise) we have dissolved. We are condemned to a disturbingly ambivalent, guilty consumption of the vast bulk of great literature. As we know, this is an inevitable experience in class societies: as one of the characters in Simone de Beauvoir's *Les Mandarins* puts it, "In curved space you cannot shoot straight."

VIII

At last we can move, as promised, from the nitty-gritty of textual analysis to the clearer air of the formal theoretical differences separating Jameson's three concentric frameworks and Sartre's "hierarchy of significations" outlined in *Questions of Method*. If Jameson has born the brunt of my criticisms here it is because, more than anyone else, he comes closest to the practical realization of the methodological ideal set out in the latter work. I have sometimes felt that my objections have risked appearing carping—for example, I have been constrained, for reasons of space and the sheer complexity of the issues involved, to restrict myself to the single and relatively minor case of Jameson's account of *Typhoon* (I believe that a similar case could be made for his lengthier analysis of *Lord Jim*); besides which, my criticisms of Jameson have been as much a jumping-off point for the elaboration of a Sartrean account of one literary text as a self-justifying exercise in its own right. But I hope that what is at stake will be clear by now: the most important single point made by Sartre, in the course of that difficult and densely written methodological blueprint for the study of Flaubert, was that *each signification is irreducible to the others:* that, for example, *Madame Bovary* (or *Typhoon*) is enveloped and conditioned through and through by the evolution of capitalism and phenomena like reification and rationalization; but that these works are *richer* than the significations or frameworks which envelop them. Now, Jameson knows this as well as anyone else.[60] But his critical practice often belies such knowledge. This is partly the unfortunate result of an excellent pedagogic or expository intention discernable in the layout of his book— the decision to illustrate his three concentric frameworks by the works of three different authors (Balzac, Gissing and Conrad) in three separate chapters. The result is an inevitable blurring of the essential heterogeneity between the three frameworks *within* the overarching historical temporalization of which they form distinct if heteronomous moments. Besides which, there is the omission—whether methodologically principled or imposed by the exigencies of writing a book in which there could be little room for consideration of the "strictly biographical," I cannot say—of that existential dimension of freedom (a fourth concentric framework, if one likes). A dimension which I have tried to restore, and the indispensability of which to any materialist

60. See, for example, *The Political Unconscious*, 225–26.

account of Beauty or the Utopian I have tried to demonstrate.[61] Is it not, in the case of Jameson's account of *Typhoon*, the restriction of the discussion of one author to the limits of a single framework or signification—in this instance, the capitalist mode of production and its attendant reification and rationalization—which inevitably maneuvers Jameson into the failure to theorize the notions of "response" and "transformation," which do appear in his argument, in terms which go beyond a recourse to a debasing, merely contingent (ultimately reifying!) biological *soma* which is contained within the notion of the *libidinal*? I say "maneuvers" because there is evidence everywhere in Jameson's work as a whole that he is far from subscribing to the classic reductionisms of an older period of orthodox Marxism, or Freudianism. (In fact, it would be deeply unjust to make these objections without simultaneously recognizing the incomparable rôle which Jameson is playing in the constitution of a vital and wonderfully flexible, free-ranging Marxist criticism whose impact, if its historical influence is on a par with its excellence, should be considerable.) So that it would seem to be the failure to oscillate *between* his three frameworks—a possibility foreclosed in *practice*, if not in theory, by the choice of three different authors as his objects of analysis—which I see as the primary cause of this tendency to reductionism. A tendency which Sartre taught us to avoid by the constant to and fro, backwards and forwards movement between the different significations of his hierarchy in a "progressive-regressive method" which never reduced any one signification to any of the others, and yet which remained faithful to their intimate reciprocal conditioning.

Finally, the absence of a problematic of freedom in Jameson's *The Political Unconscious* (so strange, given its implicit presence in the article *Reification and Utopia in Mass Culture*), gives rise to an overall *tone* to the work (of course, he is not alone in this, and it is curious given

61. In this respect I have attempted to take up and vindicate Jameson's speculations, quoted earlier (p. 22), about the possibilities still to be exploited in the earlier work of Sartre; although his dismissive remarks about the "shortlived classical period of Sartrean existentialism . . . etc." (see above, p. 39) might lead one to suppose that his speculations were not intended to be pushed as far as I have taken them. There is nothing to prevent us, however, from endorsing these remarks as long as one makes the proviso that the early existentialist hermeneutic was ideological *only insofar as it was presented as an autonomous and complete method of analysis*, or final cut-off point. Once it is incorporated into the historical temporalization within the absolute horizon of Marxism as a subsidiary moment (*even though* the existential lived, freedom itself, remains itself an irreducible absolute)—as I have tried to show here—there should be no problem. I can conceive of no other way of the uncompleted fourth volume of *The Family Idiot* being written, for example.

his final chapter which makes essentially the same plea I am about to make) which I can only describe, at the risk of sounding both sententious and dreadfully old-fashioned, as *disrespectful*, unjust even, towards literature. Now, it is true, it has been one of the major contributions of Marxist criticism (and structuralism and its variants) to be *distinctly* disrespectful towards literature—pushing it around, demystifying it, forcing it to make all kinds of nasty and rude noises, demoting established canons in favor of brash new unrespectable ones, and so on. This tendency has been a necessary moment in the dispelling of illusory sacrosanct halos in the interests of historical truth and the dismantling of forms of ruling-class hegemony; but the moment has come to correct the balance *in the interests of those self-same objectives which the above negative or critical attitude set out to serve.* The critical authority, the power and scope, the fidelity to the complexity of historical truth of Marxist criticism would all be considerably enhanced by the mobilization of analytic procedures capable of recognizing authentic moments of freedom in even the most reactionary of great works of literature. Of course, this dimension, this attention to the complexity of the dialectic has always been present in the work of the finest practitioners: from Lenin's articles on Tolstoy and Trotsky's account of Dante, through Lukács on Balzac, Adorno on modernism, down to Marcuse's *The Aesthetic Dimension* and Jameson on the Utopian elements in mass culture, some notion of freedom in artistic production has always been *implicit;* but, outside of Sartre's work, no *theory* of freedom (which is also *necessarily* a theory of historical conditioning) really exists. It is Sartre's "universal singular" which, to date, has provided us with the most precise theoretical instrument for the detection and description of these dialectical ambivalences in such a way as to do justice to them.

It would be a mistake, however, to see the implications of Sartre's work as being restricted to a purely literary domain. As is well-known, Marxism and the Left as a whole have, historically, always had to maneuver between the Scylla and Charybdis of "economism" and "voluntarism," as is borne out, for example, by the differences in theory and practice between the Second and Third Internationals. The theoretical oscillations between these two alternative emphases have generally been a function of the perceived possibilities in the contemporary political conjuncture of socialist revolutions in the West: thus ranging from Rosa Luxembourg in post-First World War Germany to the darkly pessimistic visions of "total systems" implied by the work of Althusser or Foucault in contemporary France. Bourgeois ideology itself bears the mark of these oscillations (significantly in direct inverted dialectical relation to the shifts of emphasis on the Left, which itself points to the absence of theoretical mastery among the latter)—invoking a discourse of "freedom" in periods of prosperity and relative working-class docility, and a "realistic" submission to "natural economic laws" in periods of economic crisis and political unrest. We can be sure that Marxists will continue for a long while yet to be confronted by the contradictory imperatives generated by these varying emphases, both at the level of theory and practice; and it would be naïve to imagine that these problems can be whisked away by the waving of a theoretical wand: the historical conjuncture, as always, will continue to impose on us the same perennial difficult alternatives and choices; but, whatever the failings of the second volume of the *Critique of Dialectical Reason*, the first volume alone—especially with regard to its attempt to articulate the relations between freedom and necessity in a dialectic of reciprocal interaction which goes beyond the artificial antinomy of these notions which has so often plagued Marxism up to now—has far-reaching, "revolutionary" even, to use that much-abused term, implications at the political level; and, if given the serious attention it has largely lacked, should come to have lasting consequences for revolutionary theory and practice, affording us at the very least the minimal mastery to be afforded by theoretical understanding. Which is not to suggest that Sartre provides us with some universal panacea: full of unexplored potential as it may be, the *Critique* itself contains no *solutions* as such; rather, we have the first rigorous and as yet most complete exploration of the problem of how to *talk* about this intransigent problem of the place of freedom in history (*the* problem, surely, to which Marxists or revolutionaries, whatever their ilk, should be addressing themselves); besides which, Sartre, no less than anyone else, was of his age: the *Critique* was written a quarter of a century ago, and we already live in a world which has undergone major changes. Theoretically, however, we have not even advanced to where Sartre was in the late fifties. It is time to catch up!

Part II

HOWARD DAVIES

Les Mots as *Essai sur le Don:*
Contribution to an Origin Myth

Both Marshall Sahlins[1] (in passing) and Jeffrey Mehlman[2] (in detail) have recalled that on the threshold of his career Lévi-Strauss chose to view his predecessor, Marcel Mauss, as "Moses leading his people towards a promised land, the splendor of which he would never witness."[3] It is appropriate that structuralist anthropology, which teaches us not to look for origins but to see evocations of the past as expressions of the present, should provide itself with such a potent origin myth. *Les Mots*, in which Moses also makes an appearance, resembles the "Introduction à l'oeuvre de Marcel Mauss," in that it assigns origins great force but does so polemically. I want to suggest here that Sartre's autobiography appropriates some of the objects of study central to the European anthropological tradition—notably, exogamy, rites of possession and the gift—in order to establish a context favorable to the autobiographer's liberation from the familial and from the psychologistic.

As the name of Freud also appears in what follows, it is worth making clear that my intention is not to submit *Les Mots* to psychoanalytic investigation. Much has been written on this[4] and it is not an area in which I wish to linger. Instead, I propose to remain primarily in the zone of intertextuality which may be said to be anthropological. Sartre's psychology is relevant only inasmuch as his attitude to the

1. M. Sahlins, *Stone Age Economics* (London: Tavistock, 1974), 154.

2. J. Mehlman, *A Structural Study of Autobiography* (Ithaca: Cornell University Press, 1974), 210.

3. C. Lévi-Strauss, "Introduction à l'oeuvre de Marcel Mauss," in M. Mauss, *Sociologie et anthropologie* (Paris: PUF, 1950). xxxvii. All translations, unless otherwise indicated, are my own.

4. For example: A. J. Arnold and J.-P. Piriou, *Genèse et critique d'une autobiographie: "Les Mots" de Jean-Paul Sartre, Archives des lettres modernes*, no. 144, 1973, and J. Pacaly, *Sartre au miroir* (Paris: Klincksieck, 1980).

intextextual is one of apparent intolerance, so much so that his own autobiography, like others in which he displayed great interest (that of André Gorz, for example), might be represented as a desired progression from a collection of voices to the unity of a single speaker, from chorus to hero.

In order to be able to proceed by allusion and association and to facilitate reception of what is at first sight extraneous material, I intend to make only infrequent reference to other texts by Sartre. Marcel Mauss, after all, is hardly mentioned in the works published by Sartre prior to his death in 1980; only in the posthumous *Cahiers pour une morale*[5] is a debt made explicit—and I hope that my discussion of *Les Mots* will clarify the context and the motivation of this reference. Indeed, what is particularly interesting in the autobiography is that the rigorous use of the Sartrean conceptual apparatus(es) is suspended. In this existential self-analysis there is no explicit designation of a *projet fondamental*. In what clearly anticipates "Questions de méthode" and *L'Idiot de la famille* there is no formal procedure of regression and progression. The Jaspersian distinction which underpins Sartre's methodology throughout his career—that between *Erklären* (explication, explanation) and *Verstehen* (compréhension, comprehension)—loses nothing of its importance but much of its visibility.

I shall dwell briefly on this last distinction, because while naïve expectations might well allow the autobiographer licence to invoke causal factors and to relive empathetically the experiences of a former self, a Sartrean reader—committed, that is, to fulfilling the literary contract proposed in *Qu'est-ce que la littérature?* or to answering the *appel* theorized in the *Cahiers*—is likely to wish to espouse the movement of *Verstehen* rather than to hypostatize in moments of *Erklären*. Hence, therefore, a need to reconstruct the Sartrean text rather than to deconstruct it, crediting its writer with considerable understanding of the forever provisional and partial success enjoyed by those seeking to present themselves as unified subjects. My own project is to retell his founding fiction and to remotivate it, in a mode that is best described as *compréhension avec les moyens du bord* [understanding by the means at hand] and in a manner that does not set out to diminish the power of his reflexivity. My contention is that once the Sartrean theoretical apparatus is put into abeyance, the words of *Les Mots* are allowed to display the extent to which they derive from elsewhere. At the level of the narrated, the writer shows how the great author emerged from the *je*

---

5. (Paris: Gallimard, 1983); see in particular 382–95.

designated by others as Jean-Paul Sartre. This he does in order that his origins in the words of others might be located, thus facilitating an eventual exorcism and a redemption from discursive polymorphism.

But what of the *moyens du bord* mobilized at the level of the process of narration and offered as emblems of reciprocity to the reader? Sartre's project of self-definition seems to involve, if we are to read it and understand it, relating the story of those who gave him his identity and who haunt him still, such that he need no longer relate to them. He would require, in this case, notions of *hantise* [haunting] and *don* [gift]; both are readily available—prominent, indeed—in the French anthropological tradition and await utilization. I hope to show, therefore, that the absence of theory is more apparent than real, and that this is consistent with the main burden of *Les Mots*, namely, that the absence of verbal and intellectual progenitors is likewise illusory. At the same time, the authorities invoked obliquely and allusively by Sartre promote his liberation by being caught up in what I would like to call a limited democratization of the intertext. At the level of the narrated, the *géniteurs* [begetters] are sacrificed; at the level of the narration, they are invited to embrace the status of *congénères* [congenerics].

Discussion of *Les Mots* in terms of *hantise* and *don*, and in terms therefore of its transactions with anthropological texts, requires a development of digressive aspect in which other names are mentioned, not anecdotally, but by way of identification of some of the participants in the possessions and exchanges. There is no reason why Moses should not continue to play his part, since what is proposed here is a sort of *mosaic* in the triple sense of the term—a patterned distribution of voices, arbitrarily heard but, by process of cross-fertilization, coalescing into verbal authority.

For all may be said to begin with him. It is often forgotten by commentators on Sartre's attitude to Freud that in May 1949 *Les Temps Modernes* published substantial extracts from the latter's *Moses and Monotheism*. This event might be construed as a contribution to the understanding of antisemitism, since this project had and has always been one of the most consistent features of the review. The accompanying note of introduction, signed *TM*, reveals otherwise. It rehearses the integration of psychoanalysis to what was then existentialism, a procedure with which readers of Sartre are familiar:

> As is always the case, it is legitimate to think that several of Freud's interpretations are narrow. Instead of *explaining* human conflict by sexual conflict, we could consider hatred of the father in the broader terms of human aggressivity. Simone de Beauvoir's essay in this same

number [extracts from *Le Deuxième Sexe*] shows precisely in certain respects how sexuality is part and parcel of human conflicts which do not transcend it but which, so to speak, give it its force. It must be said, however, that these very considerations were not unknown to Freud and that, in any case, they have been rendered possible only by his work—to which, by publishing these texts, we wish to pay homage.[6]

Let us remember that about the same time Simone de Beauvoir produced a similarly recuperative response (but one displaying even greater goodwill) to *Les Structures élémentaires de la parenté* of Lévi-Strauss.[7] The latter had in turn integrated *Totem and Taboo*, as origin myth, into the ethnographer's object of study, thus resisting Freud's attempt to psychologize anthropology. It is out of such interactions as these that the mosaic of *Les Mots* is built—and for this reason it is worth following Moses where he leads.

In *La Vieillesse*, Simone de Beauvoir comments on Freud's later years and remarks that "his *Moses*, a sequel to *Totem and Taboo* which had been written twenty-five years earlier, seemed to him more or less a rehash."[8] This, however, is a very free paraphrase of Freud's own commentary and misleads considerably. In fact, *Moses and Monotheism* brings Freud much closer than does *Totem and Taboo* to an analysis of the religion of his own community and of the beliefs to which he chose not to subscribe. It reveals, moreover, a degree of inhibition in which Sartre and Beauvoir should really have been interested. One might say of Freud what Lévi-Strauss said of Mauss: "at the most crucial moment [he] thus falls prey to hesitation and to scruple."[9] Just as Mauss failed to appreciate fully the implications of his sociology and its proximity to structuralist milk and honey, so Freud failed, publicly at least, to address himself to his own problematic relationship with Moses.

"I have not been able to efface the traces of the unusual way in which this book came to be written," said Freud: "it haunted me like an unlaid ghost."[10] The first two parts of *Moses and Monotheism* (the discussion of the nationality of Moses) were published not merely in advance of Part 3 (the psychoanalytic account of monotheism) but as a compromise with his reluctance to publish the whole. As he traces the history of monotheism, Freud experiences inhibitions which, observed in Hamlet or in Leonardo, would have been placed at the forefront of his

6. *Les Temps Modernes*, vol. 3, no. 32, May 1948, 1996.
7. Idem, vol. 5, no. 49, November 1949, 943–49.
8. S. de Beauvoir, *La Vieillesse* (Paris: Gallimard, 1970), 551.
9. C. Lévi-Strauss, op cit., xxxix.
10. S. Freud, *Moses and Monotheism* (London: Hogarth Press, 1939), 164.

investigations. It is true that publication was delayed for tactical reasons (his unwillingness to expose psychoanalysis to further attack), but these seem secondary if one accepts the full recursive possibilities of the text: Moses and his monotheism, both murdered in private by an Oedipal hero who shrinks from publication of the deed. Only after the crime has already been committed by another agency (Nazi invasion of Austria, persecution of the Jews and defeat of the antifascist Austrian Catholic church), does Freud release his text—from England and fearful of the reactions of his hosts.

It remains to be seen whether Sartre's scenario for the John Huston film *Freud: the Secret Passion* constitutes an existential psychoanalysis of the founder of psychoanalysis. As far as the response of *Les Temps Modernes* to *Moses and Monotheism* is concerned, it is disappointing. Given that the phenomenological ontology wished to incorporate elements of Freudian theory, it might well have designated as *projet fondamental* a prior identification with Oedipus, declaring psychoanalysis, in the manner of Lévi-Strauss's treatment of *Totem and Taboo*, to be a self-fulfilling prophecy with only a limited claim to the generalization of its findings. In the name of the *anthropologie synthétique*,[11] it should really have demanded of Freud maximum reflexivity. This, after all, is the Sartrean criterion which makes of *Les Mots* a work far more ambitious than *Moses and Monotheism*, for it is the latter which is more inhibited and which fails to lay its ghosts. The fact that this type of incorporation (incorporation by reduction) does not take place suggests that another tactic is used by Sartre. It seems to be the case that the Freudian anthropology is allowed to enter the intertextual space of *Les Temps Modernes* in order that it might subsequently be the object of the movements of expulsion undertaken in *Les Mots*.

In this connection, it is worth noting that Freud's Moses—"an Egyptian whom a people needed to make into a Jew"[12]—resembles Lévi-Strauss's *shaman*[13] as well as Sartre's Genet.[14] Not only does he resemble them, but in *Les Temps Modernes* he is their contemporary. All three are deviants or outsiders elected by a community to embody, in one way or another, its aspirations and its anxieties. The following assertion is of relevance here:

11. Cf. *"Présentation des Temps Modernes,"* Les Temps Modernes, vol. 1, no. 1, October 1945.

12. S. Freud, op. cit., 29.

13. C. Lévi-Strauss, "Le Sorcier et sa magie," Les Temps Modernes, vol. 4, no. 41, March 1949, and in *Anthropologie structurale* (Paris: Plon, 1958).

14. J.-P. Sartre, "Jean Genet," Les Temps Modernes, vol. 6, nos. 57–62, July–December 1950, and in *Saint Genet* (Paris: Gallimard, 1952).

Any given society is thus comparable to a universe in which only discrete masses are highly structured. In every society, therefore, it is inevitable that a variable percentage of individuals find themselves placed, so to speak, outside the system or between several systems which are irreducible to each other. These individuals are required, and even forced, by the group to embody certain forms of compromise which are not open to collective realization, to feign imaginary transitions and to personify incompatible syntheses.[15]

This quotation is a rewriting by Lévi-Strauss of Mauss's observation that acts of magic have to be sustained by the community at large: "Behind Moses when he touches the rock stands all of Israel and, if Moses's conviction wavers, that of Israel does not."[16] It is striking that when Lévi-Strauss comes into line with Mauss he is similarly in agreement with Sartre; the latter *quotes his formulation in full* in *Saint Genet*[17] and accords it total authority.

The young Sartre of *Les Mots* is marked by a microsocial equivalence with Moses, the *shaman* and Genet. Marginalized in a context of incompatible ideological systems (Catholicism and Protestantism, for example, or skepticism and mysticism, or "high" culture and "low" culture), he is at the same time, and more importantly, gradually drawn as a key participant into a closed system of exchange. We shall see that the autobiography taps the Maussian corpus much less as an outline of a general theory of magic, and much more as an essay on the gift.

Not for long, however, do Mauss, Lévi-Strauss and Sartre constitute a consensus. True, the Mauss endorsed in the *Cahiers* is reintroduced into circulation and revalued, as it were, by Lévi-Strauss at a time when existentialism and embryonic structuralism still live in peaceful coexistence. The composition of *Les Mots*, on the other hand, postdates the complicity so hopefully announced by Simone de Beauvoir. Between the two events comes the polarization of the Lévi-Straussian and Sartrean points of view, again in *Les Temps Modernes*, by Claude Lefort.[18] *Les Mots* is a polemical *essai sur le don* in the sense that it sharpens the differences between the phenomenological and the structuralist. One might say, in anticipation, that Sartre uses Lévi-Strauss against Freud at the same time as he uses Mauss against both Freud and Lévi-Strauss.

15. C. Lévi-Strauss, "Introduction à l'oeuvre de Marcel Mauss," op. cit., xx.
16. M. Mauss, op. cit., 124.
17. J.-P. Sartre, *Saint Genet, op. cit.*, 58–59.
18. C. Lefort, "L'Echange et la lutte des hommes," *Les Temps Modernes*, vol 6, no. 64, February 1951.

One final point, before examining *Les Mots* in some detail, makes it clear why it is productive to persist with Freud's figure of speech and to consider intertextuality as *hantise*. Both Lévi-Strauss and Sartre, in the texts already mentioned, show great respect for the antipositivist ethnographer Michel Leiris. Indeed, Sartre, to a degree much too high to be documented here, allows himself to be possessed by the Ethiopian *zar*, the spirits encountered by Leiris in *L'Afrique fantôme*.[19] These occult agencies (together with the Haitian *loa* of Alfred Métraux), whose beneficence is expressed in their ability to maximize ethnographic reflexivity, are later mobilized in the struggle against colonialism. In *Les Mots* they are present in the chorus, active parties to the labor of what might be called disallusion and dispossession, available to be visited upon whomever Sartre seeks to exorcise.

Sartre's declaration, in *Les Mots*, that absence of father was equivalent to absence of superego and to absence of obedience and aggression, is well-known. Consideration of the anthropological intertext suggests that his ability to cancel paternal antecedence is erroneously construed as liberation precisely because it lacks a Maussian understanding of itself as a transaction in an ongoing cycle of exchange. In the discussion that follows, I shall endeavor to represent *Les Mots* as an anti-Freudian gesture that gains substance only when a sociological perspective is developed to counter the psychologistic. Ultimately, however, it will be philosophy that delivers the final blow.

Let us note first of all that the family romance, from which father so obligingly absents himself, occupies a social space considerably larger than the failed nuclear family of which Sartre would have been the son. "L'insolent trépas de mon père" ["But my father's insolent decease"][20] is not a prime cause but an untoward incident in the genealogy of a primal horde. For what is actually instituted by an unnamed "instituteur accablé d'enfants" ["a schoolteacher with more children than he could afford"] (3) is a parody of Freudian Darwinism, an ironic celebration of the birth of a community. Rather than one patriarch, whose old age and murder will usher in regimes of exogamy based on deferred obedience, we are offered two lusty old-timers, apparently irrepressible, whose joint supremacies mark out the endogamic horizons of their grandchild. In particular, the spotlight falls on Charles Schweitzer, who

19. Michel Leiris, *L'Afrique fantôme* (Paris: Gallimard, 1934).
20. J.-P. Sartre, *Les Mots* (Paris: Gallimard, 1964), 9. English translation, *The Words*, trans. Bernard Frechtman (New York: George Braziller, 1964), 17. All subsequent quotations are from these editions, and will be indicated in the text.

monopolizes his daughter and "se plaît à emmerder ses fils . . . ce père terrible a passé sa vie à les écraser" (20). ["takes pleasure in being a pain in the ass to his sons. That terrible father has spent his life crushing them" (30).]

The history of such a deviant primal horde effectively subverts the phylogenetic model supplied by *Totem and Taboo* and by *Moses and Monotheism*. Indeed, in the famous footnote (41), Sartre aligns himself with the position that emerges in *Les Structures élémentaires de la parenté*, namely, that it is the incest prohibition that preexists desire rather than vice versa. He thus gives himself as origin myth a narrative which undermines the story proposed by Freud.

At the same time, the ironic *incipit* of *Les Mots* is much too hasty when it celebrates what is later described as the "absence du rude Moïse qui m'avait engendré" (91) ["the absence of the stern Moses who had begotten me" (112).] Quite simply, Moses is wrongly identified. Elimination of the intervening generation by the rampant patriarch in no way creates a power vacuum. When literature is at issue, that is to say something about which Charles Schweitzer cares particularly strongly, then grandfather on mother's side becomes father figure: "pour la première fois, j'eus affaire au patriarche . . . c'était Moïse dictant la loi nouvelle" (131). ["For the first time, I was dealing with the patriarch. . . . He was Moses dictating the new law." (158).]

It is true that when the profession of writer is equivocally stripped of its glamor by grandfather, the prohibition is delivered so ambiguously that the grandson is impelled into that which is prohibited. Nevertheless, the case of mistaken identity represents the revenge of Freud and the return of the repressed. With one disillusion, however, comes another; Sartre has to realize that the perception of mother as sister makes of him not a grandchild but another son. The primal horde is stood once again on its feet. If Sartre does not share the fate of all the other second generation males, it can only be because he is the favored youngest son, he who has greatest access to maternal love, precisely because he arrives when paternal wrath is on the wane.

But however benign the regime has become, the obligation of parricide is not obviated. This, one might say, constitutes the necessity of *Les Mots*. The dual elimination of Freudianism and of father figure has only been apparently successful; it is when the dead prove not to be dead at all that the exorcism must go on. "On m'a cousu mes commandements sous la peau," says Sartre (136) ["My commandments were sewn into my skin" (164)], reminding us that his perception of parenthood has always been associated with visitations and rituals of possession. The preface to Gorz's *Le Traître*, in which children are clothed forcibly in the skins of their ancestors, is perhaps the most succinct example. *Les Mots*, for its part, provides ample corroboration; the child is motivated by the projects and the spirits of its parents, such that when he finds expression it is as a modulation of the already articulated. It is this work of reanimation that has to be undone if ever an original eloquence is to be heard.

L'Etre et le néant gives considerable space to possession, yet it is only in the postwar period that French ethnography makes its presence felt in the language of Sartre. The figure that enters the mosaic at this point is that of the horse rider. It makes its most vivid appearance beside the parental piano: "Comme un tambour vaudou, le piano m'imposait son rythme . . . j'étais possédé . . . A cheval! J'étais cavale et cavalier; chevauchant et chevauché . . . " (103–04) ["The piano forced its rhythm on me like a voodoo drum. . . . I was possessed. . . . To horse! I was mare and rider, bestrider and bestridden . . ." (126).] Both the *zar* of Leiris and the *loa* of Métraux haunt the intertext by virtue of haunting *Les Temps Modernes;*[21] both effect equestrian possession and make their own contribution to the famous Sartrean designation of fathers—"ces géniteurs invisibles à cheval sur leurs fils pour toute la vie" (11) ["these invisible begetters who bestraddle their sons all their life long" (19).] This particular primal horde seems almost to conduct its business in a hippodrome. The patriarch has a marked taste for "écuyères" (4) and considerably more staying power than the next generation. Jean-Baptiste Sartre, for example, that "parasite sacré" (13) who, had he lived, "m'eût habité" (70), ran only the briefest of races—"fit un enfant au galop, moi, et tenta de se réfugier dans la mort" (8).

It is relatively easy to move from echoes of Leiris and of Métraux to echoes of Mauss. Sartre makes the correlation quite explicit: as well as "cavale et cavalier" he is also "donateur et donation" (22). The correlation is that of, on the one hand, the reality of the power relations and, on the other, the apparent absence of constraint. This primal horde is based on a network of transactions which allow it to be offered not only as a counterexample to *Totem and Taboo* but also as evidence supporting Mauss's contentions in his *Essai sur le don*. In particular, it exemplifies "the voluntary character, so to speak, of these prestations, apparently free and gratuitous yet constrained and not at all disinterested."[22] It is a regime in which possession is perceived as gift.

21. Michel Leiris was an editor of the review in the immediate postwar years; Alfred Métraux made contributions in February 1950 and in June 1957. Cf. also J. Pouillon, "Vaudou, zâr et possession," *Les Temps Modernes*, vol. 14, no. 156/7, February/March 1959.

22. M. Mauss, op. cit., 147.

It is true that the continued dominance of the ageing patriarch has preserved endogamy and that there is little scope for external exchange. This does not mean, however, that the domestic business cycle is any the less active for all that. The conjugal life of the grandparents is represented as "une suite infinie de sacrifices" (8) ["it was an infinite succession of sacrifices" (16)], into which is reincorporated the briefly exogamic Anne-Marie, "glacée de reconnaissance" (9–10) ["chilled with gratitude" (17)], whose withdrawal from outside circulation is merely transfer from one economy into another. Sartre is keenly interested in the system of prestations that bind together the members of this small community, for it offers him the chance to chart their interaction in terms of a phenomenology of giving.

Mauss had shown that at the level of the gift social interaction presupposed the coordination of three distinct obligations: to give, to receive and to give in return. He drew attention at the same time to the necessarily public dimension of these transactions. The Schweitzer-Sartre family corroborates his assertions. Attitudes, postures, expressions and gestures pass from person to person (and particularly between grandfather and grandson) such that peaceful coexistence is assured by the recognition, by all, of the apparent autonomy of each. Each, on the other hand, is constrained by the expectations of the others and responses rapidly become ritualized: "notre vie n'est qu'une suite de cérémonies et nous consumons notre temps à nous accabler d'hommages" (23)["No matter: our life is only a succession of ceremonies, and we spend our time showering each other with tribute" (32–33).]

The spirit of Mauss, it seems, is invoked for the sake of confirming something previously intimated by the phenomenological ontology—that generosity tends to carry a negative moral value and cannot automatically institute interactions characterized by the positive value of reciprocity. As has already been indicated, Sartre is prepared to endorse Lévi-Strauss against Freud, but he is not prepared to allow him to appropriate Mauss's *Essai sur le don;* it is a possession that is contested. *Les Mots* does not seek to represent generosity as the organizational principle of an egalitarian social group, a principle operating in the unconscious and finding expression, as a total social fact, at all levels of social reality; instead, generosity is a course of action with certain ideological antecedents, one chosen in concrete situations which are contingent in that they might have been other than they are (had the biological father, for example, not been absent).

When Sartre refers to the institutionalized "débauche de générosité" (22)["What a riot of generosity" (32)] binding grandfather to grandson, he is not exactly describing potlatch, for the objects given and received are not necessarily destroyed. There is, on the other hand, limited destruction of the recipient. The transactions between feudal lord and the privileged serf destined to succeed him (for feudalism is the regime most characterized by patronage and by generosity) give both parties the chance to deploy their affective-economic power and to survive possession by the other. This is much more the Mauss of Lefort than of Lévi-Strauss and much more consistent with the ontology. To be generous is to give in order to possess the person to whom the gift is given; it is to saddle the recipient with something that is held to be intolerable—subordination. Every donation is an assertion of power; every reception is the recognition of temporary inferiority. An agonistic cycle is set up but it is not at all a system of eternal recurrence; the balance of power changes through time and according to tactical and circumstantial considerations. Purpose and constraint continually call each other into existence.

The problem experienced by the child Sartre is that he does not enjoy the status of agent to the same extent as others in the system. As "don gratuit et toujours révocable" (15) ["as a gratuitous and always revocable gift" (23)], "don providentiel" (78) ["a gift of providence" (96)], "don du ciel" (91) ["a gift from heaven" (112)], "don de la Providence" (92) ["a gift of Providence" (113)], he enters the cycle initially as a commodity rather than as a dealer. He is given to, or appropriated by, the grandfather. He is a miracle child (another Moses) called upon to bear witness to the marvels of life in the context of the patriarch's laborious progress towards the grave. But such imposed passivity (which in other cases—the young Flaubert, for example—might have been assumed by choice) here impels a movement of self-preservation which makes of the gift a giver. Even this, however, is to adopt the mode of defense appropriate to and dictated by the nature of the attack. It is to react "dans l'orgueil et le sadisme, autrement dit dans la générosité. Celle-ci, comme l'avarice ou le racisme, n'est qu'un baume sécrété pour guérir nos plaies intérieures et qui finit par nous empoisonner" (92) ["into pride and sadism, in other words, into generosity, which, like avarice or race prejudice, is only a secret balm for healing our inner wounds and which ends by poisoning us" (112)].

It is thus in the context of an *essai sur le don* that one encounters once more the existential necessity of *Les Mots*, for the gift, like paternal authority, is the object of initial misapprehension. The original decision to write and to become a great author is finally perceived to

have been founded on dual error: not only was it not completely autonomous, but neither did it represent the end of the generous exploits of the
phantasy hero. If *Les Mots* is necessary, it is because "les grands auteurs
s'apparentent aux chevaliers errants en ceci que les uns et les autres
suscitent des marques passionnées de gratitude" (139) ["great writers
are akin to knights-errant in that both elicit passionate marks of gratitude" (167–68)]. Its appearance, in this light at least, may be said to be
due to the persistence of a vicious cycle of preethical exchange. The
writer, who required "des obligés et non pas des lecteurs" (150)
["wanted gratitude and not readers" (180)] and who willfully confused
"l'art d'écrire et la générosité" (141) ["the art of writing and generosity"
(169)], must now dispossess himself and offer, to those with whom he
would like to enter into a relationship of reciprocity, an essay on the gift.

Sartre, however, unlike Mauss, imports no exotic *mana* to account
for the power of the obligations to give, to receive and to give in return.
The purposive assumptions of the phenomenology make such an explanatory factor unnecessary. At the same time, because Mauss is both
source and recipient of Sartrean insights, he does not have to become the
object of a violent homage such as was paid to Freud.

As an *essai sur le don*, *Les Mots* is a study of vertical relationships in
a hierarchy of age. Tributes and orders are given and received, and these
are items which have no significant horizontal action. That is to say
that if they imply relationships of equality, then they have failed in their
purpose. The writing of the autobiography constitutes an attempt to
reverse this tendency and to favor the horizontal at the expense of the
vertical. The reader learns, for example, that "quand on aime *trop* les
enfants et les bêtes, on les aime contre les hommes" (21) ["when one
loves children and animals *too much*, one loves them against human
beings" (30).]

There is one factor, however, that makes this enterprise particularly problematic. It is the bond that defies categorization—the fraternal relationship of mother and son. Is it reasonable to infer, with Lévi-
Strauss, that reciprocity exists only within the context of an exogamy
which is here absent? Or is one to conclude that the real reciprocity is
synonymous with incest? It is certainly legitimate to expect *Les Mots*,
as Maussian and anti-Freudian origin myth, to provide an answer to the
question.

Mauss, in his moral conclusion to the *Essai sur le don*, quotes "a
beautiful Maori proverb . . . 'Give as much as you take and all will be
well.'"[23] The quantitative criterion and the primacy of the continua-

23. Ibid. 265.

tion of exchange are not proposed explicitly by Sartre as components of a definition of reciprocity. Instead, one particular mode of conduct is advanced as a key to the problem. It is something which in a different theoretical context might be called the *projet fondamental* of *Les Mots*. It is resentment, and it is occasioned by a breakdown of an interaction construed as reciprocal: breast-feeding. "Les veilles et les soucis épuisèrent Anne-Marie, son lait tarit, on me mit en nourrice non loin de là et je m'appliquai, moi aussi, à mourir: d'entérite et peut-être de ressentiment" (8–9) ["The sleepless nights and the worry exhausted Anne Marie; her milk dried; I was put out to nurse not far away and I too applied myself to dying, of enteritis and perhaps of resentment" (16).] The *peut-être* may be taken as a modest introduction to what later matures into an "âcre plaisir" (105) ["pungent pleasure" (128).]

This would make of reciprocity something much more than equitable exchange. It now appears to consist of subjectivity shared to such an extent that it becomes a symbiosis. (A striking feature of the *Cahiers* is the degree to which the giving of drink is used to exemplify much more general propositions concerning generosity and demand.) Its termination in premature weaning permits resentment to be the rational origin of the desire to be *ens causa sui* and of the desire to write an autobiography which eliminates all other voices. Grandfather had asserted that "le génie n'est qu'un prêt, on finit par entendre des voix et l'on écrit par la dictée" (49) ["genius is only a loan . . . . One ends by hearing voices and writes at their dictation" (63).] *Les Mots* is embarked upon in order to put those vampires to flight.

At this particular stage in the narration it is too soon to say whether Sartre is successful or not. Certainly, as we have seen, he involves the *zar* and the *loa* in the hope that these spirits will assist in the exorcism of others. As yet, however, the origin myth has no happy ending and Sartre might well agree with Freud who notes that "the distortion of a text is not unlike a murder . . . the difficulty lies not in the execution of the deed but in the doing away with the traces."[24] *Totem and Taboo* and the law of Moses have proved unexpectedly resilient and there is now, in addition, an intractable suggestion of *complexe de sevrage* [weaning complex] which has to be confronted. An ally is needed, a benign spirit to banish the bad: not Mauss, Leiris or Métraux this time, but the philosopher Max Scheler.

In the recently published text "L'Engagement de Mallarmé,"[25] there may be found, in a polemical form which anticipates "Questions

---

24. S. Freud, op. cit., 70.
25. *Obliques*, nos. 18/19, April/June 1979, 169–94.

de méthode," an analysis of Mallarmé as *homme de ressentiment*. There is no room to discuss it here, except to say that, in a manner so close to *Les Mots* as to make it appear that the text is a sibling or a rehearsal of the autobiography, reciprocity is associated with breast-feeding and resentment with weaning. Scheler's *L'Homme du ressentiment*[26] is interesting in that it runs parallel to certain parts of Freud's thought but is phenomenological rather than psychoanalytic. Ostensibly a commentary on Nietzsche (the Nietzsche that Freud chose not to read), it offers a description of resentment as an anxious brooding consequent upon the forced repression of a spontaneous reaction. If Scheler's spirit is summoned up in *Les Mots*, it is as a force capable of moving psychoanalytic concepts to a phenomenological and to an ethical level. To this extent, *Les Mots* can be viewed as a continuation of the quest for the ethic, the quest implied in *"TM"* 's note of introduction to *Moses and Monotheism* and pursued simultaneously, albeit privately, in the *Cahiers*.

Even more striking is the fact that in *L'Etre et le néant* Sartre refines Scheler's description in a way that makes the autobiography intelligible as existential project. The passage runs as follows:

> . . . the sense and the function of what Scheler calls the "man of resentment" is the No. But there exist modes of conduct which are more subtle, the description of which would carry us further into the intimacy of consciousness: irony is one of these. In irony, man annihilates, in the unity of a single act, that which he posits, he leads to believe in order not to be believed, he affirms to deny and denies to affirm, he creates a positive object which has no other being than its nothingness.[27]

All of this suggests the following scenario. When reciprocity, physiological symbiosis of mother and son, comes to an end in the process of weaning, any possible spontaneously aggressive response to this situation is suppressed. A new parent-child relationship is established, in which the father figure plays a much more dominant part than the mother. This relationship is one of possession. At the same time the suppression of spontaneous courses of action leaves resentment as the only available option. It is resentment that permits participation in acts of exchange in which possession is disguised as generosity and from which reciprocity is absent.

For the young Sartre, the act of giving is positive in that it at least

26. Max Scheler, 1912; French Edition published by Gallimard in 1933 and proofread by Sartre.
27. J.-P. Sartre, *L'Etre et le néant* (Paris: Gallimard, 1943), 85.

allows him the possibility of being something more than merely a gift. He comes to enjoy the appearance of equality with other givers in the system. On the other hand, it is negative inasmuch as it accepts to be constrained to represent constraint as freedom. Resentment, in other words, is that which links *possession* and *don:* it is that which allows participation in the latter to disguise and to limit acceptance of the former.

To return to irony for a moment, one can surmise that if the history of the primal Schweitzer horde is generally held to be ironic, it is because it is motivated initially by resentment. The acceptance of possession is narrated with apparent detachment. But it is a detachment that is soon apprehended as not being real. It is then that *Les Mots* is spurred into greater reflexivity and that it begins to lift the repression of the spontaneous modes of conduct that should have followed the breakdown of reciprocity. Irony recedes as the project of transcendence and transformation gains momentum. It does not disappear altogether, for that which remains is displaced on to the self that writes,—in a crucial moment of the Sartrean *conversion*.

The whole project may be represented as a concerted effort involving other members of the anthropological and philosophical intertext. The autobiography invokes a theorist of the gift in order to liberate itself from destructive generosity; it mobilizes exotic spirits identified in French ethnographic fieldwork and uses them to exorcise parents and Freud; it enlists a theorist of resentment to free itself both from those who are resented and from resentment itself. If there is *mauvaise foi*, it is only as a necessary stage in the attempt to institute *bonne foi*; in the same way, appropriation is a re-appropriation and a move towards solidarity. In this light, *Les Mots* offers a rare view of Sartre as *bricoleur;* far from displaying massive misrecognition of Oedipal tensions, blinded in his own theoretical perspectives, he can be seen negotiating these tensions at the level of the narration by coming to terms with a plurality of intellectual authorities.

The fact remains that these voices are not those of Sartre. The expulsion of threatening ghosts creates a void into which enter other spirits, possession by whom is benign and perceived as reciprocity. The Holy Ghost may have been banished in anti-Pentecostal fashion: what subsists is a controlled and a limited glossolalia. In the end, a certain tolerance of intertextuality is found to be necessary and desirable. When Sartre alludes to Zola's famous *"nulla dies sine linea"*[28] he aspires to a corporate and even a corporatist identity, in which Zola, Scheler,

---

28. Id., *Saint Genet*, op cit., 448, and *Les Mots*, op cit., 211.

Mauss, Leiris, Métraux, Lefort, and the anti-Freudian face of Lévi-Strauss all participate. Together, in *Les Mots*, they constitute an intertextual community that is not without authority, but in which authority is equally and horizontally distributed. From this particular point of view, *Les Mots* appears as the work of a writer who has his origins in feudal tributes, who then transcends them and who proceeds to set up a regime based not on tributes but on contributions. If I referred to this above as a limited democratization of the intertext, it is because it clearly remains masculine, collegiate and stubbornly adult.[29] This is nevertheless the regime for which Sartre devoutly wishes, for it will accord him the status of "tout un homme, fait de tous les hommes et qui les vaut tous et que vaut n'importe qui" (213) ["A whole man, composed of all men and as good as all of them and no better than any" (255)].

29. What, after all, has been the fate of the *génitrice?* Was she merely the prize in this context between the hierarchy-bound males opearting at the level of the narrated and the fraternal comrades who together orchestrate the process of narration? All that one can say is that she subsequently becomes a party to another cycle of exchange, audited not in *Les Mots* but in the *Carnets de la drôle de guerre* (Paris: Gallimard, 1983). It is in this latter text that a younger author and an older son jointly mediate between the childhood and the period of the composition of *Les Mots*. Whether posthumous publication signifies lifelong disavowal is a problem for a biographer. Suffice it to say here that when generosity is allowed, in the *Cahiers*, to acquire a positive sense, it is as acceptance of the extent to which history distorts the purport of one's actions, acceptance that the idea might become other *in the hands of friends*. If therefore death and the *Carnets* render *Les Mots* even more problematic, they should also render it still less amenable to reductive and explanatory readings.

VICTOR BROMBERT

Sartre, Hugo, a Grandfather

Spanking literary figures was one of Sartre's favorite occupations. "I have spanked Maurice Barrès," Roquentin records, on the Mardi Gras, in *La Nausée*. True, it was only a dream. The outrageously chauvinistic Barrès, in that dream, tells a soldier with a hole in the middle of his face that he should put a bouquet of violets in that hole. Roquentin and his two fellow soldiers, after indulging in an obscenity, proceed to take Barrès's pants off, spank him until he bleeds, then draw the face of Déroulède on his buttocks.

This dream-wish has many extensions in Sartre's work; Barrès is not the only victim. Metaphorical spankings occur in almost every text dealing with literature. The more famous victims are called Baudelaire, Flaubert, the brothers Goncourt, Leconte de Lisle. The list is in fact much longer; it includes all those major and minor writers who in one way or another have promoted and embodied the institution of Literature as it came to flourish in the nineteenth century.

Why then, one might ask, such relatively gentle strictures against Victor Hugo? How come Sartre grants what amounts almost to impunity to the figure who perhaps more than anyone else in his time symbolized the *cléricature* of letters, who in fact presented himself to his contemporaries and to posterity as nothing less than its high priest, or as the Word incarnate.[1] Why is such privileged treatment granted to the one writer whom Sartre, only half-ironically, calls the supreme lord of his epoch, the "incontestable souverain du siècle"?[2] One would, on the contrary, imagine Sartre to have had little sympathy or tolerance for

---

1. Jeffrey Mehlman appropriately speaks of Hugo's role in the French nineteenth century as "metonym of Literature itself," as "Literature incarnate." *Revolution and Repetition, Marx, Hugo, Balzac* (Berkeley: University of California Press, 1977), 44–46.
2. *L'Idiot de la famille* (Paris: Gallimard, 1972), v. 3, 383.

a man of letters capable of proclaiming that France is a supreme spiritual power because of its "literary priesthood" ("*clergé littéraire*") and its great writers who are the modern Popes![3]

The answer lies in part in the specific diagnosis of the nineteenth-century writer, and of his situation, as it appears in Sartre's study of Baudelaire, in *Qu'est-ce que la littérature?* and in that summa, *L'Idiot de la famille.* The main points are worth recalling. According to Sartre, when the aristocracy collapsed at the time of the Revolution, the French writers, who until then had been the parasites of a parasitic class, showed themselves unable and unwilling to express solidarity with what was, on the whole, their own class, the bourgeoisie. This mythical rupture with their own origin, this tearing themselves away from their own class, were necessarily accompanied by bad faith, alienation and a permanent sense of betrayal. The need to reconstitute a fake aristocracy in a vacuum led to a mystic integration into a self-created aristocratic order (the institution of Literature), as it also led to a literature of negativity founded on doubt, denial, and contestation—a literature of revolt, though not of revolution. The nineteenth-century writer, filled with duplicity, wants to consider universal man; but in his desire to be above it all, he becomes a stranger to the here and the now. He is attracted to the newly glorified notion of the *Peuple,* as a potentially great subject; but, filled with contempt and fear, he avoids real contact, and remains incomprehensible to the proletariat. He enjoys the metaphysics of curse and damnation (leading to the notion of the *poète maudit*), yet he refuses to confront the reality of suffering and evil. Perhaps even worse: in spite of his willed separation from his own bourgeois class, he secretly espouses its repressive ideology insofar as it allows him to justify his aesthetics of opposition and resentment.

In discussing Baudelaire and Flaubert, Sartre defined the vocation of the nineteenth-century French writer in terms of a spiritual freemasonry, an atemporal communion of saints, an at homeness in the vast cemetery of culture, a viewing of oneself as already posthumous while still alive. The rights of genius replaced the divine rights of monarchy, just as the sacralization of the collegium of artists instituted an extrahistorical order in which each writer took his place side by side with the great figures already dead, or still to be born, in the cultural necropolis. Flaubert's particular obsession with the posthumous stance (the word necropolis occurs repeatedly in his writings) explains in part why Sartre singled him out as foremost among the Knights of Nothingness.

3. "Le Rhin," *OEuvres Complètes* (Paris: Le Club Français du Livre, 1967–1970), v. 6, 535.

Surely Sartre could have used Hugo to illustrate the desire for a communion with an atemporal elite, as well as the postulation of a presence-in-death which gives a privileged status to the point of view of posterity. In *William Shakespeare*, which Sartre knew well enough to quote from it in *L'Idiot de la famille*, Hugo indeed extols in a self-serving manner the dynasty of men of genius who, coexisting in a nonsequential time, belong to the "region of Equals," and who, their work accomplished, join what is described as the "famille dans l'infini."[4] The same text—but about that also not a comment from Sartre—proclaims the coming reign of the poet-prophet and glorifies communion in the absolute of art. More strikingly even than Baudelaire or Flaubert, Hugo affirms the genius's ontological presence-in-death. "To be dead is to be all-powerful". Again, and even more tellingly: "Having been, they are."[5] And could Sartre have forgotten that Hugo, in a well-known preface, specifically asked that *Les Contemplations* be read as "le livre d'un mort" ["the book of a dead man"], that he never tired of presenting himself as vatic poet and *sacerdos magnus?*

Sartre could certainly have made use of Hugo for polemical purposes. Yet he chose not to do so. The superficial reason may well be that, no matter what his sins, Hugo did not fit into Sartre's theoretical schemes of alienation and negativity. In discussing the metaphysics of failure in *L'Idiot de la famille*, Sartre suggests that Hugo's vitality and success must necessarily have made the Knights of Nothingness ill at case. Feeling accursed neither by destiny nor by his mother, Hugo appears to them as triumphant, at ease in his fame, prestigious in his political exile—in fact a political party all by himself: " . . . il possède je ne sais quelle puissance surhumaine [" . . . he possesses an unfathomable superhuman power."]"[6] It is hard to tell whether this sentence is a free indirect discourse (expressing the awe of the confraternity of writers), or whether Sartre speaks in his own name, and once again only half-ironically. Might it not be that it is Sartre himself who is made ill at ease by Hugo?

Interestingly enough, if one is to trust *Les Mots*, Sartre's awareness of Hugo goes back to his earliest childhood memories. Just as his interest in Flaubert's problem with words has its origin in his own childhood experience of "idiocy" when he first encountered *Madame Bovary* and the opaqueness of language, so a private family mythology had early crystallized around the figure of the Guernsey patriarch. Only Hugo

---

4. *William Shakespeare*, ibid., v. 12, 170, 242.
5. Ibid., v. 12, 294–95.
6. *L'Idiot de la famille*, v. 3, 162–63.

precedes Flaubert by a good twenty-seven pages in the Gallimard edition. This anteriority, or priority, of Hugo is, however, not a simple matter of textual strategy. Hugo is clearly associated with even earlier childhood memories than Flaubert, associated specifically in fact with the figure of Sartre's grandfather, a substitute for the absent-dead father. The grandfather himself takes the grandfatherly figure of Victor Hugo as a model to imitate in thought and gesture. Charles Schweitzer not only had a cult of Hugo (for him, all of literature led straight from Hesiod to the author of *La Légende des siècles*), he lived in a state of symbiosis with him. Photogenic, like Hugo he enjoyed being photographed and he assumed Hugo-like poses in front of his family. To the point where it is hard to tell whether it is to his beard or to Hugo's that Sartre refers as he evokes the childhood impressions of Poulou (the little Jean-Paul). Both Schweitzer and Hugo had perfected the art of being a grandfather; both were inebriated by their own theatricality. Schweitzer's inebriation (producing poses, attitudes, a sense of petrification, "moments of eternity" when he becomes, as it were, his own statue) corresponds to Hugo's inebriation with himself. Playing on Cocteau's famous quip, Sartre states that his grandfather was a nineteenth-century man who, like many others, like Hugo himself, took himself for Victor Hugo.[7]

"Un homme du XIXe siècle . . ." ["A nineteenth-century man . . ."]: the formula is clearly meant to suggest a significant anachronism which, in the case of Poulou the boy and Jean-Paul the adolescent, is first lived out at the family level. The heavy presence of the substitute father, who has replaced the dead/eclipsed begetter, corresponds to the intrusion of, and return to, the past. The child comes under the spell of a figure belonging to another century, who imposes on him—and this fifteen years after the death of Mallarmé!—ideas that were currency under Louis-Philippe.[8] One may well wonder whether Sartre did not recall the dramatic relationship, in *Les Misérables*, between Marius and his grandfather, Monsieur Gillenormand (defined as a man of the eighteenth century!), who also replaced and displaced the eclipsed father (first banished, then dead), and imposed on the childhood of Hugo's young hero (himself a retrospective projection of Hugo's own childhood) the conservative views of another century.

The problematic bond between family structure and ideology obviously complicates Sartre's judgments as well as his silences concerning Hugo. Blended and confused with the image of the grandfather,

7. *Les Mots* (Paris: Gallimard, 1964), 15–16.
8. Ibid., 49.

Hugo remains an oppressive, paradigmatic, and very intimate presence. Mention of his name sends contradictory signals. On the negative side, he strikes Sartre as the embodiment of idealistic humanism and spiritual arrogance. God's self-appointed interlocutor, the "favorite interviewer of God"[9] appears to him hardly as an intellectual subversive, a questioner of the order of things. His repeated claims to be the teacher of the invisible world all seem to derive from a self-publicized, unmediated contact with the voice of darkness. Sartre might have been amused—in case he did not know it—that Hugo himself inscribed under one of the countless photographs taken by his son Charles (on this one, he was perhaps just dozing): "Victor Hugo écoutant Dieu" ["Victor Hugo listening to God."] In any case, the "superhuman power" and undeniable "sovereignty" to which Sartre alludes clearly indicate misgivings about the *vates* posing as spokesman for transcendence.

What he must have known, however, though he chose not to dwell on it, is that Hugo had expressed himself against a certain notion of militant art (*l'art enrôlé*) and that history, when it was not strictly speaking raw material (very raw) to be changed by and into art, remained for him, in spite of his lifelong fascination with it, an ominous and evil force. If Enjolras, the revolutionary student-leader in *Les Misérables*, dreams of an exit from the forest of events, it is no doubt because Hugo came to question not only the historical perspective, but the historical process itself. In "La Pitié suprême," he denounced "inexorable history" ("l'histoire où le sang reparaît" ["history where blood reappears"]) as the accomplice of crime. History is darkness and violence. The "grand sanglot tragique de l'histoire" ["great tragic sob of history"] bewails the reenactment, in various forms, of the eternal crime of Cain.[10]

Equally disturbing to Sartre must have been Hugo's continued fear of the popular masses. For in spite of his abstract glorification of the *Peuple* (a concept to be given concrete form by none other than the artist), in spite of his courageous defense of the repressed Communards, Hugo felt hostile to the *peuple* as a social, physical and historical reality, and regularly allowed his pen to glide from the word "people" to the French equivalents of crowd, mob, plebs, rabble, scum. Sartre must have been in some sympathy with Proudhon, Marx, and Lukács, all of whom criticized Hugo for espousing a liberal utopian view which was essentially a justification of the bourgeois order, and for not understanding, or not wishing to understand, the class struggle and underlying socioeconomic problems of the industrial age.

9. *L'Idiot de la famille*, v. 1, 841.
10. *OEuvres complètes*, v. 10, 300, 308.

The gentleness of Sartre's treatment of Hugo remains noteworthy, colored as it is by an only partly concealed admiration. "Cet homme étonnant" ["this surprising man"], he calls him in *L'Idiot de la famille* (3, 383). Once more, Sartre's recorded childhood memories are telling. Hugo was ubiquitous; he was on all the shelves, manifest in all the genres. "Victor Hugo le multiple nichait sur tous les rayons à la fois" ["The multiple Victor Hugo was on all the shelves at once."] And Poulou had cried over the destinies of Jean Valjean and Eviradnus.[11] The admiration, in depth, is however closely linked to Sartre's own destiny or vocation as writer, in so far as *Les Mots* is centered on the relation between *lire* and *écrire*. The most remarkable feature of the phenomenon called Hugo is indeed, as Sartre seems to suggest, his readership: he may not have been the only one to intuit the existence of a new potential reading public—the proletariat; but this bard of the disinherited and the underprivileged (Sartre surely knew "Les Pauvres gens" as a schoolboy) was and still is the only one to be read by the working classes.

In this context, Sartre almost forgets about Hugo's camouflaged complicities with the dominant ideology; he remembers only that Hugo turned against art for art's sake, that he became the "chantre des pauvres," and that this astonishing individual, this sacerdotal anarchist who had and still has a popular readership, expressed as his last wish the desire at once "childish, theatrical, and sublime," to be brought to rest in the "corbillard des pauvres," to be given a pauper's funeral.[12]

It is thus a kind of *engagement* after all that Sartre values in Hugo; a commitment and sense of mandate confirmed, it would seem, by a proletarian reading public. Sartre's own notions of the writer's responsibilities are, as is well known, explicitly set forth in *Qu'est-ce que la littérature?* and in the short manifesto introducing the first issue of *Les Temps Modernes:* the writer must not miss out on his time; he must espouse his period; he must avoid indifference, and understand that silence can be a scandal. Flaubert's decision not to protest made him an accomplice of the repression which followed the Commune. More fundamentally still—and more permanently—the writer must give society an uneasy conscience (*conscience malheureuse*), and thereby necessarily clash with all conservative forces. Ultimately, *engagement* is of course philosophical: the acute awareness that evil is not a simple product or by-product; that it cannot be avoided, reduced, or assimilated by the rhetoric of idealistic humanism; that evil remains absolute, and that

11. *Les Mots,* 50, 145.
12. *L'Idiot de la famille,* v. 3, 203, 382–83.

literature therefore has an obligation to deal with "extreme situations."[13]

By Hugo's definition, too, there can be no innocent bystander. "Qui assiste au crime, assiste le crime" ["Whoever is the witness to a crime, abets it."] Any bystander is necessarily an accomplice. Hugo's aphorism has, by anticipation, a Sartrean ring. There is in fact much in Hugo—and Sartre well knew it—that is a praxis of involvement. *Le Dernier Jour d'un condamné*, partly the oneiric projection of a psychodrama, is a polemically charged, militant plea against capital punishment and the inequities of the Law. It is a novel clearly designed, as the Molièresque dialogue-preface suggests, to create maximal unease (Hugo's equivalent of the *conscience malheureuse*) in the reader. It is a book which, moreover, projects its powerful and creative shadow over all of Hugo's subsequent writings. Hugo's capacity for social and political indignation was alive indeed. We hardly need speculate about whether he would have remained silent or not on the subject of concentration camps and genocide. Certainly he would not have waited several decades to discover that there had been such things as the Stalinist purges, the Holocaust, and the Gulag archipelago! Sartre knew very well that, even though Hugo had inveighed against *l'art enrôlé*,[14] he had denounced the autonomy of art, precisely in the name of progress. Sartre even quotes from *William Shakespeare* about "l'art pour le progrès."[15] And he knew that for Hugo also evil was not just a metaphysical shadow, an idea to be dissolved or dismissed in and by an abstraction, but an immanent reality which galvanized the salvational mission of the writer.

The soteriological impulse of the writer, the assumption that he has a mandate to save the world, was of course not Hugo's monopoly. For Sartre, it was a very personal subject—almost too personal for comfort. If society needs to be given a *conscience malheureuse*, it is no doubt because the unease is first and foremost the writer's own deeply painful experience insofar as his mandate—about which he feels both doubt and guilt—seems to imply, on his part, a condescending sollicitude which he judges with severity. In his "Présentation" of the first issue of *Les Temps Modernes*, Sartre stresses the importance, for the writer, of binding himself to a social class, of not allowing himself to look down (*se pencher*) from a privileged, lofty position. *Se pencher* over problems and human beings means, figuratively, to take interest and to show concern; but it unavoidably suggests the more concrete image of bend-

---

13. *Situations 2* (Paris: Gallimard, 1948), 12–13, 246–250.
14. *OEuvres Complètes*, v. 5, 38.
15. *L'Idiot de la famille*, v. 3, 203.

ing down, of condescending. Where, after all, was the writer to begin with? "In the air?"[16] And is that not the preferred position of Victor Hugo, the vatic poet, writing in his glass encased "lookout" all the way on top of Hauteville-House on the island of Guernsey?

But what about Sartre himself? Does he not also, like the false prophet Clamence, in Camus's *La Chute*, feel irresistibly drawn to heights and supreme summits? In *Les Mots*, he in fact admits to his delight at living and writing at a great height; he refers to his childhood reading and writing obsession as an early desire to live in the rarefied air of the upper spheres, "parmi les simulacres aériens des Choses."[17] Even the desire to *come down* is perceived ironically as the obverse of the vocation of verticality and altitude.

But the feeling of guilt accompanies not only the climb to the cîmes, it sticks more stubbornly still to the writer's yearning for private salvation—and in particular to the opportunistic desire to be saved by politics. In *L'Idiot de la famille* (3, 91), Sartre makes a revealing comment about how Hugo, "lost" to poetry in 1848, was "saved" by the coup d'état of Louis-Bonaparte in 1851. The implicit accusation is one of political parasitism. Obliquely, the accusation is self-directed. Sartre knows that his relation to History is problematic; that no matter what his proclaimed intentions, he too remains dedicated to the institution of Literature. He cannot forget (nor quite forgive himself) that many years earlier, exactly at the time he confused the beard of his grandfather with that of Hugo, he "gave himself to Literature," and by so doing "took holy orders" (" . . . j'entrais dans les ordres"), banking on a "posthumous beatitude."[18] Even as he reminisces and writes his autobiography in front of a tenth floor window symbolically overlooking a cemetery, he confesses to feeling something akin to terror at the thought of the eventual cooling of the sun, a catastrophe, which would deprive him of the millions of survivors whom he would like to continue to haunt and to save. The end of the world would deprive him of his posthumous stance!

With little indulgence for Poulou, Sartre recalls how he never doubted for a moment that a place was reserved for him in the Pantheon.[19] Next to Hugo, perhaps? He does not tell. It is clear, however, that if the image of Hugo continues to serve Sartre's self-incriminating bent, it also mirrors a permanent longing. Sartre denounced in others,

16. *Situations 2*, 10.
17. *Les Mots*, 47.
18. Ibid., 208.
19. Ibid., 146.

and in himself, the big lie of any literary *cléricature*. Yet he was never to give up the ambition he describes, as he nostalgically evokes his friendship with his fellow Normalien, Paul Nizan: the hope of bringing about salvation, "notre salut et, avec un peu de chance, celui des autres" ["our salvation, and with a little luck, that of others."] The hope, and the shame that went with it, were intimately related to the use of *words*, quite specifically—though both he and Nizan were atheists—to a religious vocabulary: "Nous gardâmes longtemps, lui et moi, le vocabulaire chrétien . . ." ["For a long time he and I retained the Christian vocabulary."] But words were also to be terrorist weapons: ". . . ces bombes, mes paroles ["these bombs, my words"]".[20] Revealingly and ironically, Sartre titled his autobiography *Les Mots*, a title that becomes even more ironic if one remembers that it was Hugo—and this precisely in a poem that stands next to the famous assertion concerning the explosive, revolutionary impact of his own literary language—who proclaimed the transcendence of the *Word*: "Car le mot c'est le Verbe, et le Verbe c'est Dieu."[21]

20. "Avant-propos" to Paul Nizan's *Aden Arabie* (Paris: François Maspero, 1960), 33.
21. This is the final line of the poem "Suite" which follows the well known "Réponse à un acte d'accusation" *OEuvres Complètes*, v. 9, 81.

Part III

RONALD ARONSON

Sartre and the Dialectic: The Purposes of *Critique, II*

Today, more than ever, we need Sartre—we who live at a time when the future itself is in question, when the human world has never seemed more out of human control. Uniquely among this century's great writers, Sartre's body of work points towards understandings and actions which may possibly return the world to its creators and so let there be a future. But how so, since at first glance the harsh judgement of neglect mounting even before his death might appear justified by the extraordinary topicality of his writings? After all, what other great twentieth-century thinker has given himself so unstintingly to his specific historical situation? A body of writings, even as bequest, is only in situation. This simultaneously Marxist and existentialist concept, developed by Sartre as early as 1939[1] and then enriched and deepened by him over the next three decades, suggests that changing times may quite appropriately diminish his own importance for us. Most of his plays, for example, deal with problems of the moment, as does much of his fiction. The ten volumes of his political and literary essays read mostly as precisely dated interventions: the postwar call for the writer's *engagement*, discussions of contemporary writers and artists, moral and political wrestlings with Communism and colonialism, the cold war and Cuba, De Gaulle and the New Left. Only a few "timeless" works stand out to sustain his claims before "posterity": *La Nausée, L'Etre et Le Néant, Huis clos, L'Idiot de la famille*, and now his *Lettres au Castor*. Is not Sartre falling under the sway of history's pitiless process of sorting out, destined as it is to leave a few major works alive and in the foreground of continuing general interest, while consigning the topical works to the near oblivion of doctoral dissertations and specialist studies?

1. See Jean-Paul Sartre, *Les Carnets de la drôle de guerre* (Paris: Gallimard, 1983), 56–57.

This might be an appropriate posthumous trajectory if the world had resolved the political problems which preoccupied Sartre. But, alas, we have not yet become free of colonialism and its heritage, the capitalist-communist confrontation, or the blockage of hope represented by the Communist states. For half his life Sartre searched, and struggled, for a meaningful politics of liberation: for those who still care, the search and struggle continue today. Along his way Sartre sought to reflect on, and develop appropriate forms of intellectual involvement. He also sought to recover theoretical Marxism's revolutionary force by a grounding and reshaping which would found it as *the* human science. Certainly no better answers to these political-intellectual problems lie ready to hand today, and the problems themselves have hardly lost their interest. On a more purely theoretical level, Sartre's abiding concern with freedom, which yielded a lifetime of exploration of the ways in which the individual is shaped, shapes himself and takes shape, has not been rendered obsolete by recent wisdom on the subject, any more than his studies of the individual's relationship with society and of the dynamics of social formation have been dated by later research.

If Sartre's work is largely ignored today, it is not so much because his questions have been better answered elsewhere, but because they are not being asked.[2] This says less about their intrinsic importance or the merits of his answers, than about today's intellectual fashions. When interest reawakens in such questions, there is no doubt that the paths to be taken by those who ask them will lead in each case, through Sartre's works. His insights, his concerns, his answers may or may not in any case be definitive; but politically and theoretically, he will command attention for having lived and thought them so fully, so courageously, so deeply.

Yet even since Sartre's death times have worsened. The development of the atomic bomb, which Sartre indicated in the late 1940s in the *Cahiers sur la morale* as having transformed our world,[3] has indeed changed everything. The threat has broadened, deepened, become part of our daily lives. The kind of terror mentioned only briefly by Sartre at the darkest days of the cold war,[4] is imposed on us at every moment of every day by strategic policies making us all hostages during "peace-

---

2. For a cogent description of the process in France, set within a wide-ranging sketch of the overall intellectual scene today, see Perry Anderson, *In the Tracks of Historical Materialism* (London: Verso, 1983).

3. Paris: Gallimard, 1983.

4. See "Merleau-Ponty," *Situations* 4 (Paris: Gallimard, 1964), 247–48; trans. Benita Eisler, "Merleau-Ponty," *Situations* (New York: George Braziller, 1965), 286.

time." Similarly, Sartre's pitched struggle for political hope chronicled in his changing attitudes towards Communism and his efforts to create a New Left can be seen as remarkably optimistic in the face of that New Left's subsequent collapse everywhere, of martial law in Poland, of the—at least momentary—exhaustion of the forces for social change in the West, their containment in the East, and the general absence of any hopeful alternative in the Third World. The zones of hope for which Sartre searched and to which he attached his support and analysis have become, one by one, cancelled by events, leaving us today facing the greatest danger in memory and with the greatest sense of disarray. As a consequence, hope itself has not been more in jeopardy since the beginning of the modern world.[5]

Yet if the situation has deteriorated, our darker time only makes Sartre's work more relevant. In repeatedly trying to understand the worst, and indeed to make way for change within it, he is one author who provides keys and encouragement.[6] In extreme situations Sartre again and again points not towards paralysis and confusion, but radical clarity and commitment. As he wrote, so did he act: moving towards the most intractable and painful problems of his lifetime, locating the point of most extreme tension between threatened hope and crushing reality, working within the tension, and from there insisting on finding a way forward.[7]

The theory of this practice of radical hope in extreme situations is perhaps the most important of all of Sartre's ideas: that human beings are the source of the human world. If we live entranced by a network of material and ideological mystification which raises our creations beyond our control, Sartre insists on revealing the *praxis* at their origin.[8] Both those who would demonize the human world on the one hand and

5. For an elaboration of this and the next three paragraphs see the author's *The Dialectics of Disaster: A Preface to Hope* (London: Verso, 1984).

6. I have criticized Sartre's ontological individualism as a structurally pessimistic mode of thought, unable to grasp, or foresee the transformation of, a sociality which it excludes from the outset and in any event sees primarily as negative. Such qualifications should not, however, keep us from the great riches of Sartre's thought, especially in a period when so few other thinkers wrestle with such fundamental questions.

7. Sartre was self-conscious about this approach. See Simone de Beauvoir, *La Force des choses* (Paris: Gallimard, 1963), 280–82; *The Force of Circumstance*, trans. Richard Howard (New York: G. Putnam's Sons, 1965), 261–62.

8. Earlier, when his social philosophy was less developed, Sartre's key idea in this respect was *responsibility:* that we have to assume the world's weight, whatever its source, inasmuch as we internalize it as a decisive step of our own action. *Praxis* points to the prior level, as Sartre seeks to understand the human actions and intentions in which the world first takes shape.

those who would remove its human, *moral* dimension, on the other, can be educated by Sartre's emphasis on human responsibility and intentionality, on choice and action even in the most difficult situations: neurosis, for example, is the path chosen by the organism "in order to be able to live an unlivable situation."[9] With such concepts Sartre can help us to grasp the logic of evil and defeat: nuclear madness, the destructiveness which has so marked our century, the partially realized but repeatedly betrayed hopes of socialism, the dispiriting course taken by Third World revolutions.

If times have indeed darkened since the optimistic postwar decade and a half of Sartre's richest productivity, a way out will not be found by abandoning his chosen terrain for various modes of sophisticated evasion. Compared with the ambitions of other thinkers much in vogue today we can only be struck by Sartre's courage, his conviction that anything human can be understood, his indefatigable insistence on seeing human action and intention, however deviated, as the world's source. If we are, indeed, to survive, it will probably only be by a concerted intellectual-political practice paralleling his own: of deconstructing the fixed, frozen, menacing entities—above all, the Bomb—created by us but placed beyond our control by determinate *and comprehensible* human institutions and intentions; of reconstructing the world so that human intentionality prevails with as few deformations as possible. The only hopeful politics for today and the future will seek to return this world gone mad to its human source.

I

With these thoughts in mind we turn to one of his richest works, *Critique de la raison dialectique*, II, in the hope of contributing to the revival of interest in Sartre by making the arguments of this unpublished work available. It will and must be criticized; but first it must be understood and appreciated; and before that, it must simply become known. Here I will take a modest first step in the detailed presentation of Volume Two by describing Sartre's purposes as he spells them out, both throughout Volume One and in the first pages of Volume Two.

Considering the notorious difficulty and complexity of the published first volume of the *Critique*, the guiding question of its second volume appears as clarity itself. How, Sartre asks at the outset, can we "conceive that a struggle between individuals or between groups is

9. Sartre's foreword to R. D. Laing and D. G. Cooper, *Reason and Violence* (London: Tavistock, 1964), 7.

dialectically intelligible?"[10] What enables us to view each side's action according to the terms of dialectical thought—as participating in the creation of history, as leading to progress and development, as proceeding by contradiction and transcendence? The issue is a simple yet absolutely basic one: how can a meaningful larger whole emerge "when we are in the presence of *two* actions, that is of two autonomous and contradictory totalisations?" (II, 3).

Those who have studied the published portion of the *Critique* will readily feel at home within the tone, register and conceptual universe of such questions. The first pages of the second volume, indeed, begin precisely where the first leaves off. Unlike the beginning of Volume One they reveal no sense of starting out afresh, no need to create a place for the entire undertaking in the world of human praxis and discourse—or indeed in the history of thought—but rather they seem merely to pose, after a pause, the next question of a sustained line of thought whose basic concepts and frames of reference have already been carefully established. To be sure, we shall see later in this essay that Sartre devoted considerable energy in Volume Two's opening two dozen pages to specifying, focussing and circumscribing this line of thought, and we shall travel this path with him to understand better the work and its significance. But, as we shall also see, it is clearly indicated as being no more than the continuation and completion of Volume One.

In a remarkable parallel with *L'Etre et le Néant*, the final paragraphs of the published *Critique* had posed a series of questions to be taken up by the sequel. Yet the sequel to the first, the *Cahiers pour une morale*, also unfinished and unpublished during Sartre's lifetime, point towards a fundamentally new work, stamped by an entirely new problematic, written at the time of a personal-political transformation. The second half of the *Critique*, on the contrary, is a single, coherent and well-developed manuscript, unlike the *Cahiers*, which are a series of preliminary studies and notebooks.[11] It reflects a stable conceptual universe, not one undergoing challenge and transformation.[12] To be sure, it drops

---

10. *Critique de la raison dialectique*, tome 2 (manuscript), 2. All references are to the New Left Review / NLB typescript. Gallimard will publish the manuscript in 1985.

11. Their editor, Arlette Elkaim-Sartre, has perhaps exaggerated their unfinished state by proclaiming that these "notes," if "they have a thread and are often more that half-written," "do not have structure", 5. As Perry Anderson has pointed out in his discussion of it, Sartre unambiguously sets out the project's overall structure on 484–87, and it takes only the briefest study to see the internal logic linking the various issues treated.

12. On the other hand, it is also true, as André Gorz has written to the author, that "the ms. is not only unfinished but unpolished, had never been reread and is full of wandering (though interesting) digressions and excursions sometimes leading nowhere."

off unfinished at the end, and it seems to turn radically from its main purpose at least once.[13] Yet in it Sartre does pursue, with great vigor and clarity, at considerable length and in detail, the project announced early in Volume One. In taking up "the same structures as those brought to light by regressive investigation," he indeed seeks "to rediscover the moments of their inter-relations, the ever vaster and more complex movement which totalises them and, finally, the very direction of the totalisation, that is to say, the 'meaning of History' and its Truth."[14] The structures laid out in the first volume—individual *praxis*, the practico-inert, the series, the fused group, the sworn group, the institution, social classes—are intended in the second as "the condition of a directed, developing totalisation" (I, 69).

II

This is, after all, the daunting terrain of the *dialectic*. The very term serves to remind us of the deeper complexity lying within the relative simplicity and clarity of Sartre's project in Volume Two. "Relative" indeed: just to attack one of the key terms of dialectical reason, "totalization," in order to clarify Sartre's meaning, would require a massive essay necessarily exploring a number of other key terms, precious few of which could be defined succinctly at the outset. After all, under the rubric of the dialectic, we are dealing with a process of ever more complex self-development. Even the study's formal categories cannot be spelled out in advance, because they are intended as the emerging substance and structure of the study itself (and indeed of reality), and so must bear a considerable weight of ambiguity, serving more than one purpose and often changing over time. And finally, no key term can be understood without the others, in an analysis destined for complexity and lack of analytical precision by its very focus on a region synonymous with "totalization" and the "truth of history."

Access to the area of reality which Sartre seeks to describe—*the* dialectic, but as created by the multiplicity of *individual praxes*—requires persistent, and often confusing, acts of abstraction. Thus even

13. Perry Anderson suggests that the text wanders off after Sartre's discussion of Stalin (*Arguments within English Marxism* [London: Verso, 1980], 53), a position with which I agreed in my *Jean-Paul Sartre—Philosophy in the World* (London: Verso, 1980), 284. But is not the first wandering the very study of the Soviet Union itself (hardly a "totalisation *without* a totaliser"), and the return, Sartre's ontological speculations at the end? Michael Sprinker has suggested this in discussion: a fuller analysis will have to wait the conclusion of the study of which this is the introduction.

14. *Critique de la raison dialectique*, vol. 1 (Paris: Gallimard, 1960) trans. Alan Sheridan Smith, *Critique of Dialectical Reason* 1 (London: Verso, 1976), 69.

Volume Two is not intended to lead us "to the absolute concrete, which can only be the individual (*this* event and *this* date of *this* history) [but] at least to the absolute system for applying the determination 'concrete fact' to the fact of one history" (I, 69).

In such a study, self-consciously seen as a process paralleling the self-development of human reality itself, the reader will be challenged to determine just what is at stake in any particular discussion. And indeed, once a moment of precision is attained, the next stage of discussion may necessitate shifting ground and require yet another act of self-situation before the reader is again sure of its direction—whereupon, once again, the ground may shift, forcing yet another retaking of bearings, far now from the original moment of clarity. Moreover, it should be evident from the quotations above that Sartre's agenda for Volume Two simultaneously contains, and may even confuse, a number of separable if interconnected purposes. If he will indeed focus and narrow the direction of Volume Two at its outset, let us first establish its place in the *Critique* project, allowing the part and the whole to illuminate each other mutually.

Why, we may ask, does the central thrust of the *Critique* call for an attempt to decode both individual struggle and "the complex phenomenon which has to be described as a *praxis*-process and which sets classes in opposition to one another as circular totalisations of institutions, groups and serialities?" (I, 806). The most obvious part of the answer lies in Sartre's description of the two halves of the *Critique* in the terms announced in *Question de Méthode*, as a *regressive-progressive* project. *Critique*, I, as the regressive component has sought to deconstruct social reality into its abstract elements, categories and processes, its synchronic structures, to demonstrate "the intelligibility of practical structures and the dialectical relations which interconnect the various forms of active multiplicities" (I, 818). But this achieved, "we are still at the level of synchronic totalisation. . . . " It is time for the progressive study, in which the researcher turns back towards reconstructing the concrete by considering "the diachronic depth of practical temporalisation"—"whose aim will be to rise up the double synchronic and diachronic movement by which History constantly totalises itself" (I, 818). In other words, having first revealed "the static conditions of the possibility of a totalisation, that is to say, of a history," it is time to "progressively recompose the historical process on the basis of the formations in question" (I, 68) in order to learn whether the complex interactions, including struggles, "reveal an intelligible (and thus directed) totalising movement" (I, 68).

In asking about History with a capital *H* Sartre is, however, pointing to another goal of the project's second part: "it will attempt to establish that there is *one* human history, with *one* truth and *one* intelligibility. . . ." One history? Althusser's attack on the first volume was precisely his denunciation of the "historicist" reading of Marxism, dominated as it was by "the shade of Hegel."[15] But Sartre's unflinching purpose was indeed "to establish the dialectic as the universal method and universal law of anthropology" (I, 18). This strategy entailed establishing "the permanent necessity for man of totalising and being totalised, and for the world of being an ever broader, developing totalisation" (I, 21). Marxism's Immanuel Kant would "explore the limits, the validity, and the extent of dialectical Reason," allowing it "to ground itself and to develop itself as a free critique of itself, at the same time as being the movement of History and of knowledge" (I, 21).

The dialectic: method, structure of reality, vision of universal History being unfolded through our acts. With a breathtaking Hegelian ambition and sweep so uncharacteristic of the latter half of the twentieth century, Sartre then sought, in laying the a priori basis for Marxism, simultaneously to claim the dialectic as *the* method of any study of human reality and "to discover the basic signification of History and of dialectical rationality" (I, 818). But besides accepting Marxism as providing the decisive keys into the meaning of history and the overarching logic by which that meaning is grasped—as well as illuminating and advancing the struggle by which the historical process advances—Sartre's project was to be shaped and driven forward by yet another commitment, also falling under the rubric of the dialectic. He criticized Hegel and Engels for dogmatically and onesidedly making the dialectic external to, and imposing it on, the individuals who create it.

> So, in a sense, man submits to the dialectic as to an enemy power; in another sense, he *creates it*; and if dialectical Reason is the Reason of History, this contradiction must itself be lived dialectically, which means that man must be controlled by the dialectic in so far as he *creates it*, and *create* it in so far as he is controlled by it. Furthermore, it must be understood that there is no such thing as man; there are people, wholly defined by their society and by the historical movement which carries them along; if we do not wish the dialectic to become a divine law again, a metaphysical fate, it must proceed *from individuals* and not from some kind of supra-individual ensemble. Thus we encounter a new contradiction: the dialectic is the law of totalisation which creates *several* collectivities, *several* societies, and *one* history—realities, that is, which impose themselves on individuals; but at the same time it

15. Louis Althusser, *For Marx*, trans. Ben Brewster (London: Verso, 1977), 116.

must be woven out of millions of individual actions. We must show how it is possible for it to be both a *resultant*, though not a passive average, and a *totalising force*, though not a transcendent fate, and how it can continually bring about the unity of dispersive profusion and integration. [I, 35–36]

Paradoxically, then, while seeking the most general and abstract laws of self-unifying human social development—laws whose existence many thinkers, some Marxists among them, would deny—Sartre simultaneously insists on their origin in the activities of individuals:

> Thus, there is no *one* dialectic which imposes itself upon the facts, as the Kantian categories impose themselves on phenomena; but the dialectic, if it exists, is the individual career of its object. There can be no pre-established schema imposed on individual developments, neither in someone's head, nor in an intelligible heaven; if the dialectic exists, it is because certain regions of materiality are *structured* in such a way that it cannot not exist. In other words, the dialectical movement is not some powerful unitary force revealing itself behind History like the will of God. It is first and foremost a *resultant*; it is not the dialectic which forces historical men to live their history in terrible contradictions; it is men, as they are, dominated by scarcity and necessity, and confronting one another in circumstances which History or economics can inventory, but which only dialectical reason can explain. Before it can be a *motive force*, contradiction is a result; and, on the level of ontology, the dialectic appears as the only type of relation which individuals, situated and constituted in a certain way, and on account of their very constitution, can establish themselves. The dialectic, if it exists, can only be the totalisation of concrete toatlisations effected by a multiplicity of totalising individualities. [I, 37]

Sartre seeks *the* dialectic, rooted in *individuals:* the striking originality of the *Critique* lies in his adherence to *both* poles and all they imply. It lies above all in his determination to see the second as the source of the first: "it is no more than ourselves" (I, 39, tr. changed). The still dubious reader can perhaps glimpse the immense scale of Sartre's ambition by considering that these twin commitments intend not merely to present, but to integrate, the most radical ontological and sociological individualism and the most sweeping sense of the oneness of human history. In short, Sartre seeks both to trace the dialectic back to its source in individual action and to view it, writ large, as the meaning of history.

Whatever its difficulties, and indeed whatever its subsequent weaknesses and structural improbabilities, Sartre pursues this ambition with a consistenty, force, and honesty which mark it as a truly great intellectual adventure. The entirety of Volume One is a remarkably bold and sustained effort to explain basic structures of social reality without recourse to the "hyperorganicism" of *Society*, an independent being seen to move and act on its own—by demonstrating how each structure under consideration depends on a multiplicity of individual actions. The materiality thereby created—as product, as tool, as organizational structure of the producers themselves—absorbs the separate actions of the multiplicity, holds them in its inertia, and then in turn imposes itself as the given of future actions, redirecting and reorganizing them according to *its* logic. Indeed, this brilliant concept, the practico-inert, points to a socialized dimension of individual activity without conceding the existence of Society.

Given these purposes, however, it will be in volume two that the wager is won or lost. In addition to its more genial formal purpose of allowing the structures adduced in Volume One "to live freely, to oppose and cooperate with one another" (I, 818), it bears the urgent substantive burden of establishing that the scattered and separate multiplicities do indeed produce a single History. "In Volume Two, which will appear later, I shall approach the problem of totalisation itself, that is to say, of History in its development and truth in its becoming" (I, 824). Were he not to meet this challenge we would indeed be left viewing a series of elements with no sense of whether or how they combine, a sense of those focused and directed moments of historical rupture and their congealing into institutions, but no understanding of how separated and even hostile multiplicities combine to create *a* History. Lacking Volume Two, we have many histories, but no History. In Sartre's eyes this result would drain each history of its meaning, depriving the dialectic, totalization and even Truth of their sense, destroying any hope of achieving *an* anthropology. Volume Two, then, is more than fully half of the project—it is its completion, its culmination.

Until now, readings of the first volume have had to assume a self-sufficiency and completeness not inherent in its pages but imposed by Sartre's subsequent decision to break off the project before its completion. As a result, understandably, specific structures have been emphasized rather than the larger historical process into which they are to be inserted;[16] or indeed, the (reversible) passage from one structure to another is mistaken as a kind of totalizing study of History itself rather than a highly abstract study of its elements and their modes of combina-

---

16. See for example Pietro Chiodi, *Sartre and Marxism* (London: Harvester, 1976).

tion and transformation.[17] I hope this discussion of the *Critique*'s purposes—mostly drawn from Volume One, but framed by Volume Two,
has so far suggested new angles of vision into the published portion. As
knowledge of Volume Two becomes more accessible, and especially
after its publication and translation, the first volume can for the first
time be widely read in light of the project as a whole. Knowledge of the
second volume may impose new lenses through which to view the
purposes and analyses of the first. New evaluations and appreciations
may become possible, allowing in turn a fuller understanding of the
Critique in Sartre's overall philosophical trajectory and, above all, of the
scope of his considerable contribution to twentieth-century thought.

With these considerations in mind, Volume Two helps place in
appropriate relief the most monumental aspect of the *Critique:* its attempt to dissolve the frozen, fixed givens of social life—virtually all of
the human world—into the process of its constitution. Sartre does not
merely proclaim that *"praxis* creates the world" but sets out to *demonstrate* it. And the first volume shows evermore complex realities being
built up from simpler ones, beginning with individual *praxis*. Indeed,
his concern is to reveal how and under what conditions our products
become forces beyond our control and in turn dominate the *praxis*
which creates them. In a sense, nothing is given, all is created, even in
its genielike escape from its creator's control—and by the end of the
second volume this focus will be extended to the very meaning and
direction of History itself. Volume One concerns itself only with the
elements and first-level products of action, or with structures which, in
one form or another, have been specifically intended. But no less important, and absolutely essential for completing the map, are the products
intended by *no one*—on the first level, the results of class conflict, and
on the furthest reaches of study, the direction of history itself.

Sartre's great ambition is to explain precisely how separate and
even opposed individual actions can add up to a meaningful history,
enabling it indeed to be described as a "totalisation without a totaliser."
But however extraordinary, these are not merely philosophical ambitions, coming as they do from a political thinker-activist aware that
"the dialectic is both a method *and* a movement in the object" (I, 20). As
"the living logic of action" (I, 38) it can only appear in its true light, as
"the rationality of *praxis*" (I, 39) to one who performs the *Critique* "in
the course of *praxis* as a necessary moment of it . . . " (I, 38). What is
Sartre's *praxis?* Most evidently, to ascertain the limits of the dialectic

17. See for example Mark Poster, *Sartre's Marxism* (London: Pluto Press, 1980).

after Stalinism, "the *abuses* which have obscured the very notion of dialectical rationality and produced a new divorce between *praxis* and the knowledge which elucidates it" (I, 50).

Such a critique makes sense only *after* the dialectic "was posited for itself in the philosophies of Hegel and Marx," then had become the algebra of twentieth-century socialist revolution, and then "Stalinist idealism had sclerosed both epistemological methods and practices. It could take place only as the intellectual expression of that re-ordering which characterises, in this 'one world' of ours, the post-Stalinist period" (I, 50). If the "totalising activity of the world" had led to a "divorce of blind unprincipled *praxis* and sclerosed thought, or in other words the obscuring of the dialectic," the movement of de-Stalinisation now makes a critique of dialectical reason both possible and necessary, indeed urgent.

But these formulations from Volume One suggest a still more contemplative approach than would satisfy the thinker whose work on these questions was framed by his sustained contribution to the Algerian struggle for independence, on the one hand, and his attempts to create sympathy for revolutionary Cuba menaced by the United States, on the other. Most readings of the *Critique*, I have grasped its formal and metatheoretical Marxist ambitions. But the imposed self-sufficiency of Volume One has forced them to miss the concrete political purpose which, for Sartre, lay at the heart of the project:[18] to determine why the Bolshevik Revolution followed the course it did, and to explore the prospects of its thawing into a genuine socialism. This had indeed been one of Sartre's great obsessions even before his formal adherence to Marxism, to be explored time and again in the ten years before beginning the *Critique* in plays (*Les Mains sales* [1948], *Le Diable et le Bon Dieu* [1951], and the screenplay *L'Engrenage* [1946]) and in extended political essays (most notably in *Les Communistes et la paix* and *Le Fantôme de Staline*). In the *Critique* he finally poses the question of revolutionary success-cum-deterioration as, remarkably, the central question of social theory.

While his specific analysis begins with the storming of the Bastille, and most of his references are drawn from the French Revolution, the study of the passage from the fused group to the Terror to the institutionalization of the revolution, to bureaucracy and the cult of personality ends up by focussing not on Napoleon but on Stalin.[19] Whereas

18. The exception confirms the rule: it is based on a study of Volume Two. See Anderson, *In the Tracks of Historical Materialism*, 70–72.
19. See 660–63.

considered by itself, Volume One may not allow us to say confidently that in its central sections Sartre meant to understand the Russian Revolution through the French, this impression is strengthened not only retrospectively, by the remarkably anticipatory analyses in *Les Communistes et la paix*, but above all by the central sections of Volume Two. There, Sartre discusses first the general problem of contradictions and opposition within a revolutionary group, then the Trotsky-Stalin conflict, then Stalin's political practice in the 1930s (including collectivization and industralization), and finally the question of Stalin's anti-semitism. This sustained four-hundred page work on the Soviet Union is both theoretical and political, finally asking—and answering—the question of questions: why Stalin? In it Sartre's ambitions as political thinker rival his ambitions as social philosopher, as he reflects not only on how the dialectic became "obscured" under Stalin but also on whether the Revolution's positive results can now be freed from its negative ones.

In these monumental analyses we see Sartre exerting intellect and commitment with all his considerable might, insisting not only on the dialectical character of the blockages of the dialectic,[20] but also on the *praxis*-process at the heart of some of the grimmest facts of the century. A labor of hope as I termed it in my introductory words, it is a pitched struggle on behalf of socialism and against all political and intellectual tendencies which would confirm human products as forces *beyond* human control (and reversal). Sartre here combats both bourgeois and Stalinist outlooks which would separate our (however alienated) product from us and would impose it back upon us as the creation of laws, Society or fate. One senses in these analyses—and, through the retrospective light they throw, in the entire *Critique*—a heroic single-handed effort to move heaven and hell (indeed to expose both as human creations), in order to restore our ability to think about the world as *ours*.

How radical, then, how ambitious is the *Critique!* This sketch of its purposes in light of its second volume may enable us better to appreciate it, especially if we set it in its environment in a postwar period marked by growing cynicism and narrowing horizons. A sense of how vast are Sartre's goals may help to explain why he wrote it as a man obsessed, under the greatest strain, helped along by corydrame capsules.[21] And it may encourage forgiveness of the project's failings, of the chaotic char-

---

20. And implying a sense of progress he had rejected in his first reflections in *Cahiers sur la morale*. See *Critique*, 1, 660.

21. See de Beauvoir, *Force of Circumstance*, 385.

acter of much of Volume One, and the difficulty it imposes on the reader.

This sketch of the project's purposes may also indicate how much depends on Volume Two. Few of the *Critique*'s major goals as I have outlined them have been met by the pause at the end of its first volume; most of them must await the completion of the second. Early on, Sartre himself poses four questions which must be answered "if the dialectic is possible":

> (1) How can *praxis* in itself be an experience of necessity and of freedom since neither of these, according to classical logic, can be grasped in an empirical process?
> (2) If dialectical rationality really is a logic of totalisation, how can History—that swarm of individual destinies—appear as a totalising movement, and how can one avoid the paradox that in order to totalise there must already be a unified principle, that is that only active totalities can totalise themselves?
> (3) If the dialectic is comprehension of the present through the past and through the future, how can there be a historical future?
> (4) If the dialectic is to be materialist, how are we to comprehend the materiality of *praxis* and its relation to other forms of materiality? [I, 79]

Solutions to questions (2) and (3), it will be obvious, cannot even be attempted before the second volume. Numbers (1) and (4) can be posed, but the first can certainly not be completed without exploring and establishing the meaning of History as a joint production of necessity and freedom. Only the last question might have been answered—but was not—in the first volume. The point is that through the pause we have understood certain elements of the dialectic, have seen the way they may combine, but have not yet observed them combine to form the irreversible and large-scale entities which emerge in and seem to direct our history. And so we must accordingly turn to its second volume.

III

Given that the overall purpose of the *Critique* is to philosophically anchor and delimit the dialectic as method of comprehension, course and meaning of history and guide to concrete political action, Volume Two has been seen to bear most of its burdens. It must, to return to our first and simplest formulations, show how and whether totalization does take place even at the heart of conflict, which is to say, how history's positive direction takes shape and sustains itself even within negativity. If, as Sartre in agreement with Marx says, "[t]he history of all hitherto existing society is the history of class struggles,"[22] he seeks to explain, on the most rudimentary theoretical level, why those struggles yield human development, rather than—nothing at all.[23]

Sartre makes these questions more precise at the end of Volume One, and because of their great interest they are worth quoting even at the risk of some repetition.

> We have seen how the mediation of the Third party realizes the transcendent unity of positive reciprocities [That is, how individuals each engaged in the same practice form themselves into a coherent single fused group through the mediation of a third person engaged in the same activity]. But is this unity still possible when each action is aimed at destroying that of the Other and when the observable results of this double negation are nil—or as usually happens—when the teleological significations which each adversary has inscribed in it have been partly erased or transformed by the Other, so that no trace of concerted activity is any longer to be seen? [I, 816–17]

Taking the example of individual combat, how are we to understand that significant results are produced in a situation in which "each blow dealt by the one is dodged or parried or blocked by the Other—but not completely, unless they differ greatly in strength or skill" (I, 817). In the face of the complex totalization which is History we are left trying to understand efforts which "have to be comprehended not as the realization of a project, but in terms of how the action of each group (and also of chance, accident, etc.) prevented them from realizing that of the Other, that is to say, to the extent that they *are not* practical significations, and that their mutilated, truncated meaning does not correspond to any one's practical plan so that, in this sense, they fall short of being human."

At stake in the next stage of analysis is nothing less than the nature and meaning of History itself, seen as:

> the totalisation of all practical multiplicities and of all their struggles, the complex products of the conflicts and collaborations of those very diverse multiplicities. . . . This means that History is intelligible if the different practices which can be found and located at a given moment of the historical temporalization finally appear as partially totalizing and as connected and merged in their very oppositions and diversities by an

22. Karl Marx and Frederick Engels, *The Communist Manifesto, The Collected Works* (London: Lawrence and Wishart, 1976), vol. 6, 482.
23. A position he explored with considerable sympathy in *Cahiers sur la morale*. See 47–49.

intelligible totalisation from which there is no appeal. It is by seeking the conditions for the intelligibility of historical vestiges and results that we shall, for the first time reach the problem of totalisation without a totaliser and of the very foundation of this totalisation, that is to say, of its motive-forces and of its non-circular direction. [I, 817]

And so we come, after a pause, to Volume Two. In its first pages Sartre further clarifies and refines his goal, throwing considerable further light on what *Critique*, II is to be about and why. In a step by step introductory discussion he both indicates what Volume Two is *not* about and deepens our sense of its tasks and importance. In following him closely we can observe his remarkable intellect at work shaping the terrain of study, and perhaps complete this introduction to Volume Two.

If the question is to understand *contradiction*, at the outset Sartre indicates and dismisses the kinds of contradictions he does not have in mind: those arising "at each moment of action" (II, 2) of a single, coherent *praxis* as, for example, it must inevitably oppose this or that section of a practical field to the others, or as it necessarily seeks to go beyond its initial results and limits. Indeed, "contradiction" may well be used in an a priori fashion to assimilate two opposing sides—a "double *praxis* of antagonistic reciprocity"—as "a given moment of totalisation" (II, 2). But wherein lies the unity? Dialectical intelligibility, after all, starts with totalization; and totalization is the product of a unifying *praxis*. A given region is intelligible *because* human intentionality itself shapes its structures and history. But what if, on the contrary, *conflicting* intentionalities are at play:

> in fact there is, if one wishes, a single movement of the two bodies but this movement is the result of *two* enterprises which oppose each other. It belongs at the same time to two practical systems but precisely because of this, it escapes in its concrete reality—at least partially— each of them: if the plurality of the epicenters is a real condition of *two* opposed intelligibilities (insofar as there is comprehensive intelligibility in each system and starting with each *praxis*) how could there be *one* dialectical intelligibility of the process in course? [II, 3]

We may certainly regard a boxing match as *a fight, an object* to appreciate, to find tickets for, to remember, "but this unity is imposed *from the outside on an event*" (II, 4). The point demands closer attention:

> Object for individuals, groups, collectives, defined as totality by language, by the press and the organs of information, and then subse-

quently, in the past designated as a unity in its being-past by memory (it was *the day of the* Carpentier-Dempsey *fight*) the fight, in itself, appears as one of those mathematical symbols which designate an ensemble of operations to carry out, and which figure as such in the series of algebraic equivalences without the mathematician ever being troubled to really carry out the indicated operations. It is an object to be constructed, to be utilized, to be contemplated, to be designated; in other words it figures as such in the activities of others; but no one is troubled to know whether this reality—noematic and unified correspondent of individual and collective *praxis*—is in *itself*, as internal operation to be carried out by two individuals in the reciprocity of antagonism, real unity or irreducible duality. [II, 4–5]

Sartre admits without reservation that *the* match exists, for many people and for many purposes; his goal is "to know if as struggle, as objective fact of reciprocal and negative totalisation, it possesses the conditions of dialectical intelligibility" (II, 5).

Appreciating this question as relevant, legitimate and important is critical to grasping Sartre's purpose. We see here, on the level of struggle (but not yet class struggle), *the* questions of the progressive synthesis: how do separate, antagonistic actions yield *a* history; how do individual totalizations lead to Totalization (and also progress, the direction of history, its truth and meaning)? Here more than anywhere in his *oeuvre* Sartre directly and unflinchingly approaches the master problem, of the passage from Descartes to Marx, the cogito to society, individual *praxis* to collective membership.

But before continuing to approach it directly, Sartre embarks on a lengthy methodological reflection whose purpose is to distinguish the dialectical analysis of struggle from the study of battles usually undertaken by analytical reason, for example in military schools. His goal is to define his terrain of analysis further. Rationally and in a systematic manner, the instructing officer "again goes over all *possible* maneuvers in the envisaged situation to determine whether the one which was done in reality is indeed the *best possible one*, as it should and claims to be" (II, 6). The point is that this approach does not give us the whole, as struggle, but rather as a "complex whole of possibilities which are rigorously linked to each other" (II, 6). Whatever its utility for practical purposes, an approach which concentrates on "a multiplicity of relationships between possibles" (II, 7–8) has abandoned the plane of dialectic. This is the gravamen of Sartre's criticism of analytical reason: it evades "the scandal of irreducible antagonism in order to fall into conditionings in exteriority" (II, 8).

Why must this approach be described pejoratively? Because here as elsewhere in the *Critique* analytical reason is seen as a mode of rational analysis which is unable to grasp both the individual specificity and the larger social processes with which Sartre is concerned. Because it is an abstract and external understanding, carrying us "far from what could be called the irreducible singularity of the epicenters" (II, 8). To elaborate further, "it has definitively abandoned every characteristic which makes the historic reality and the temporal individuality of a given conflict" (II, 9). Under the rubric *dialectical* Sartre has in mind understanding which would both center itself in the perspective of either of the combatants rather than claiming a—necessarily external—neutrality, and illuminate the individual situation of that combatant. Nothing could be further from the military schools' abstract calculus of possibilities than the "blind and passionate" combatant, under threat, urgently forced to respond.

> A real combatant is a violent and passionate man, sometimes desperate, sometimes ready to seek death, who risks everything to destroy the adversary but who maneuvers in a time which is measured for him by the rhythm of the other's attacks (and by a hundred other factors of every order). In having at his disposal (for example) a limited number of men and arms (which forbids certain operations) and who struggles in a variable but always profound ignorance (ignorance of the enemy's real intentions, of the relationship of real forces, of the real position of reinforcements—for the adversary and for him, etc., etc.) this obliges him to take risks, to decide upon the most probable without having the necessary elements for being able to calculate it, to invent the maneuvers which take account of several eventualities (if the enemy is disposed in such a fashion, the operation will take place in such fashion or such manner, if it is discovered in the course of action that he is otherwise disposed the operation is conceived to be able to be instantaneously modified, etc., etc.). It is this blind and passionate inventor who gambles in uncertainty in trying to limit risks, and whose every action is conditioned by external and interiorised scarcity, this man we call a battler [*lutteur*]. [II, 11–12]

Ignorance, urgency, blindness, passion, scarcity—may be obstacles to an analytical reconstruction of the map of possibilities; a dialectical understanding on the contrary understands our action "*in its insufficiency, in its imperfection*, in its mistakes beginning with the negative determinations which it conserves in transcending them" (II, 10). For in fact no action, in its historical reality, can be understood in terms of "the best possible solution since the best possible solution can only be found if one possesses every element of the situation, all the time necessary to regather them into a synthesis which transcends them, all the calm and objectivity necessary for self-criticism" (II, 10–11). In short, a dialectical understanding of a struggle is constructed *in terms of*, not in spite of, these various negativities, and therefore takes place "at the very level of struggle" (II, 11).

For Sartre, then, intelligibility, if it exists, appears in and through the individual project—it is a function of subjectivity in action. Sartre's famous individualist starting point is here above all a commitment to an internal, concrete and thus dialectical understanding. If the match indeed "should be revealed as a unity," the point is not to posit it a priori, which would force us to pretend that each *praxis* is somehow a determination of that larger unity (which would thus be a hyperorganism operating on its own and imposing itself upon individuals from the outside). The point is, rather, to observe how each specific unity is indeed created in "a very particular *praxis*-process" in which "the process is here defined as the deterioration of one *praxis* by the other" (II, 12).

Having further clarified the nature of a dialectical, as opposed to an analytical understanding, Sartre now formulates "the two essential problems." First, to return to the notion of *contradiction*, he now asks about conflicts which "can be, in the interior of a group, the real actualisations of a developing contradiction." In other words, the collectivities studied in Volume One suggest that we may think of *a* battle in terms of a contradiction, and its adversaries as the terms of a contradiction-in-the-making. But to do so, in addition to being able to find in each struggle "the three characteristics of dialectical intelligibility, that is, totalisation, particularisation and contradiction" (II, 12), the opponents "must be able to be considered as the transitory determinations of a more ample and more profound group one of whose present contradictions their conflict would actualise . . ." (II, 12). And, at the same time, the group would have to transcend the "struggle towards a new synthetic reunification of its practical field and an internal reorganization of its structures." In other words, no matter how bitterly opposed might be the adversaries, the real secret of their struggle would be *the group's* self-development.

The second essential problem receives far more development, obviously because of its greater difficulty and complexity. It concerns the products and residue of struggle—the "ambiguous and insufficiently developed" events, incomprehensible objets which become "the factors and conditions of further history" (II, 13). A certain intention—to create the Ateliers Nationaux in 1848—may have been conceived to meet a social need of the moment, but was generated by, and became the object of, class struggle. The products of such struggles appear "as *aporias* since they stand at one and the same time as results of a common enterprise and testify that this enterprise has never existed unless as the inhuman inverse of two opposed actions each one of which aims to destroy the other" (II, 13). The original intention has not been met, but "in spite of the deviations and partial annullments, something remains of the original project and the enterprise conserves a confused efficacity which leads to unforseen results" (II, 14).

Here we reach *the* problem: to make sense of history as totalization, and thus of each struggle in turn as *a* totalization, we must be able to grasp "individuals or groups in struggle as collaborating in fact on a common work. And as the work is perpetually given, as residue of the struggle—be it the devastation of a battlefield, insofar as one could consider the two adversaries as having together burned and sacked the fields and woods—it must be grasped as the objectification of a group at work, itself formed of two antagonistic groups" (II, 14). Not as achieved by their concerted *praxis*, but as in the case of the Ateliers Nationaux, having indeed become "historical realities only to the degree that they do not conform to any of the projects which have achieved them in reciprocal antagonism" (II, 14–15). Remarkably, then, they are historical to the degree that they are made by men, escaping from their makers without thereby becoming unworked matter. "To the degree, in sum, that they deviate from every route one wants to assign them, themselves taking an unforseen route and producing results that could not be guessed" (II, 15). They deviate, that is, not because of the exteriority of materiality as such, of seriality or alienation—but rather because "each one steals his act from the other" (II, 15) in a history based on a plurality of epicenters in conflict.

Social objects formed in such processes and bequeathed to future generations would thus "contain as internal structure the double negation of themselves and of each component by the other" (II, 15). Every social whole contains "a certain aporia": "the apparent unities and partial syntheses cover over lacerations of all orders and sizes; from a distance the society seems to hold all by itself [*tenir toute seule*]; from up close it is riddled with holes" (II, 16).

What is the deeper source of these strange objects and the conflicts which produce them? All conflicts are "conditioned by scarcity, negation of man by Earth, interiorised as negation of man by man" (II, 16). Thus struggles "are never in any way accidents of human history: they represent the very manner in which men live scarcity—in their perpetual movement to transcend it" (II, 16). That is, the original relationship to nature—*there is not enough*—is interiorised, translated onto other levels and transformed into permanent struggles, and into classes. Some societies, as Lévy-Strauss and American sociologists have shown, may transform original scarcity through "rigorous systems of mediations-compensations" and thus "correct chance by a redistribution of certain goods" (II, 17). But then, conflict being prohibited, it remains present as tension and as latent conflict, the malaise of the entire society.

Still, the necessity and universality of scarcity is no more demonstrable a priori than that of history: no one can say "that every practical ensemble should secrete a history, nor even that all possible histories should be conditioned by scarcity." Sartre limits his claims by insisting that such developments "arise with all the contingent richness of a *singularity*" (II, 18). It happens that *our* history, internalizing *our* society, has been one of class struggle: "in the framework of scarcity, the constitutive relationships are fundamentally antagonistic; from the point of view of their temporal development they come under the form of this event which is struggle" (II, 18). This, then, is the very definition of the specific historical process whose intelligibility we seek: first, its strange products "will become the material circumstances which will have to be transcended by other generations torn by other conflicts" (II, 18). Second, these products refer us "wholly and from every point of view" to the conflicting *praxes* in which they originated; but thirdly, the product "overflows the adversaries and by them becomes other than what each one projects" (II, 19).

In this sense, with Marxism, we can regard the class struggle as "the motor of history." For indeed, it reveals "to us the dialectical development of the historical process" (II, 19). Framed in Marxist terms, we can now pose the question of Volume Two: "Is there a unity of different classes which sustains and produces their irreducible conflicts?" Certainly, at the theoretical level, this is the question of questions. Given (a). the primacy of the active *cogito* on which the *Critique* is founded, and given equally (a). that history is a dialectical process, how does (a). produce (b).? If the class struggle is intelligible to dialectical reason, "it must be possible to totalise classes in struggle, and this amounts to discovering the synthetic unity of a Society torn completely apart" (II, 19). Indeed, Marx himself was aware of this problem, as is evidenced by his discussion of the capitalist process as "an anti-social force *in society*. But on the other hand he always refused—and for good reason—to give a reality to this verbal entity that one calls society. He saw there only one form of alienation among others" (II, 19). Neither he nor subsequent Marxists, appropriately concerned as they were with material results, explored such formal problems of intelligibility. But it is today, "at the very moment when the machine seems to jam that it is fitting to clean up the formal difficulties which have hitherto been neglected" (II, 20). It is time today to ask whether struggles are totalizing or detotalizing—that is, whether they create a larger, meaningful and developing whole, or whether they amount to nothing at all or indeed dissolve previous totalizations. Marxism itself is at stake, as Sartre indicates in this trenchant summary:

> Marxism is rigorously true if history is totalisation; it is no longer so if human history is decomposed into a plurality of particular histories. Or if in any case within the relationship of immanence which characterises struggle, the negation of each adversary by the other is on principle *detotalising*. Certainly, we have neither the project nor the possibility of showing here the full truth of dialectical materialism— which we will without doubt attempt elsewhere, in a book devoted to anthropology, which is to say to struggle as such. Our single goal is to establish whether in a practical ensemble torn by antagonism (whether there are multiple conflicts or they are reduced to a single one) the breaks themselves are totalising and entailed by the totalising movement of the ensemble. But if in fact we establish this abstract principle, the materialist dialectic, as movement of history and of historical understanding need only be proven by the facts it illuminates, or if one prefers, need only be itself discovered as a fact and through other facts. [II, 20–21]

But if such a totalizing movement exists, "it occurs everywhere"— leading Sartre to the important new idea, central to what follows: "that each singular event totalises in itself this whole [be it planetary or indeed were it to become interplanetary] in the infinite richness of its singularity" (II, 21). Which suggests indeed that each particular struggle may itself be seen as a "totalisation of every struggle." Before asking, later, about the nature of history or its truth, we must first seek to comprehend a single irreducible conflict, such as the boxing match, "as totalisation of the whole of contemporary irreducibilities and splits . . ." (II, 21).

And so, in the next paragraphs, Sartre launches into his analysis of a particular conflict—a boxing match, for which his introductory discussion has carefully prepared us. The study proper begins. By now its question has been given precision, its outer limits and internal structure shaped, and its significance indicated. I have let Sartre speak at length in order to allow the reader maximum access to the manuscript. We now know what we must look for and why. It is, I said at the outset, a clear yet decisive question. Indeed, we have seen the same question amplified, lent meaning from a number of angles, and representing a rather remarkable self-challenge to Sartre's conceptual universe. We may now be prepared to enter the study from within, understanding and sharing Sartre's purposes—and perhaps even his enthusiasm and urgency.

JULIETTE SIMONT

The *Critique of Dialectical Reason:* From Need to Need, Circularly

"Everything is to be explained through need."[1] So says Sartre at the beginning of the first chapter of the first volume of the *Critique of Dialectical Reason*. And in the last pages of the manuscript of the second volume: "The determination of action in its entirety by the need it transcends in order to satisfy it, such is the foundation of historical materialism."[2] The point of departure turns out, in accordance with what appears an eminently dialectical circularity, to be a point of arrival as well, at the end of an itinerary involving the progressive disclosure of what was nevertheless disclosed from the beginning. It is precisely for this circularity at once unfolded and folded back again upon itself, for this return to a *déjà-là*, that Ronald Aronson reproached Sartre in his critical review of the manuscript of the second volume.[3] He indeed detects in the text something like a break, a schism, a crack, which he situates at the exact spot where Sartre, after studying the concrete evolution of the U.S.S.R. up to the Stalinism of the fifties, returns to the notion of *need* as the very foundation of historical materialism. Far from understanding this return as the dialectical unveiling of an evolved truth, Aronson sees in it the sign of a radical impoverishment of Sartre's thought—perhaps the depletion or exhaustion of the dialectic to which Sartre himself alludes.[4] He sees Sartre suddenly lapsing into tautology, redundancy, the rehashing of an outmoded conception of Being, the sluggishness of argumentation. The abrupt change, from the brilliant

1. *Critique of Dialectical Reason* trans. Alan Sheridan-Smith, (London: New Left Books, 1976), 80.
2. *Manuscript*, 500. The pagination is that of the typed version of the text.
3. Ronald Aronson, "Sartre's Turning Point: The Abandoned *Critique de la raison dialectique*, Volume Two," in *The Philosophy of Jean-Paul Sartre* (The Library of Living Philosophers, 1981), ed. Paul Arthur Schilpp, 685–706.
4. *CDR*, 519.

analysis of the history of the U.S.S.R. to the flat and repetitious text of the last pages of the manuscript, testifies, according to Aronson, to a profound internal drama in Sartre's mind, to an impassable breach in his thought, the impossibility of his project become manifest, the discovery of the inaccessibility of his goal given the premises he had posited. Whence a circular and emptily circulating panic of the dialectic, whence psychic upheaval and shipwreck.

The goal was to provide an intelligible foundation, a founded intelligibility, for History or common action. The premises stipulated that the attempt to do so should be based on constituent *praxis* in its primordial translucence, on the *praxis* of the free individual organism; and that common *praxis* possessed no being irreducibly its own, but always found its intelligibility in constituent *praxis*. It is, according to Aronson, the absolute primacy accorded to individual *praxis* that, on principle, dooms Sartre's undertaking to failure, and it is the manifest ineluctability of this failure that leads Sartre to a very profound crisis, which translates in the text as an obstinate, almost obsessional repetition of the problematic *in its very impossibility:* the fundamental, preeminent character of the individual organism in the genesis of common action. . . . The return to the notion of need as the very Being of History would represent Sartre caught in his own trap, condemned to turn infernally in a circle whose closure he himself has determined, prisoner of that false absolute—individual *praxis*—which bleeds and kills the possibility of his project. For Aronson, this failure is beyond doubt. The proof is that Sartre, in the pages devoted to the U.S.S.R., had set himself the task of elucidating the intelligibility of class conflict, and that, ever obsessed by the fact of free individual *praxis* alone, he deviates from the prescribed itinerary and misses his mark; while he should have applied himself to studying the relations of different practical multiplicities and to showing how they can be totalized to form *one* History, he focuses anew on individuality and studies the *praxis* of a dictator, Stalin, or how the *praxis* of a single individual can enslave an entire society and divert that common project, socialism. Thus, Sartre's intention, swayed by his fascination with individual *praxis*, is reversed: it is no longer a question of how multiplicity can become one in the unity of a historical totalization, but of how the unity of an individual *praxis* can reduce a whole society to itself. At the end of this deviation from his objectives, Sartre, at once discovering and denying the impossibility of the whole undertaking, falls into a weary repetition of the problematic of need and of the relations of the organic and the inorganic with which he had inaugurated this work, a work of whose pointlessness he is now aware.

"'Society' is in fact the missing term of the entire project,"[5] concludes Aronson, who seems to believe that he thus administers an infallible panacea capable of relieving all of Sartre's discomfiture. If Sartre
believes that the *praxis* of the roadmender and of the gardener, even if
they are reciprocal, *"will always remain separate,"*[6] it is because he
chooses to ignore the prior cooperation that unites them even in their
separation and that consists in their belonging to a society that comprises estates large enough to require the work of a gardener and public
thoroughfares requiring regular maintenance. By degrees, the relation of
the roadmender and the gardener expresses the social whole and exists
only on its basis. In brief, why does Sartre, proposing to study common
action, not begin from the right end, that is, the community? This
would have spared him a good many setbacks. . . .

One immediately sees the paradoxical character of this critique,
which amounts to reproaching Sartre not for this or that point of his
project, but for what is at stake in it. The critique appears as a reaffirmation of the necessity of a hyperorganicism, which Sartre continually
refused, denouncing it as illusory. It is apparently less a matter of an
internal critique of Sartre's ambition than of a pure and simple opposition to what it entails. Sartre supposedly fails to reach the level of
common action . . . but to propose as a remedy what Sartre endeavored
to show would inevitably fail is perhaps to attach too little importance
to the relentless rigor with which he pursues and sustains his own
failure. This latter is perhaps a triumph of thought, and conversely, to
try to make it good through recourse to the agency of community or
society is perhaps to rely on an apparent plenitude deeply undermined
by failure. The sense of the last pages of Sartre's manuscript will accordingly be understood either as the frantic babbling of thought in distress,
or as an implacably rigorous and lucid conclusion, one which is perhaps
desperate but whose desperation derives from a flawless respect for
reason rather than from its collapse. This is a debate that can only be
decided if we examine the pages attacked by Aronson, while trying to
bring to the fore what is at stake and the way in which the argument
progresses.

Sartre places himself in these pages at the level of an *ontological*
problematic. He intends to ground therein the *reality* of the dialectic, or,
which amounts to the same, the being-real of the totalization of envelopment, that is, of History as it has unfolded in dialectical discourse.

5. Aronson, op. cit., 704.
6. *CDR*, 114. [The French reads: "elles *resteront toujours deux*," and the English
translation: *"there will always be two* of them."–Tr.]

The stakes therefore are as follows: to prove that the dialectic cannot be accused of idealism, that it is never simply a method or a theory of knowledge, but that it *is* and that Being is dialectical, that the dialectic has being and that this being is that of Being itself. It is apparently a matter, therefore, of a decisive moment in the economy of the project, at which the legitimacy of the project as a whole is subjected to scrutiny. According to Aronson, this move to the ontological plane, to the quintessential level of philosophical discourse, is only a show designed to mask Sartre's inability to solve the central problem: how can *practical* multiplicities *concretely* become *one* historical totalization? In moving to the plane of the *being* of the totalization of envelopment, Sartre forgets that he has not even elucidated the possibility of this totalization, and proceeds as though, having solved all the problems, he could at last raise himself to this culminating and conclusive stage of thought. This false self-assurance actually conceals a core of absolute uncertainty. . . .

Let us try, then, in order to test this critique, to evaluate the importance of this ontological problematic. Sartre has established that History has a *meaning*, which is its objectification as produced by the historian. If History is intelligible or possesses a *meaning* that the historian can and must grasp, this is because the *comprehension* he summons is practical, homogeneous with all practices, and hence with common, historical practice. The historian comprehends History, that is, gives it a meaning, because he does his work—research, reading of archives, of historical accounts, etc.—through the very movement of temporalization, which is also that of History: the present is illuminated and becomes past on the basis of its self-projection toward the future. The historian's relation to History becomes the internal relation of *two praxes* separated by a temporal lag, and the individual *praxis* of the historian is directly related to the common *praxis* of History to the extent that it is itself enveloped by the common *praxis* of History in progress. The danger of idealism inherent in the status of comprehension is plain to see. How can the historian, who grasps the past comprehensively in giving it a meaning, who is situated by the historical process of his own era, by its methodological prejudices, by the lacunae and the specificities it manifests in its apprehension of the real—how can the historian avoid reducing the being of History to his own, partial point of view, reducing Being to being-known, how can he avoid producing but an idealistic extrapolation of his own limits to the totality of Being?

To put it plainly: what is the status of the *Critique of Dialectical*

Reason, of this situated discourse which purports to explain the intelligible foundation of History? Has it no other status than that of a purely formal system? Must it be considered a nominalism? In brief, must one see an irremissible contradiction between situation and enveloping totalization, between situated individuality and History? It is on this question that the being of the dialectic depends, to the extent that—if Sartre's ambition proves justified—this being is Being itself.

Sartre endeavors, then, to show that if History assumes a meaning through the comprehension of the historian, it is certainly not to the extent that this meaning is *relative* to the knowledge gleaned from History and receives its being from it, but, on the contrary, that it is Being itself that expresses itself in knowledge. It is at this point that Sartre begins his "refutation of idealism," that the debate is brought to a properly ontological level, and that Sartre announces that he must confront the question of *the being-real of the being-meaning* of the totalization of envelopment. It is not situated comprehension that reduces the totality of Being to itself, it is Being that opens situated comprehension to the future. That the historian has only a partial view of Being does not prevent this view from being totally true and from bearing the truth of *Being*. To be sure, any epistemological practice—and, as we shall see, any practice whatsoever—is limited by an *external ignorance:* techniques of apprehension not yet invented, the totality of future sociocultural relations whose advent will allow a transformation of historical disciplines. But far from enveloping Being by reducing it to itself, this basic limitation of knowledge marks its own envelopment in the enveloping totalization. The situated character of comprehension does not make Being relative to being-known, but is the guarantee that knowledge is always relative to Being. The limitations of a given historical synthesis necessarily inscribe it at the heart of future historical syntheses, to the extent that the latter will themselves be conditioned by the modifications of History in progress.

But it is also necessary to understand the reverse of this movement. If, in the relation of the situation to the totalization of envelopment, that is, to History, the situation has no autonomy of being that would allow of its reducing the whole of Being to its being-limited, neither does Being have any such autonomy, nor is there any supreme envelopment of all situations that would reduce them to being but epiphenomena without any consistency of their own, entirely determined by the whole that envelops them. The being of the totalization of envelopment is nowhere but in what is made of it by situated comprehensions extending beyond themselves. Being is everything the situation is not, the external limit of situated comprehension. But the latter can be limited only inasmuch as it is internally affected by its limit; a limit purely exterior to the limited would annul itself, since the limited is limited only by encountering its limit, by being internally related to it, without which the limit could not constitute the positivity of the limited. The external limit of the situation is therefore its internal limit as well, already exceeded by that which it should contain. That which limits— exteriority or envelopment—has no autonomous being by which it would dominate enveloped situations, but is only the movement by which those situations are transcended, or by which, outside themselves within themselves, they push back the borders of this false outside by expanding their interiority. Thus, the relation is two-way: exteriority is only the movement by which interiority constitutes itself by interiorizing its limit, interiority is only the movement by which exteriority is repropelled. Situated comprehension is at once enveloped and enveloping, and the totalization of envelopment at once enveloping and enveloped, in an indefinitely revolving spiral where each term expresses the vanishing perspective immanent to the other. *Made history*, the result of a given historical synthesis, *meaning* as the sedimentation of common *praxis*, is therefore also *history in the making*, just as history in the making ceaselessly makes of itself the past of what it is and deposits itself in totalizations enveloped by its own movement. Knowledge is the *being-past* of Being, or the movement by which Being becomes what it has been.

At present, it is proven that situation and totalization of envelopment, rather than being contradictory and mutually exclusive, so that a situated point of view could never constitute more than an ideal extrapolation unduly claiming to say the last word on being, are in a relation of mutual envelopment and reciprocal implication. What indeed emerges at this stage of the argument is that there is an unavoidable relation between situation and totalization. But the problem has only slipped back a notch: although, in a dialectical logic, situation and totalization are inseparable, this does not yet prove that *the logic of this relation itself* is not idealistic, or that this relation as it has been logico-dialectically established, as the very being of *praxis*, is not actually cut off from the being-real of Being. In other words, even if the partiality of the situation is eliminated in favor of the double, spiral envelopment of situation and totalization, nothing yet says that this double movement itself is anything other than a "theory of knowledge," one which is simply a bit more flexible and supple than others, but which for that does not reach the fundamental level of Being. The question therefore is raised again: "What matters for us is to determine if we must view the totalization of envelopment through a positivistic nominalism or in the perspective of a radicalizing realism."[7] It is clearly the second way that Sartre chooses, and to test its pertinence he uses—still affirming paradox to the extreme—what seems poles apart from realism, namely, myth or science fiction. An interplanetary traveler—a Martian—astonished, watches humanity bustling about with a relentlessness whose inanity it does not for a moment perceive. This Martian is the expression of the superior indifference of Being to the surface disturbances of the human world. He grasps human activity and its totalizing claims as mobilizing an infinitely limited sector of Being, a proof of that limit being the knowledge the Martians acquired long ago of a cosmic catastrophe whose advent will reduce humanity to dust. For this absolute witness, how could human *praxis*—the relation of mutual envelopment between situation and totalization—not appear as an absurd commotion having nothing to do with the most profound being of Being, how could it not seem quite similar to the abrupt movements of puppets oblivious to the strings that pull them or to the complacency of the dove that ignores its dependence on the air that bears it? The reciprocal immanence of interior and exterior, of situation and totalization, changes, before the cosmico-synthetic gaze of the absolute witness, into illusion and dream, into absolute exteriority with regard to the absoluteness of Being. In brief, it seems that the Martian, while grasping our ends, does not comprehensively reactualize the movement by which we project ourselves toward them, that he grasps them as pure *exis* and not as *praxis*.

But actually, the absurdity of the bustle of the human anthill for the Martian is itself absurd. Such an external point of view is possible only inasmuch as it becomes internal to what it supposedly looks down upon, as it therefore negates itself, situates itself by the very negation it produces of every situation. If the Martian were absolutely transcendent, really outside of our practical field, he would absolutely not be; if he grasped our *praxis* only as *exis*, he would not grasp it at all. It is clear that the Martian could not see human *praxis* as being-already-past in view of the cosmic catastrophe to come if he did not identify with human ends before differentiating himself from them. Yet this still does not suffice to prove the impossibility of the Martian's transcendence, for he could carry out this identification only in order decisively to detach himself from it, and such would be precisely the definition of the

7. *Manuscript*, 445.

superior point of view. It must therefore be shown that, for the Martian, the simple fact of having to pass through the identification with human ends as with his own exteriority involves him in a relation of definitive immanence with the terrestrial world. The proof of this is easy to come by. In order to be really *extra*terrestrial, the extraterrestrial would have to assert himself through a properly unheard of mode of self-production, befall the world as an absolute strangeness, that is, exhibit an absolute independence in the matter of temporality. Ultimately, his gaze would have to strike the world with the instantaneous and blinding violence of the cosmic catastrophe itself. But if this gaze relates an unveiling of the future and a present unveiled on the basis of this unveiling as already-past, if this gaze effects an opening and a reflective distancing, then the Martian does not do otherwise than the situated and very human historian who turns back upon made history on the basis of that which declares itself in history in progress. If the Martian's operation is identical to that of the historian, this homogeneity, which entitles the extraterrestrial to objectify the *praxis* of humanity, also entitles the historian to objectify the Martian in return. What this means, finally, is that the Martian *is a man* like all and like any, who, in unveiling an as yet unknown future, attests to no absolute transcendence but reveals himself only as an inventor more daring than others: he who has enlarged the practical field by introducing into it the cosmic catastrophe and by adapting past *praxis* to this knowledge, he who has pushed back the frontiers of external ignorance.

By its very absurdity, by its necessarily mythical or fictional character, the myth of the Martian will have served to show the absolute irreducibility of the relation of the situation to the totalization of envelopment. This relation is unsurpassable, and to try to surpass it by locating it in a superior envelopment is always to resituate oneself within it. This relation is Being, and to be is necessarily to be this relation. It is to be noted that one finds the translation of this apparently childish myth in great philosophical theories that are, throughout the critique, Sartre's appointed adversaries: principally Leibniz and Spinoza, and through them every theological or materialist determinism. For these are forms of thought based on the attempt at a radical desituation, on a conception of the relation of situation and totalization, of the parts and the whole, such that the whole always acquires a kind of autonomy or sufficiency of being that enables it to absorb the parts. "There are two ways to desituate oneself in relation to the object: one is to become Nature; the other, less easily detectable, is to refuse the situation as reciprocity. . . . The first desituation leads to the dogmatism of the outside, the second to positivist idealism."[8] To become Nature or to understand man as a fragment of the adventure of the universe, such is Spinoza's substantialist determinism. Positivist idealism is only a modernization of Leibnizian idealism: the positivist abstracts himself from his object in order to consider it as constituted by a myriad of irreducible punctualities, or *facts*, but at the same time he must, in order to confer a meaning upon his undertaking—which might seem destined to lapse into a pure and simple passivity—assume a horizon of reconciliation, an optimistic progressivism which appears precisely to be excluded by the careful respect for the single, isolated fact. The hand of a God incomprehensibly sorts out from on high the brute incomprehensibility of facts. . . . In Leibniz as well, the supreme Monad harmonized, with a view toward the best, a multiplicity of monadic isolations *sans portes ni fenêtres*, cut off from any mutual relationality.

Both Spinoza's substantialist determinism and Leibniz's theological determinism are characterized by an *absence* of the relation of the whole and the parts, of totalization and situation. In Spinoza this relation is absent through an *excess of immanence:* any distance between the substance and its intensive manifestations is abolished, so that there is no longer a relation but a pure compactness of being, so that what is lacking is that lack of being or that distension in being which is the very freedom of relation. This pantheism of absolute immanence is a dogmatism of the outside, a form of thought consigned purely to exteriority, a ruthless determinism, since the compactness of Being, always fully present in a totalitarian manner in the least of its expressions, reduces the latter to an immediate, fused identity with the whole that excludes any inventive circularity or mutual readjustment. In Leibniz this relation is absent through an *excess of transcendence:* no longer absorbed through excessive proximity in a confusional immanence, but broken by the infinite distance that separates its terms, a relation so dissociated and dualized that one no longer sees how it might hold together. On the one hand, there is the infinite dispersion of a-relational monads *sans portes ni fenêtres*, the exacerbation of a principle of atomistic individuality; on the other hand, there is the level of the whole or of God's relating of these monadic entities. Spinoza-Leibniz, two impossible non-relations, each becoming its opposite by the simple fact of its occurrence. That the substance multiplies itself in an infinity of finite self-expressions means that it must never cease leaving itself in

8. Ibid., 446.

order to be itself, that it must exteriorize itself in order to reinteriorize itself, therefore that this pantheism which assumes the immediate, fused identity of the whole of Being is actually mediated by a circularity that is at bottom nothing but the very *life* of nature. And as for the harmony established by the supreme Monad, it is enough to examine it to see it negate itself at once: either there is a relationality of monads, in which case God, in order to produce it, must become internal to them, become their multiplicity, and therefore relinquish his transcendence and become immanent to the monads, so that he is nothing but *their* relation; or else, in the hypothesis of an absolute transcendence of God, who would confine himself to his pure being-exterior with regard to the world, harmony would never be the harmony *of* the monads and the best of all possible worlds would go up in smoke.

There is no desituation; there is neither Martian, nor substance extending itself unitarily as the whole of Being, nor is there a great operator or divine hand harmonizing from on high the monads or facticial punctuality. There is a necessary relation of the part and the whole, or rather of situation and totalization, a relation which is simultaneously Being and the intelligibility of Being. In the end, all the preceding developments lead back to this single conclusion: there is no absolute objectification, no "point of view of the whole"—and moreover, the very expression, contradictory in itself, is enough to reveal its own impossibility. Indeed, how could the whole, if it is everything, abandon itself to that partial activity of taking a point of view on. . . . how could its power of inclusion not be self-sufficient, a full positivity having no need to adopt a perspective on a limited sector of itself. If knowledge as such is the objectification of Being as *meaning* or as being-past, if objectification has no autonomy, no irreducible specificity, but must always become internal to that in relation to which it purports to maintain a relation of exteriority, then it is indeed in a *problematic of Being* that we are involved with the dialectic of situation and totalization and not in a theory of knowledge. Still, it is necessary to produce from this problematic an intelligibility that is not simply negative, that is not defined by what it *is not* (*neither* Spinozist idealism *nor* Leibnizian idealism, *neither* confusional immanence *nor* inaccessible transcendence). It is now a question therefore of clarifying, in its specific originality regarding the idealisms it refutes, the dialectic of situation and totalization, of the part and the whole, as Sartre upholds it throughout the critique.

Sartre wishes in fact to avoid the danger of a further misunderstanding. If one understands things too quickly, it might seem that this dialectic is only a mixture of Leibnizianism and Spinozism, their simultaneous mobilization, their contradictory union: at once the whole is the parts (Spinoza) and is not the parts (Leibniz). What else is at issue in the dialectic of the mutual envelopment of situation and totalization than this double movement? Every situated practice is irreducible in its singularity (the monadic universe), and at the same time it is the human totalization or "human milieu" that expresses itself in each of these singularities (the substance multiplying itself in its modes). And yet it cannot be the union of these two idealisms, each refuted for itself, that enables Sartre to escape all idealism. He therefore specifies that although in fact he often uses such turns of phrase or lines of reasoning, although he frequently adopts a certain formalism concerning the relation of the whole and the parts, this must be seen only as a *metaphor* and not understood literally: "This language, as one can tell, is our own, it is the language of all dialecticians, and in fact it presents no danger if one sees in it only a set of efficient, figurative locutions that save time and that cancel themselves in the very act of comprehension. But if one takes it literally, it plunges us back into an idealistic optimism"[9]—into that optimism which considers that the human relation that links the parts to the whole, situated individuals to society, is always and everywhere first. The relaxation of the thought of Leibniz and Spinoza through their mutual balancing is a form of idealism, as is that fluid and circulating double relation through which the whole is and is not the parts, the parts are and are not the whole. It is a humanist idealism, since it is always a question of the *human* project and of its inscription within the total horizon of human realizations. Sartre returns, then, to the original source of his project, namely, the free practical organism and need, and recalls the profound truth of this highly spiritual and ethereal flexibility, to wit, that the latter is always only metaphorical with respect to an eminently concrete relation, one which is linked to a fundamental material rooting.

It is this fundamental materiality of *praxis* that could be clouded by the "levity" of the formal relation. It must therefore be emphasized that this excessively pure relationality is not the substance of the human act, that "the 'substance' of the human act is on the contrary the nonhuman (or at most the pre-human) to the extent that it is precisely the discrete materiality of each human being."[10]

This does not mean that Sartre returns to a positivist materialism—which is, as we have seen, only a facet of idealism—that he subjects

9. Ibid., 452.
10. Ibid.

freedom to a facticial given. It is simply a matter of showing the *emergence* of the totalizing relation *at its primary and most elementary level*, that beyond which intelligibility cannot go, that of the very advent of historical humanity. The biological organism is the site of this advent and the absolute guarantee of the *reality* of the dialectic. Sartre then finally develops what he had begun rather abruptly with in the first chapter of the first book of the *Critique*. Humanity cannot survey itself, there is no point of view that might attain to the inhuman while retaining the unifying and synthetic power of the human. But although this elevated inhumanity is impossible, one must affirm the necessity of a prehuman inhumanity which is not a desituation but an a-situation, which is not a superior synthesis but an external dispersion: matter, or the *being-in-itself* of the totalization of envelopment. It is in matter, that is, at the crudest and most opaque level of reality, on a plane of being that seems governed by pure laws of exteriority, that "one must consider as an absolute reality the appearance of practical, toolmaking organisms, with their own temporalization, and the transformation of this sector by the improbable physico-chemical systems these organisms engender."[11] Being-in-itself or unsurpassable facticial dispersion cannot be reduced to an inert succession of exterior, material *states*, precisely because it includes those complex systems, highly improbable in light of natural mechanisms, constituted by organisms with their circular structure, their feedback reactions, their relation of interiority to exteriority. This is where the *Critique of Dialectical Reason* began, this is where it ends; and what could be more justified, whatever Aronson may think, since it is here that the *dialectic as such* begins, and here as well that it stops: "It goes without saying that, although the real existence of organic totalities and totalising processes reveals a dialectical movement, the existence of organic bodies can in no way be derived from the dialectic. However biology may develop in future, organic bodies can never be regarded as any more than *de facto* realities; we have no means of establishing their existence by reason alone."[12] The paradoxical tension between situation and totalization that Sartre sustained throughout the text, that tension which is but dialectical discourse itself and whose being-real he now turns back to examine, finds its ultimate and quintessential expression in this *emergence* of the dialectic—the human organism—which is at the same time the *arrest* of the dialectic—the impossibility of establishing the appearance of this organism by reason alone. There is an absolute reality of the dialectic

11. Ibid., 459.
12. *CDR*, 91.

through the absolute reality of the dialectical functioning of the organism, but an absolute contingency of that absoluteness through our external ignorance as to the genesis of this functioning, as to the "why" of this leap out of itself toward itself of being-exterior interiorizing itself as organism.

The dialectic finds the ultimate guarantee of its being-real in this, that far from being a discourse masking the contingency of Being beneath the fluidity of its conceptual perfection, it is radically situated with regard to that contingency by the very inexplicability of its emergence. Thus, just as we established that there was an exterior of every interior *in* the dialectic, so there is an exterior *of* the dialectic itself which prevents it from becoming an idealist overview of Being. But also, just as *in* the dialectic the exterior of the interior was interior to the latter, so the exterior *of* the dialectic is interiorized by the dialectic itself, which constitutes its internal limit. Consequently, if the dialectic interiorizes its outside, there is no difference between what is *in* the dialectic and what befalls it *from without.* In other words, although the dialectical functioning of the organism is limited by the opacity of its own appearance, although it is bounded on all sides by external being-in-itself, it interiorizes in return this being-exterior, modifies it practically, situates it in relation to its own circularity. Or again: the circularity of the organism's activity cannot enclose itself within a limited sector that would not summon the totality of external being-in-itself. Therefore it is indeed the whole of Being that the practical organism totalizes—be this in the mode of a fleeting and inaccessible whole—and hence the totalization of envelopment *is* absolutely: Q.E.D. But we must still provide the ultimate demonstration of this, which Sartre develops through the notion of *need.*

"Thus, the reality of the totalization stems from the presence of these two absolutes and from their reciprocity of envelopment."[13] The two absolutes are external being-in-itself and the interiorizing activity of the practical organism. What must finally be reached is the intelligibility of this apparently untenable paradox: that of *two absolutes.* It seems that the absolute, in order to be absolute, must be total and unitary, that a duality of absolutes could only reciprocally limit itself and therefore cease to be absolute. In brief, this question must be answered: how can *two* absolutes guarantee, by their dual presence, the absolute reality of the totalization, when their very duality appears to imply that they mutually condemn themselves to contingency and can

13. *Manuscript,* 466.

therefore found nothing absolutely? What must be understood is that these two absolutes are of course contingent, but that this contingency in no way detracts from their absoluteness. *Need*, which is closest to the emergence of organic practice outside of external being-in-itself, is what gives a contracted, purified visibility to this absolute duality of the absolute. "Everything is to be explained through need." Through need, the external absolute of scarcity or the threat of death that weighs upon every organism, and the internal absolute of the reproduction of organic life, confront each other absolutely. Through it, that which—in a universe where scarcity was masked by a *relative* material abundance—was lived as an uninterrupted, cyclical immanence of life to nature, of nature to life, is suddenly revealed as antagonism and *exteriority:* nature is what represents to the organism its impossibility, the organism is what represents to nature the impossibility of that impossibility. This is the moment at which the two conjoined absolutes seem to impose upon themselves a mutual limit or to rob each other of their absoluteness, it is the moment at which the tense relation between the organism and the universe seems to explode. Yet such an explosion cannot take place, for it would in fact abstract the unsurpassable exteriority *of* the organism. The organism cannot, in response to the need that assails it and enjoins it to negate the negation imposed upon it by the world, produce from itself, through purely organic processes, what will fill the gap; the simple fact that it is "assailed" by need is enough to prove this, for if the organism had a self-sufficient power of synthesis, it would be a pure, self-creative springing forth, never letting itself be affected by any negativity. The duality of the two "states of matter,"[14] external being-in-itself and the practical organism, that duality which constituted the absolute duality of the absolute of Being, is to be found therefore *within the organism*, as the necessary relation it must maintain with the inorganic in order to reproduce itself. The organism must become inert in order to act upon the inert, or it chooses directed passion as a means of action. What this means is that, through the very limit that being-in-exteriority imposes upon it, through the break that this latter introduces into the smooth harmony of life, the organism, in moving from function to action, from reproduction in immanence to the expanded implementation of means in view of ends, interiorizes this being-exterior or expands into a totalization that extends to the very confines of the universe. The organism, echoing *within itself* that scission of the two states of matter which is the absolute of Being,

14. *CDR*, 87.

comes to be such that it can absolutely totalize Being, such that its own movement of self-pursuit is the movement *of* Being. Thus, the two absolutes do not exclude but rather imply each other *to the extent that organic interiority is its own exteriority.* It is to be noted that this mediation required by the practical organism does not relativize the absoluteness of being-in-itself, since it is only when provoked by it, when threatened by scarcity, that the organism will become the duality it is and thus project itself in an action that totalizes Being itself. The organism has no *de jure* privilege (this would be yet more idealism), there is simply the *de facto* impossibility of freeing ourselves from the absolute fact of organic circularity, the impossibility of claiming that it is not through interiority that being-exterior befalls us. But being-exterior is everywhere, it is the very depth of our practice, the infinitely infinite relations our practice forms with the whole universe, the necessary horizon of its movement.

It is thus shown that the two absolutes, by the very limits they impose upon each other, by the "contingentization" each attempts to inflict upon the other, reciprocally propel each other back into their absoluteness, in a spiral which is but the totalization of envelopment or Being itself. Let us try now to assess the significance of all these developments with regard to our starting point, namely, Aronson's critique of Sartre. This critique was twofold: it concerned at once the text of the manuscript whose development we have attempted to reconstruct and Sartre's general ambition, the text being denounced as redundant and quasi-neurotic, the ambition as impossible, the second denunciation supporting the first. In trying to follow closely the meanderings through which Sartre delimits more and more precisely, from the most abstract to the most concrete, from historical knowledge to organic reproduction, the double envelopment that characterizes the totalization of envelopment, we have perhaps already invalidated the first critique. Invalidating the second will be easier as a function of the distance already covered. This critique holds that the agency of society is the "missing term" of the *Critique.* To be sure, it is missing, but only in the sense that this lack is not the sign of any failure, and expresses the movement of the mutual envelopment of the two absolutes, that is, of the totalization as Being itself. He is not an idealist whom one thinks to be. According to Aronson, Sartre idealistically abstracts the material infrastructure of society, the whole concrete play of the social relations of "prior cooperation," when, undoing the totalization he has just produced, he breaks the reciprocity of the *praxes* of the roadmender and the gardener with this irrevocable verdict: "they *will always remain separate.*" But what sort of concrete, material infrastructure would this be that would bring the two men together in an indissoluble community? Does it not dangerously resemble an otherworldliness of ends in themselves, a fantasmatic domain of pure recognition, of the "communication" of minds"? Does it not deny the very being of matter, namely, discontinuity? Is it not a pretext masking a kind of Leibnizian or idealist-positivist aspiration to harmony? What could be the difference between preestablished harmony and "prior cooperation"? As for the supposed impossibility of Sartre's project, we have seen that it was the necessary condition of its own possibilization. Now that the dialectical relations of situation and totalization have been elucidated as relations of *being*, the task of understanding common *praxis* on the basis of constituent *praxis* becomes implacably coherent. The internal bond that ties the interiority of the organism to its exteriority, to the very depth of the universe, makes possible the being-real of its attempted totalization of Being. Stalin's *praxis* is internally linked to that of his era and of his society, according to the double, contingent absoluteness of envelopment already evoked, just as *Madame Bovary* concentrates and expresses the whole drama of 1848. Not only are there singular absolutes, there are *only* singular absolutes, totalizing by their very situation, "programs" summarizing in a foreshortened temporalization the development of a broader, historical temporalization. Enveloping-enveloped, enveloped-enveloping, we cannot attain to any realm of recognition, we can but infinitely pursue the broken relation of totalization. No, matter is not yet immaterial, no, "we are not angels and we do not have the right to understand our enemies, we do not yet have the right to love *all* men."[15]

Translated by Thomas Trezise

15. Sartre, Saint Genet: comédien et martyre (Paris: Gallimard, 1952), 202.

Part IV

DAVID S. GROSS

Sartre's (Mis)Reading of Flaubert's Politics: An Unacknowledged Dialectic of Misanthropy and Utopian Desire

> Gradually I have come to realize what every great philosophy up to now has been: the personal confession of its originator, a type of involuntary and unaware memoirs. . . .
> The anchorite does not believe that any philosopher (assuming that all philosophers were once anchorites) ever expressed his essential and ultimate opinions in a book. On the contrary, one writes books in order to conceal what is concealed in one. He will doubt, in fact, that a philosopher *can* ever have an "ultimate and essential" opinion. He will suspect behind each cave a deeper cave, a more extensive, more exotic, richer world beyond the surface, a bottomless abyss beyond every bottom, beneath every "foundation." Every philosophy is a foreground philosophy. . . . There is something arbitrary in the fact that the philosopher stopped *here*, that he looked back and looked around, that *here* he refrained from digging deeper, that he laid aside his spade. . . .
> Each philosophy also *conceals* a philosophy; each opinion is also a hiding place; each word is also a mask.
> —Nietzsche, *Beyond Good and Evil*

I

Jean-Paul Sartre writes with Nietzsche's irony toward philosophers and historians—toward, one might say, intellectual endeavor in general, when applied to human existence and its motivating forces—very much in mind. Yet, I shall argue here, his own monumental study of Flaubert needs to be questioned in just the way that Nietzsche suggests.[1] For despite the awesome length of Sartre's *Flaubert*, important things are left out; for all his digging, Sartre too soon lays aside his spade. The source of the problem seems to be in Sartre's use of history, or, rather, in an unacknowledged conflict in his works between the representation of the active, ever-changing historical process and the static, artificial rigidities of certain categories from Sartre's conception of literary history.

1. Jean-Paul Sartre, *l'Idiot de la famille: Gustave Flaubert de 1821 à 1857*, 3 vols. (Paris: Gallimard, 1971–72). All citations will be from this edition, abbreviated as *Flaubert* rather than as *Idiot*. It will be generally cited in the text. All translations from the French, unless otherwise indicated, are my own.

In this essay I will use a historical method in an attempt to deconstruct Sartre's conception of history. I shall muster facts about Flaubert and nineteenth-century France, especially in and around the revolutionary praxis of 1848, not in order to assert the primacy of such empiricist evidencing over Sartre's theoretical armature, but rather to suggest a crucial lack in that theory when it comes to literary history.

Since at least the 1948 *What is Literature?* Sartre operated from an ironic and, I shall argue, a truncated, ahistorical view of modernism. From a point of view which persists with very little change through the *Flaubert* Satre describes French literature after 1848 as an absolutely negative phenomenon, in which the "best" writer must "write on principle *against all his readers.*" Such a writer "was up in the air, a stranger to his century, out of his element, damned," and uselessness was a necessary condition for beauty. "The extreme point of this brilliant and mortal literature was nothingness. Its extreme point and its deeper essence. There was *nothing positive* in the new spirituality. It was pure and simple negation of the temporal," "a parasitic aristocracy of pure consumption" in ineffectual permanent rebellion against the bourgeoisie: "The bourgeoisie let him carry on; it smiled at these monkey shines."

The problem is that Sartre makes this provocative partial view into a comprehensive, fundamentally static, ahistorical category within his brilliant, tour de force literary history in these pages. Perhaps because his own fiction, especially in *Nausea*, his best novel, is so much a part of the negative, critical modernist movement he describes, his criticism is one-sided, his view incomplete. He fails to acknowledge the tension within such texts. Had the writer, says Sartre, sided with the proletariat "his style would have regained an inner tension," his art would have taken root in "generosity, the original source of the work of art, the unconditional appeal to the reader." Only in the *future* can Sartre see literature as he says it ought to be, "a synthesis of Negativity, as a power of uprooting from the given, and a Project, as an outline of a future order; it will be the Festival, the flaming mirror which burns everything reflected in it, and generosity, that is, a free invention, a gift."[2]

I believe that the very tension that Sartre describes—a dialectical, complex response to the constant flux of history—exists within the discourse of modernism, where he refuses to see it. I think he is wrong to assert that there is "nothing positive" in such literature. For all the

---

2. Jean-Paul Sartre, *What is Literature?* Trans. Bernard Frechtman (New York: Philosophical Library, 1949). Emphases added. 117; 127; 128–29; 130; 134; 86–114. (In less than sixty pages Sartre takes us from the seventeenth century through the middle of this century); 148; 159.

sense of pointlessness in *Nausea*, for example, the feeling of absurdity in all projects (including, of course, the historical biographical project of the protagonist, so similar to Sartre's own project twenty-five years later in the *Flaubert*), and the irony toward the "humanism" of the self-taught man, the intuitive rush of sympathy at the end of the novel toward the self-taught man alone in his agony, gives signification to Roquentin's existence. But Sartre will not acknowledge the Utopian aspect of modernism, in his own work or in Flaubert's. I use the word "Utopian," following Ernst Bloch and Fredric Jameson, to mean the largely unconscious desire for a better world, desire having its source in the libido.[3]

In the totalization which Sartre constructs around Flaubert's project to be a writer, "to choose the unreal," Sartre omits key positive elements which exist alongside, usually submerged under, the negative ones he discusses so brilliantly and at such length. Sartre refuses to admit Flaubert's connections to history, and sees *only* the withdrawal into a literary historical classification robbed of its own dialectical relation to a larger historical context. If the picture is corrected through additions which come from a further examination of history, a new totalization of Flaubert and modernism emerges, one in which the dialectical tension, the "festival" Sartre can only see as hypothetical or as in the future, can be seen within the discursive practice of Flaubert. Flaubert's fictions, like many works in the modernist canon, can then be seen to have their greatness in a rich and complex relation to history, in a dialectic tension between the Negativity Sartre makes so absolute and the Utopian generosity and hope which Sartre can only imagine as a possibility in works which do not yet exist. It is in order to add to Sartre's view and not to deny it, that I will try in these pages to insert Flaubert into history, to show that his was in fact a discourse in which the eternal present which is all Sartre can see in his work was open to "the drifts from the other ends of time."[4]

3. The word "Utopian" as used in this essay was defined and articulated by Ernst Bloch. Cf. *On Karl Marx*, trans. John Maxwell (New York: Herder and Herder, 1971), and *A Philosophy of the Future*, trans. John Cumming (New York: Herder and Herder, 1970); it is obvious from Fredric Jameson's account in *Marxism and Form: Twentieth-Century Dialectical Theories of Literature* (Princeton: Princeton University Press, 1971), "Ernst Bloch and the Future," 116–59, that *Hope the Principle* (1959) is also of central significance. In this country the term has been given significant application by the Social Text group, especially by Jameson in *The Political Unconscious: Narrative as a Socially Symbolic Act* (Ithaca: Cornell University Press, 1981).

4. Fredric Jameson, *The Prison-House of Language: A Critical Account of Structuralism and Russian Formalism* (Princeton: Princeton University Press, 1972), 187. Jameson's beautiful phrase was called to my attention by Frank Lentricchia, *After the New Criticism* (Chicago: University of Chicago Press, 1980), 123.

It is this privileging of the negative in Flaubert by Sartre which I would like to discuss in this essay, pointing out where and in what ways I think Sartre's account is wrong. I shall show that there exist in Flaubert's vision as embodied in his discourse elements in powerful opposition to the nihilistic and hopeless resignation of modernism which Sartre is alone willing to acknowledge. I shall show as well the distortions which result from Sartre's nondialectical view of this particular issue, the misleading view of Flaubert which results from the omission of certain crucial elements from the totalization which Sartre constructs. Finally, I shall attempt to account for the reason why Sartre would present such a view.

II

No concept is more central to Sartre's thought than *totalization*.[5] It is also that aspect of his theory which connects his thought most directly with the whole structuralist-post-structuralist enterprise, with its critique of the *cogito*, the privileged, centered subject, and its insistence that it is in the systemic, structural interaction and interdependence of component parts and forces that any aspect of reality must be investigated and understood. The idea that meaning and significance are relational, based on interaction and difference among forces both present and absent is always operative when Sartre speaks in terms of totalization, whether he is speaking of a historical movement or moment or of the situation of the one man, Flaubert, in nineteenth-century France.

The concept of totalization can be said to take precedence over the notions and categories of *Being and Nothingness*, and it is notable that it is in just those ahistorical existential and phenomenological aspects of his early thought that his work is most opposed by the newer structuralist and poststructuralist thought. And it is from the time of the famous "conversion" to Marxism in the late 1940s that the idea of totalization achieves the significance it continues to hold in his work. The "conversion" was really, of course, to historicity, and to a more thoroughgoing and rigorous materialist epistemology. The concept of totalization allowed Sartre to think about, to seek out what one can know about a subject in terms of the freeze-frame, momentary temporal suspension in a rich textual interaction which is the synchronic, and at

5. See the discussion in Jameson, *Marxism and Form*, 230–32. As Jameson points out "totalization" becomes in the *Critique* and thereafter Sartre's key descriptive term for dialectical situations of three sorts: those referring to history, to individual actions, and to the sort of thinking which deals with either or both of them.

the same time to see his subject inserted in the larger complex of change and interaction of history. At the heart of the idea of totalization is the Marxist dialectic, with its insistence on the holistic, historical and materialist nature of any aspect of reality which one chooses to investigate. The dialectic to which I refer is not the pseudoactivity but actual stasis of the binary opposition, nor the privileging of the economic one sometimes finds in "Marxist" thought, but the sense of constant change and mutual influence and interaction of all significant material objects and forces. This process is characterized by opposition and conflict, the movement implied by Blake when he asserts "Without Contraries is no progression."

I use the idea of "material forces"—as I understand it to have been used by Marx and the other great thinkers in his tradition—to include many forces usually thought of as lying outside that designation, aspects of desire, power, force usually labeled as being spiritual, cultural, rhetorical, etc. "Material" would thus designate something like "real" forces, those which have effects, which act, are acted upon, have the capacity to change things. Marx himself uses the notion in that way. His works are filled with accounts of the actions, effects and influences of forces usually not seen as material. The use of the idea of materialism in this way has the effect of cancelling most oppositions to Marxism, which assume a privileging of the economic and granting of significance only to crudely material forces, operating in a mechanistic and narrowly deterministic fashion.

Neither the narrative produced by the Marxist dialectic nor that based on Sartre's totalization posits any such simplistic view of reality. Indeed, like Marx, Sartre attempts always to avoid false simplifications, the privileging of any realm, from the economic through the aesthetic or spiritual, which would grant false, easy answers, reduce complexities to a more comfortable structure wherein—I think both Sartre and Marx, like Nietzsche, would agree with Derrida here—a transcendental signifier always lurks, turning real chaos, fluidity, disorder, dialectical complexity and change into a lulling, (even when profoundly ironic and depressing), ordered Center around which some economic, political, psychological or aesthetic stasis is assumed to arrange itself, outside history.

Yet for all the rigor of Sartre's understanding of totalization—and I think the very number of the nearly three thousand pages of the *Flaubert* testifies to his desire not to arrive at any false, reductionist accounts as answers to the famous question "What can one know about a man?" ["*L'Idiot de la famille* est la suite de *Question de méthode*. Son sujet: Que peut-on savoir d'un homme, aujourd'hui" (v. 1: 7).]—in one important aspect his view of Flaubert seems wrong, strangely one-sided. Sartre's view of Flaubert's politics—in particular the novelist's actions and responses in and around the ideas and events of 1848, with its terribly disillusioning failed revolution—recognizes *only* the misanthropy and pessimism, the *l'art pour l'art* escapism and the apolitical. Sartre makes *absolute* Flaubert's conviction that the eternal baseness of human nature assures that there can be no change for the better in political and social matters, that life is hopeless, imagination and nothingness always preferable to being, existence, what Sartre calls *le vécu*.

The political pessimism and misanthropy which Sartre sees in Flaubert is certainly there. The question is whether it is always dominant, and whether, even when present and powerful, it is not opposed in a relation of dialectical tension by very different attitudes and desires which Sartre does not recognize. For ten years I have seen students profoundly depressed by *Madame Bovary* and the *Sentimental Education*, agreeing with Sartre's view that for Flaubert the purpose of his art is to accomplish the work of Satan, "to injure by demoralizing."[6] Like Sartre, I have read through all the correspondence, and no one could deny the world-weary pessimism which appears very early and continues with remarkable consistency throughout his whole life. Flaubert is forever fatigued with life, disgusted with himself and even more disgusted with everyone else, nearly certain of the futility of all human endeavor.

Especially after his famous mental-somatic breakdown in 1844,[7] the misanthropic, pessimistic, alienated attitude was certainly the most obvious and predominant element of Flaubert's position on public issues. Many of his statements, the thrust of much of his published work (though it must be noted in that regard, that all his published work dates from after the 1848 revolution) place him squarely where Sartre wants to put him, as a member of what Sartre calls les Chevaliers du Néant, [Knights of Nothingness].[8] Sartre coins the phrase to describe

6. The phrase is Hazel Barnes' from *Sartre & Flaubert* (Chicago: University of Chicago Press, 1981), 243. See the discussion in Sartre, *Flaubert*, 2: 2081–88, entitled "l'Art m'épouvante," and the treatment of romanticism and the "Chevaliers du Néant" throughout *Flaubert*, 3. Barnes' book is a very useful, usually accurate treatment of Sartre's immense, three-volume work.

7. Sartre is brilliant and convincing on the sources of the crisis and on its shaping influence on the course of Flaubert's life. See *Flaubert*, 2, especially 1771–1861.

8. Sartre uses the phrase, with several variants, in much of the *Flaubert*. See especially the analysis in 3: 160–201, and the sum-up description in 3, 610. See also the perceptive discussion in Barnes, 268–78.

Flaubert's generation of post-Romantic writers—besides Flaubert, the most prominent among them would probably be Baudelaire and Mallarmé—who, says Sartre, sought to deny the real in asserting the superiority of the imaginary, to privilege nonbeing over being, the nonhuman over all messy, painful manifestations of lived human existence, death over life. They saw themselves as agents of what Sartre calls the "imaginary" as absolute beauty, absolute evil (3:181), doing "the work of Satan" in revealing the nightmare world under the smug, self-satisfied illusions of Progress and Science. Sartre sees their mission as motivated not by the desire to awaken and change things, but to reinforce the illusion that the moral and aesthetic horrors of human life have their source and inevitability outside history, in some fixed, fallen, eternal human nature.

Sartre is, of course, describing attitudes and values at the core of modernism, from Dostoevsky's *Notes from Underground* on. There is ample evidence for Flaubert's membership in the order, and that aspect of his internal dialectic is almost always the most obvious, clearly predominant. Thus what I want to argue is not that Sartre is wrong in such powerful passages. Rather I would apply to Sartre's argument his own words from another context, describing a widely held view of Flaubert's attitudes after the defeat of the Empire in 1870: "The truth is that this interpretation, without being entirely false, remains too simple and seems truncated: Gustave's conduct is richer, more secret, and more ambiguous," (3: 567).

Sartre's view of Flaubert's politics seems similarly truncated, one-sided, robbed of its dialectical conflict, its density and complexity. It seems to me that the basic error with regard to Flaubert on Sartre's part is related to and has its source in an error which has typified Sartre's thought from early on: from the early *Psychology of the Imagination* through the middle period *What is Literature?* Sartre has tended to see things in terms of absolute binary oppositions between, for example, the imaginary and the real, between poetry and prose, literary and nonliterary uses of language. In all these cases and many others, the separation is much too neat, too complete, and it leaves out the possibility of the dialectical interpenetration of such opposed elements.

In discussing the influence of romanticism on Flaubert in his youth, Sartre sees reading as the love of the imaginary, the passage into the unreal, a preoccupation with images instead of things, spellbinding, antilucid, paralyzing action rather than provoking it (2: 137–79). Certainly one familiar with Flaubert and the writers Sartre is discussing will find much to recognize in that picture. But it ignores, like the

Knights of Nothingness notion which is built on it, the existence of powerful opposed elements, the ability of a text, for example, to awaken or reveal long-repressed Utopian desire, to provoke what Blake called honest indignation and create an imperative to change the world.

In contrast to Sartre's view, which sees unrelieved pessimism and misanthropy reflected in a withdrawn, apolitical position, set in stone, at least from 1844 on, I will argue that while he had adopted a cynical, world-weary attitude before 1848, Flaubert's hopes were raised by the February days of 1848. After the Revolution's failure, its end in the bloody repression of the June days, and during the military dictatorship of the bourgeoisie after 1851, Flaubert did adopt and display the escapist misanthropy and formalist aesthetics Sartre describes. But there still persisted—though muted, deflected, denied—the hope for a better world, for change, Utopian longings which Sartre does not recognize at all. Traces of that positive side of the dialectical opposition within Flaubert's politics are evident in all his discourse, both the letters and the published novels.

When the picture is corrected, and the positive elements are added to the negative, ideological ones Sartre describes, the situation and the discourse of Flaubert are seen to typify what Fredric Jameson sees in modernism in general: "ideology and Utopia all at once."[9] There is certainly plenty of evidence for the aspects of Flaubert's position emphasized by Sartre, and he builds a powerful and persuasive case on evidence from letters and interpretations of the novels. But in addition to omitting all along the view which would alter the one he allows by illustrating dialectical tension and depth, Sartre makes several errors of fact or interpretation which display the traces of his larger error of omission. My objections to Sartre's view are based on several different (and different sorts of) texts: two statements from Sartre's *Flaubert* that I think are "wrong," a few passages from letters which Sartre ignores in constructing his skewed image, and aspects of Flaubert's novels which Sartre fails to recognize, all words of Flaubert which Sartre omits in order to omit from his own discourse words of imaginative vision, of Utopian desire, submerged under but powerfully resisting the dominant hegemonic mode, which is ahistorical, ironic and pessimistic.

On the last of his thousands of pages on Flaubert, Sartre flatly states that Flaubert "missed the rendezvous of '48," (3: 665) reiterated a few

9. Fredric Jameson, *The Political Unconscious*, 237. See also 63, 236–37, 287. My debt to this book is very large. The dialectic I see in Flaubert is clearly related to the central dynamic in modernism as Jameson describes it on the pages just cited.

times (448, 455); elsewhere he says "he did not attend the events" of the February Revolution (3: 455). And he interprets Flaubert's positive attitude toward the right-wing historian and politician Adolphe Thiers: "Thiers, there's his man," (502; 570–72) as representative of Flaubert's attitude. Both of these sets of direct statements by Sartre—on Flaubert and the Revolution, especially the February days, and on Flaubert's attitude toward Thiers—seem to me to be wrong, and to exemplify Sartre's desire to suppress the "leftist," Utopian, positive side of the dialectic within Flaubert's views.

To take first the matter of Thiers, since it is less complex: it is true that Sartre's sentence is an imitation of one of Flaubert's, approving Thiers's repression of the Paris Commune of 1871,[10] and Flaubert did join the Goncourts and most of his fellow writers in feeling that the revolt had to be put down. Sartre points out quite correctly, then, that Flaubert, as a *rentier* dependent upon the economic status quo, sided with the "party of Order" when he felt he had to. His reaction is less violently hostile to the left than most,[11] but he did accept as part of his conscious ideology that social and economic egalitarianism must be opposed.

It is true, in fact, that Flaubert's letters after 1848 contain several diatribes against socialism, egalitarianism, "levelling." His Utopian desire was almost never allowed to be foregrounded, to be present to itself, though, as I am arguing, it was present, active and formative, even though usually denied by Flaubert—always denied, or absent in Sartre's version. But in the political comments in the letters, especially in the 1860s when he was thinking a lot about the subject, working on the political, historical aspects of *Sentimental Education,* a novel in which he placed the events of the February 1848 Revolution at the very center, the strongest political animosity in his letters is not in reference to socialism. It is reserved instead for Adolphe Thiers.

Thiers had been a force in French political life since 1830. He held positions in several different governments, and also turned out many volumes of extremely chauvinistic histories of the French Revolution and the Napoleonic years. He was a member of the Academy for almost fifty years. By no means, then, a representative of some right-wing

10. Flaubert, *Correspondance,* 6 (Paris: Conard, 1930), 246, 21 juin, 1871. "Thiers vient de nous rendre un très grand service. . . ." For the letters through 1858 I have used the new edition edited by Jean Bruneau, in two volumes (Paris: Gallimard, 1980). For later letters I have had to use the old Conard edition; for purposes of clarity I will designate them henceforth as *Correspondance:* Conard, and Bruneau, and they will be so designated in the text.

11. See Paul Lidsky, *Les Ecrivains contre la Commune* (Paris: Maspero, 1970).

fringe, he had become the most respected spokesman of the party of Order. After the defeat of the Commune which he directed he was President of the Third Republic for three years. In many ways Thiers embodied those qualities which the alienated Flaubert insisted were typical of all politicians, Left or Right. He was coldhearted, manipulative and ambitious, single-mindedly devoted to the protection of bourgeois interests and the *gloire* of France—and of Thiers. His ideas were banal and complacent, yet they so perfectly responded to what the newly powerful middle-class wanted to hear that he was highly respected as a writer and thinker. Naturally, Flaubert hated that sort of ill-deserved intellectual reputation, but at the same time, Thiers was the leading spokesman for the social class of which Flaubert was a member, a leader in the fight against egalitarianism and socialism. Despite that agreement in their beliefs, Flaubert's attitude toward Thiers was unequivocal:

> Myself, I am overjoyed at the triumph of M. Thiers. In it I find confirmation of my disgust for my country and the hatred I bear for the Prud'homme. [15 décembre, 1867 *Correspondance*, Conard, 5, 344–45.]

> Peut-on voir un plus triomphant imbecile, un croûtard plus abject, un plus étroniforme bourgeois! Non, rien ne peut donner l'idée du vomissement que m'inspire ce vieux melon diplomatique, arrondissant sa bêtise sur le fumier de la bourgeoisie!

> [Can one find a more triumphant imbecile, a more abject fool, a more turd-shaped bourgeois! No, nothing makes me feel more like vomiting than does that old diplomatic fruit, depositing his stupidity on the bourgeois dungheap! 18–19 décembre, 1867, Conard, 5, 346.]

This is by far the most violent language in Flaubert's letters of this period. The excremental view of Thiers and his writings is particularly striking. For all his diatribes against socialism, Flaubert reserves his deepest anger for the Right, even in the finished novel. One reason for this hatred of a man like Thiers is his anger that such a man should be the spokesman for the ruling class, that mediocrity should be so popular. But another reason for Flaubert's opposition to Thiers or for his portrait of M. Dambreuse in the *Education* was his acute sense of his own alienation from bourgeois social practice; like so many other artists, Flaubert was very conscious of the fact that the bourgeois world view did not accord any significant place to the artist. In a letter to George Sand he speaks of having recently noted an instance of the hatred of the bourgeois for gypsies. He goes on to say:

That particular hatred is part of something very deep and complex. You find it in all the law-and-order types. It is the hatred they bear for the bedouin, the heretic, the philosopher, the hermit, the poet, and there is fear in that hatred. [15 juin, 867; Conard, 5, 309.]

This cluster is intriguing. Flaubert obviously sees himself as an example of the kind of person hated and feared by the bourgeoisie. And his analysis is persuasive. Hostility toward the groups he mentions is certainly typical of the bourgeoisie. But for all his awareness of that fact, Flaubert is frequently guilty of the same sort of thinking.

As an artist he is aware of the things he shares with those "outcasts" whose life styles and values represent a threat to the bourgeois world view. But as a member of the ruling class, in his social being apart from his existence as artist, he suffers from the same blindness and paranoia he can sometimes observe so accurately. And one should add, of course, that his perspective is such that he can only conceive of the continued existence of those things he *does* value, art and "culture," within the framework of an elitist social order, where a privileged sector is alone responsible for such matters. He thus fuses in his mind the "levelling" desires of the "socialists," their attacks on privilege of any sort, and the pragmatic, utilitarian attitudes and goals of the official spokesmen for the bourgeoisie.

Despite the contradictions in his position though, he is consistently more critical of the Right, and this is what Sartre fails to acknowledge. In fact, despite all his talk of the need to keep his opinions out of his fiction, he admits he is not going to be neutral in the *Education*. On several different occasions in 1867 and 1868 he mentions his intention to "get" the Right in his novel. After each of the remarks about Thiers which I quoted above, he speaks ironically of his intention to "insinuate a panegyric" (18–19 décembre, 1867: Conard, 5, 347) against the statesman—or simply to "fix him" (15 décembre, 1867; 1345) in the *Education*, in a dinner scene to take place after the days of June. Months later, when he had actually already written the political chapters, he wrote to George Sand, "The reactionaries, in the end, will be treated less kindly than the others, because to me they seem more criminal" (10 août, 1868: Conard 347).

Thiers enters Flaubert's fictional oeuvre itself in the collection of fragments of "stupid" discourse which he had apparently intended as an appendix to the unfinished *Bouvard et Pécuchet*; among the items to be copied by the copy clerks made rich, when, discouraged with action, philanthropy or even self-education, they decide to go back to copying, is this quotation from Thiers' *l'Histoire de la révolution francaise:*

But why, we might ask, could not a frank meeting put an end to everything the next day? Why did the King not understand the fears of the people? Why did the people not understand the difficulties of the King? But why are men men? At this last question, we must stop, submit, resign ourselves to human nature, and continue our sad tale.[12]

I agree with Richard Terdiman that such "derisive quotation" within the discourse of Flaubert functions as "the sign of a primitive, brutal deconstruction of the consecrated forms of mid-century rationality."[13] That Thiers represented, in the novelistic prose as well as in the discourse of the correspondence, the political Right, for which Flaubert held a loathing that surpassed his irony toward socialism and the Left, is ignored, denied by Sartre when he says "Thiers, voilà son homme," and proceeds for several pages on several occasions to use Thiers to signify the politics of which Flaubert approved (3: 502, 570–72). And for Sartre to ignore the fact that Thiers and the Right seemed "more criminal" to Flaubert is to distort his position in such a way as to mute, to disperse Flaubert's powerful criticism of social existence as he knew it, his conviction that Thiers and other leaders of his type were an insult to humanity.

The other assertion of Sartre's which I would like to examine and contest is that Flaubert missed his rendezvous with the Revolution in 1848.[14] The ironic reference in Sartre's phrase—the reason he uses it twice, coming back to it on the last page of the last volume—is, of course, to the scene in *Sentimental Education* in which Frederic Moreau avoids meeting his activist friends and taking part in the demonstrations which began the Revolution, because he believes he can have a long-awaited sexual asignation with Madame Arnoux.[15] He waits for hours in vain, misses out on both the political engagement he had promised his friends and the sexual/romantic satisfaction the hopes for which had caused him to forgo fulfillment of the former desire. It is a complex figure, in which Flaubert's passive-inert antihero protagonist decides against praxis; and the text, at its center, links explicitly the two causal formations of desire which Flaubert had in mind when, in the preparatory notes to the novel he told himself: "Show that Sentimen-

12. Cited in Richard Terdiman, "Counter-Humorists: Strategies of Ideological Critique in Marx and Flaubert," *Diacritics*, 9: 3 (Fall, 1979), 21.

13. Ibid.

14. See above p. 135. For a much fuller treatment of this subject see my doctoral dissertation, *The Novel and Social Change: Gustave Flaubert, the Revolution of 1848, and l'Education sentimentale* (Iowa City, 1973).

15. Gustave Flaubert, *l'Education sentimentale, Oeuvres*, v. 2 (Paris: Gallimard, Bibliothèque de la Pléiade, 1951) 308–10. (Part II, ch. 6).

tality since 1830 follows Politics and even produces the same phases of development."[16] The irony is complex, and is intended to debunk the possibilities of fulfillment in both realms, but Sartre is in error when he makes the figure of Fréderic at that moment stand for Flaubert.

Flaubert travelled from Rouen to Paris specifically in order to witness at least the events of the Revolution. He was there; he even took notes, and he made use of those observations many years later when writing *Sentimental Education*.[17] So Sartre is simply wrong to say that Flaubert was not there, that he did not "attend" the events. Since by 1848 Flaubert had already adopted his cynical pose and liked to present himself as apolitical, interested only in "art," any evidence for the reasons for his trip to Paris, any hope or desire that the Revolution be successful and accomplish significant change is largely concealed beneath large amounts of misanthropic bluster and irony. The principle that "Le pire est toujours sûr" ["The worst is always certain"] which Sartre calls his dogma, his black religion, (3: 489), is already well in place by 1848. Thus any signs of the opposite tendency in Flaubert's position are largely hidden, and are certainly ignored by Sartre.

There is not space here to call attention to all such evidence. Several letters of the period do express highly guarded hopes for change as a result of the Revolution, very tentative hopes, surrounded by disavowals.[18] There is even evidence that Flaubert and his best friend Louis Bouilhet took more direct active participation in the political process during these revolutionary months.[19] I shall take as exemplary of the sort of significant evidence Sartre ignores Flaubert's reaction to an event that was part of the Revolutionary constellation, though it took place two months before the February days in Paris, the reform banquet in Rouen on Christmas day, 1847.

The campaign of reform banquets took place all over France during the second half of 1847. Ostensibly concerned with electoral reform, they were strongly opposed to the existing regime, dedicated, in fact, to fanning the flames of discontent. Flaubert, whose letters in the months preceding the banquet had shown no interest in politics, decided to

16. Marie-Jeanne Durry, *Flaubert et ses projets inédits* (Paris: Nizet, 1950), 187.

17. Although most biographers mention this trip, and it is recounted in the memoir of Flaubert's friend, Maxime Du Camp, Sartre writes as if it simply never happened. For further elaboration and documentation on this matter and on Flaubert's participation and interest in 1848 see my dissertation, op. cit., especially Chapter I.

18. See especially those of mars, 1848, *Correspondance*, Bruneau, 1: 492–93, and 10 avril, 1848, 496.

19. Bouilhet, as apolitical as Flaubert before the Revolution, a member in good standing of the Chevaliers du Néant, even ran for election to the new Assembly in April!

attend: "There is going to be a reform banquet in my region. I shall go. The powers that be will look at me in a bad light, my name will be added to police lists . . ." (20 décembre, 1847, *Correspondance*, Bruneau: 1: 490). It really is a significant, remarkable decision—and one completely ignored by Sartre. And it certainly constituted a significant break with his previous practice. In the years before the banquet, between 1844 and 1847, Flaubert seems to have been particularly cut off from all public events; his life was filled with overwhelming private concerns. His battle to establish a significant life for himself which would be independent of his father had caused terrible suffering. The elder Flaubert had only contempt for the lazy, useless life of an artist, and Gustave was resisting desperately the legal career that had been chosen for him. All this conflict resulted in a complete physical and mental collapse. That period also marked the beginning of his affair with Louise Colet, and then the sudden deaths of his father and sister, the latter the only member of the family he had been close to. In December, the friend who seems to have meant most to him, Alfred Le Poittevin, was sick and dying. And yet, suddenly, Flaubert attended the banquet.

Certainly Flaubert's discursive practice in the letters from 1847 immediately preceding the decision to attend the banquet gives no hint of any concern with politics, is dominated by the most extreme pessimistic negativity, by the side of Flaubert's inner dialectic which Sartre is alone willing to recognize. The letters from 1847 are dominated by three themes: Flaubert's alienation and apathy with regard to the world around him; his desire to run away, to escape all the familiar and unwelcome things he knew; and, most often a sense of self-loathing, of some sort of spiritual and physical rot eating at him from the inside. In a letter where he asks the rhetorical question, "Is there anything to drink in an empty glass?" he even speaks of a desire to castrate himself! (13 avril, 1847, *C*, Bruneau, 1: 449–50). The most striking of the scores of such passages from letters of this period may be the following:

> Non seulement j'arrive à ne plus pouvoir parler, mais j'en arriverai à ne plus pouvoir écrire. Il est étrange combien toutes mes rigoles se bouchent, comme toutes mes plaies se ferment et font digue vis-à-vis les flots intérieurs. Le pus retombe en dedans. Que personne n'en sente l'odeur, c'est tout ce que je demande. [Début, février, 1847, *C*, Bruneau, 437.]

> [Not only do I end up no longer able to talk, I'm even getting so I can no longer write. It is strange how all my channels become choked, how all my wounds close and form a dike, holding back what's flowing in me. The pus falls back on itself inside. All I ask is that no one can smell it.]

We also know that sometime in the fall of 1847 he had another seizure and was bedridden for several weeks. As the revolutionary events drew near, then, Flaubert was sick, turning ever more inward upon himself, cynical and alienated from everything and everyone, and celebrating his twenty-sixth birthday with all the elan of a defeated, wasted old man.

Yet at this moment we find him politically engaged. I feel it must be seen as a sudden, guarded, but quite desperate attempt to establish some noncynical relationship to the rest of the world. Naturally, he concealed any such positive feelings with the layers of irony in his writings which Sartre takes at face value. But his action showed the opposite tendency. He must have felt that there was reason for some sort of hope in the political and social unrest so widespread at that time. And he must have wanted to ally himself publicly with the forces of change, for it is clear from his letter before the banquet that Flaubert felt it to be a significant, politically dangerous act. Why else would he break a pattern of complete political alienation and withdrawal, at a time when all the alienating forces in his life seem to have converged?

Flaubert's response to the banquet is contained in a letter to Louise Colet. For the most part it consists of a long diatribe against the wine, the food, and, especially, the speeches. Throughout his life Flaubert was obsessed by the clichés and banalities of bourgeois discourse, especially in its pompous and platitudinous public posturings. The speeches at the banquet do seem to have been very much of a kind with Homais's speech and, especially, that of the speakers at the agricultural fair in *Madame Bovary* and at the gatherings chez M. Dambreuse in *Sentimental Education*. The very fact that the discourse of the *soi-disant* opposition partook so entirely of the debased, hegemonic formulations of the established order surely enraged Flaubert all the more, even as that fact pointed—for us, and, perhaps, even for Flaubert—to the complicity between the status quo and the "opposition," to the eventual failure of the Revolution in the bloody street battles of the June days, and to the restoration to power of the bourgeois "Notables" who ruled France, under all regimes, from 1830 on.

Since Flaubert wanted the banquet to signify something different from the hypocritical and self-serving discourse and practice which he feared were to dominate the world absolutely, it is no wonder that he came home "chilled to the entrails" after nine hours of hypocritical clichés (fin décembre, 1847, *C*, Bruneau, 491–92). And yet, amazingly, he says: "Yet I still saw something noble and fine [*quelque chose de beau*] behind it all, and I am still dominated by the impression, at once sad and grotesque, with which the spectacle left me. I attended a reform banquet!" (Ibid.) Thus despite all his irony about what was said he still finds "quelque chose de beau." I think that phrase has to be a sign of what Sartre denies: the secret, unacknowledged, heavily guarded and distanced motive in Flaubert for a fundamental change in human relations, for a more human society; a motive, after all, for his attendance altogether. Generally, of course, Flaubert denies such Utopian aspirations, and after 1848 they become very rare, though flashes of the ill-formed feeling do appear in some letters, often as tag lines, throw aways, attached to misanthropic diatribes from the other side of the dialectic. It is not surprising that the positive, Utopian elements in Flaubert's discourse would be marginal, dispersed, small in quantity, nearly hidden in the letters and evident only in faint traces in the novels. Since his conscious, overt political position was based on the idea that there was no hope, since he consciously presented himself as a pessimistic misanthrope, one has to look for evidence for the other side on the edges of his discourse, where it seems to slip in accidentally, in brief flashes, when his ironic guard is down. In searching out the Utopian in Flaubert, I have had to approach his writings after the fashion of Derrida:

> I do not "concentrate" in my reading . . . either exclusively or primarily on those points that appear to be the most "important," "central," "crucial." Rather, I deconcentrate, and it is the secondary, eccentric, lateral, marginal, parasitic, borderline cases which are "important" to me and are a source of many things, such as pleasure, but also insight into the general functioning of a textual system.[20]

To read Flaubert and modernism in this way is to disrupt Sartre's literary history, to problematicize the rigid view which Sartre produces by ignoring the marginal, concentrating on the "central."

Sartre ignores all the complex and contradictory involvement with and response to the politics in and around 1848 when he says that Flaubert missed his rendezvous with the Revolution. He kept that rendezvous, as I have shown, and he observed with great interest the events of February, placing them later at the center of *Sentimental Education.* It is true that after the Revolution he felt he'd been a fool, a dupe to have had his hopes raised, and he was never again to harbor any overt expectations for change for the better through political action. Sartre is right to

20. Jacques Derrida, "Limited Inc abc . . . ," *Glyph*, 2 (Baltimore: Johns Hopkins University Press, 1977), 180. I would like to thank Professor Ronald Schleifer for calling my attention to the relevance of Derrida's position to my argument here, and for all his penetrating suggestions when this essay was in manuscript.

see the misanthropy, the self-conscious adoption of an apolitical withdrawal into "art" as increasingly dominant after the failed hopes of 1848. But surely the picture is dramatically different if his tentative adhesion to the cause of revolution in 1848 is denied. And beyond that, even after 1848, Flaubert's profound Utopian desires, now almost always deeply submerged under their dialectical opposites of misanthropy and despair, continued to affect the shape of his discursive formations, where their trace can be found despite his attempts to eradicate them, attempts which seem to have blinded Sartre to their presence.

There is simply no question but that the Right is treated worse than the Left when he represented historical forces in *Sentimental Education*, despite his more overt, overarching desire to show that all sides were wrong, all actors in the revolutionary drama either dupes or charlatans. I cited earlier his own statement that he intended to be harder on the Right, finding them to be "more criminal."[21] I do not have space here to show the ways in which his critical representation in that novel of the social existence he had known— *not* a book about nothing, but, in his own words, "the moral history of the men of my generation" (6 Octobre, 1864, *C*, Conard, 5: 158)—constituted a de-mystifying attack on the ideological strategies of the dominant powers of his day.[22] Sartre seems to take at face value Flaubert's repeated assertions that in a world where all is ersatz and absurd, any *conclusions*, on any subjects, will of necessity be false, absurd. Like Jonathan Culler,[23] Sartre sees only this typical modernist strategy of containment, denying all countertendencies. What Sartre fails to acknowledge, as Richard Terdiman puts it, is that "if discursively he [Flaubert] refused to conclude what is right, his counter-ideological strategies demonstrate, beyond any statements to the contrary however frequently repeated, that his instinct for what was wrong, and *guiltily* wrong, was unerring."[24]

Sartre seems to assume that after 1848 Flaubert *welcomed* the alienation, separation of artist and public in some simple, nondialectical way. But when in a letter of 1854 he rhetorically and sarcastically thanks Napoleon the Little, for *restoring* his contempt for the masses

21. See above, p. 137.
22. See my doctoral dissertation, Chapters III and IV, op. cit.
23. Culler flatly asserts that Flaubert's work is always "fundamentally gratuitous," that he "refused to make assumptions to be shared." *Flaubert: The Uses of Uncertainty* (Ithaca, New York: Cornell University Press, 1974), 14–16. Culler's position is even more extreme than Sartre's in his desire to represent Flaubert as entirely apolitical, one who "freed" the novel from all "social functions," 14.
24. Terdiman, "Counter-Humorists," 27.

and his hatred for the popular,[25] we are authorized to see the tacit recognition that during the Revolution's early months Flaubert's hopes had been sincerely raised, that he had not felt such complete separation, such hostility toward his fellow citizens. He's being led back to misanthropy, *from* something quite different *to* the side that Sartre recognizes exclusively. To Sartre the "real" Flaubert is speaking when, in the same letter, he describes as the dream of socialism: "to be able to place humanity, monstrous in its obesity, in a niche painted all in yellow, like those in train stations, and that it squat there over its balls, drunk, mouth agape, eyes closed, digesting its lunch, awaiting its dinner and shitting on itself. So help me! I won't die without having spit in its face with all the strength I have."

That position is certainly important, and, sadly, representative. But in recognizing only that elitist, antidemocratic and pessimistic side of the dialectic within Flaubert's position Sartre trivializes, mutes, defuses and contains the angry denunciations of the available forms of human social existence in his society; Flaubert's nightmare version of the socialist dream is crucially important in motivating his pessimistic misanthropy, as it effectively cuts him off—as Sartre recognizes—from the working class and from other oppressed groups, ensuring his estrangement. But to recognize that side alone is to deny the powerful longings for a better world, one not run by Homais and Napoleon III, which fuels the angry denunciations in *Madame Bovary, Sentimental Education* and elsewhere.

When Flaubert discusses the isolation of the artist in another letter he does not delight in it, as would be suggested by Sartre's view. His mood instead is one of regretful, wistful irony. Writing to Louise Colet in 1852 he sees writers in his day groping blindly in the shadows of a darkened corridor, the earth insubstantial, sliding away under their feet. He asks himself what literature is good for, what needs their "babbling" (*"bavardage"*) responds to: "Between us and the crowd, no ties. Too bad for the crowd, certainly too bad for us" (24 avril, 1852, *C*, Bruneau, 2: 76). The sense of sadness and loss in the letter is motivated, explained not by misanthropy and hatred which Sartre is alone willing to recognize, but by its dialectical opposite—oceanic longing. Utopian desires which motivate his hatred for life as it is lived in his day, explain his empathy for Emma's dreams, despite her weaknesses and folly.

Emma despises the smug satisfactions of Homais, of Lheureux, the

25. Flaubert, 2 mars, 1854, *Correspondance*, Bruneau, 2: 529. "Je remercie Badinguet [satirical name for Napoleon III]. Béni soit-il! Il m'a ramené au mépris de la masse, et à la haine du populaire."

shopkeeper/money lender, of Bournisien, the priest. In all cases, what's wrong with them is that they are *satisfied* with things as they are, find the available forms of fulfillment as good enough. It is interesting to note, in view of my concerns here, that the pro-status quo party in the prerevolutionary 1840s were known derisively as *les satisfaits*, for having pronounced themselves satisfied with the government's weak, hypocritical and self-serving explanations of one of the many governmental scandals which came to light during this period. Sartre recognizes this aspect of Flaubert's views in the novel,[26] but fails to recognize that passionate denunciations of the existing order are motivated by a deep longing—repressed, denied, diverted, unrecognized most of the time by Flaubert himself—for a better world, for what Fredric Jameson has taught us to see as that side of the dialectical opposition within the discourse of modernism which is characterized by Utopian desire with a heavy, if heavily repressed, libidinal investment. Nietzsche says "I love the great despisers, for they are the great adorers, arrows of longing for the other shore."[27] Sartre recognizes only the great despiser in Flaubert, denying the dialectical connection with the arrows of longing.

I have left to the last what I think is the most direct and striking statement by Flaubert of the aspects of his views which Sartre leaves out. Like so many of the letters I cited earlier in countering Sartre's presentation of him as approving of, agreeing with the right-wing Thiers, these lines are from a letter of the midsixties, when he was thinking and writing about political ideas and political practice, working on *Sentimental Education*. He is speaking of his youth, to George Sand: "When you come right down to it, we were romantic reds, perfectly ridiculous, but in glorious full bloom. The little good which remains in me comes from those days," (17 novembre, 1866, *C*, Conard, 5: 239). I believe that Sartre is probably right that there is little to indicate that Flaubert was ever a conscious leftist in his youth at school in Rouen or in Paris. That is to say, as a referent for what he *did* Flaubert's nostalgia in 1866 for political engagement in his youth may be an illusion, a self-delusion, (though in 1848, at age 26, he was far more interested and engaged than Sartre is willing to acknowledge), but it is more important for my concerns that such values were positive ele-

26. Barnes, *Sartre & Flaubert*, 345. I have had to rely on Barnes for most matters dealing with Sartre's reading of *Madame Bovary*, as we know the unpublished fourth volume of the *Flaubert* only through Professor Barnes' summaries, descriptions and commentaries on the unpublished manuscript materials.

27. Friedrech Nietzsche, *Thus Spake Zarathustra*, in *The Philosophy of Nietzsche*, trans. Thomas Common (New York: Modern Library, 1954), 9.

ments for Flaubert in what he *imagined,* dreamed, and desired. His linking of "romantic" and "red" recognizes a side of romanticism which Sartre denies entirely in his discussion of the movement's shaping influence on Flaubert, and that is the great visionary, egalitarian and messianic strain, in British romanticism especially, from Blake through William Morris.[28] Flaubert assumes not the despairing, elitist, lonely romanticism Sartre will alone allow, but the connecting, Utopian and enthusiastic impulse which Sartre wants to deny to Flaubert entirely.

The phrase "In full bloom" is a striking image for the sort of aspirations toward gratification in experience and oneness with others in the world, libidinal investment in "change the world," drawing energy from what Freud called oceanic longing. Of course he denies it simultaneously—"perfectly ridiculous"—but goes on immediately to recognize its continued persistence in him as his only "good" side. The same sort of dialectic, with strikingly similar imagery, is evident in this passage from *Madame Bovary:* "Her cravings, her sorrows, her sensuous pleasures and her ever-young illusions had slowly brought her to full maturity, and she blossomed forth in the fulness of her being, like a flower feeding on manure, on rain, wind and sunshine."[29] Both sides are there, the libidinal intensity of Emma's desire and its gratification shown in the same terms as Flaubert's image of himself as a youthful romantic red, and the sudden intrusion of the manure, which undercuts with irony the image of positive fulfillment.

Within the confines of the "romantic red" statement then Flaubert acknowledges *in himself* the dialectical coexistence and conflict between Utopian desire and irony and pessimism which Sartre never recognizes. Flaubert's statement shows that he feels in himself as a powerful, positive force a cluster of values which in other letters he ascribes to socialism and opposes. It is an attractive but (like all instinctual demands) a frightening force, which raises hopes and desires which 1848 "proved" to him to have been without foundation, impossible to achieve.

In the novel which he wrote on the subject, *Sentimental Education,* both sides are present, powerfully shaping one another in a dialectical embrace in which each defines, delineates and advances the other. The

28. Lest anyone suspect that I am projecting back onto Flaubert's use of "red" a meaning it did not then yet have, I will cite only the famous anecdote from February 1848, when the democratic Left wanted the red flag adopted as the flag of France, only to be defeated by the chauvinistic discourse of Lamartine.

29. Gustave Flaubert, *Madame Bovary,* trans. and ed. Paul de Man (New York: Norton, 1965), 140.

positive side is embodied in the young worker, Dussardier's naive revolutionary aspirations, in the "fraternal enthusiasms" of the February days, and in the rigorous moral critique and exposure of the Reaction. The equivalent of Dussardier on the Right is Louise Roque's father, the rich and grasping peasant who pronounces himself exhausted, "too sensitive," after a night spent as a member of the national guard during the June days, during which he has shot and killed a revolutionary prisoner behind bars who asked for bread.[30]

The negative side, of course, is embodied in the overall ironic and pessimistic stance, in the victory of Reaction, in his cynical view that all sides are wrong, success not possible in either love or politics. This is the "the worst is always certain" position which Sartre imposes on all of Flaubert's views, cancelling thereby any Utopian aspirations assuming a tension between the opposing forces. When Sartre leaves out the romantic red, he mutes and distorts the dialectical power of Flaubert's discourse, in which the ahistorical stasis of aesthetic withdrawal is always opposed by the urgency of desire, where the desire to write a book about nothing is countered by the desire to make of *Sentimental Education* the history of his generation, a book about everything. Sartre's view—and after him, those of Flaubert critics like Culler and Victor Brombert[31]—brings to premature closure a dialectic between political hopes and misanthropy, between life and art or the real and the imaginary, between direct statement and uncertainty, which in Flaubert's texts remains open and active, its tensions persisting, in ways crucial to the workings of his fiction.

Sartre's view trivializes Flaubert's position, removes any significant motivation for the linking of "sentiment and politics" in planning *Sentimental Education*.[32] As in the case of the moral critique of social existence in *Madame Bovary,* why pour years of effort into writing about 1848 and politics and aspirations for a better world if it's an open and shut case? Sartre's position closes an argument which Flaubert's novels leave open, "concluding" neither for the pessimism, misanthropy and retreat into the imaginary which Sartre describes so brilliantly nor for the revolutionary aspirations, the Utopian dreams, which Sartre denies.

30. Flaubert, *l'Education, Oeuvres*, 2: 370, end of Part III, chapter 1.
31. See the Culler reference Note no. 24 above, and Victor Brombert, *The Novels of Flaubert: A Study of Themes and Techniques* (Princeton, N.J.: Princeton University Press, 1966), 4.
32. See above, note no. 15.

III

In *The Political Unconscious,* Fredric Jameson uses the phrase "strategy of containment" to describe the intellectual or formal operations which are used "to project the illusion that [partial] readings are somehow complete and self-sufficient."[33] Sartre's distortion of Flaubert's relation to history as I have described it constitutes just such a position. It is just such a task I have attempted in my discussion of Flaubert and history, within and outside his written discourse, where Utopian hopes ignored by Sartre radically alter the totalization he presents of Flaubert, his works and the world. It is because such strategies of containment are even more powerful in Flaubert's discourse than in Sartre's that it has been possible for Sartre to leave the Utopian desire out of his account. It is for that reason too that the traces I have pointed to are so marginal, nearly entirely denied and concealed by Flaubert himself. The brief flashes I have shown in Flaubert's discourse and deportment of desire and hope for a better world and sympathy for those who act on such desire, when released from their containment and foregrounded in a way Flaubert never would have done, can alter our reading of Flaubert, engaging our own relationship to history and to social change.

What remains to be considered is the question of why Sartre would present Flaubert and history as he does, since the political effects of the approach I am arguing, and which his literary history, from *What is Literature?* through the *Flaubert,* effectively denies in modernism altogether, would seem to be just those which he would want. The implications of his political position[34] would lead one to expect him to want to reveal rather than conceal those things in Flaubert which acknowledge, approve of, and even cause to stir in the reader the desire to change the forms of social existence, the essential character of the reality which Sartre dedicated his entire oeuvre to ruthless critical exposure and condemnation.

I do not have the space here for the careful examination of Sartre's career which would be necessary to support definitively my conjectures—though with regard to the Flaubert specifically I shall point to some comments in a late *Monde* interview which are quite revealing— but I would suggest that from the time of the "conversion to Marxism"

33. Jameson, *Political Unconscious,* 10.
34. I do not have space here to deal with or even describe Sartre's politics at any length. While he always avoided labels in that respect, his political position as it emerges from the ninety-page interview he gave at age seventy is a libertarian socialism with anarchist overtones. "Self-Portrait at Seventy," *Life/Situations: Essays Written and Spoken,* trans. Paul Auster and Lydia Davis (New York: Pantheon Books, 1977), 3–92.

(which coincides more or less exactly with the formulation of the ahistorical literary historical reading of modernism in *What is Literature?*) Sartre was himself burdened with unacknowledged guilt with regard to his own contributions to and participation in modernist discourse, and to his situation as a privileged professional intellectual. For that reason he refused to see the Utopian aspects of modernism, whether active Utopian desire or more passive Utopian compensation. Such desire is always repressed to one extent or another, in discourse, or in our hearts. The libido fuels both sexual and political desire (the crucial connection recognized by Flaubert in planning *Sentimental Education*), and such urgings, always mediated by repression, become the stuff of the unconscious.

Sartre became convinced in the late forties by the Marxist historical view that the intolerable situation he had been describing in timeless, eternal terms—"the human condition"—was potentially changeable through collective human praxis, since that situation had a history, had itself come into existence out of something else, through such collective praxis. He has to have felt guilt about the ironic, pessimistic resignation he saw as implied by his own earlier work, wanted to fight such views. He came to see that ahistorical, timeless view of human nature as the crucial strategy of containment in modern intellectual thought, a strategy proposing "man" to be incapable of intervening in a historical process which consists only of repetition, and thus rendering political hopes and actions senseless and futile. Sartre's revulsion against such ahistorical, self-indulgent and escapist thought was the source of his conflict with Camus. He saw in modernist practice, then—and this had to include his own in *Nausea*—the unacknowledged defense of privilege which he came to see as the source of all bad faith.[35] He saw in Camus and in modernism altogether exactly the desire to injure by demoralizing—by seeing hopes as an illusion, stoicism, nihilist rebellion or refusal the only tenable positions—which he uses to define Flaubert's project.

So strongly does Sartre want to break with such views, to advance the cause of the oppressed and of change, that his guilt over his own privilege and his earlier discursive practice blinds him to the positive utopian elements in the discourse of modernism. In the 1972 interview in *Le Monde* where he discussed the *Flaubert* and his reasons for writing it, Sartre describes his early encounters with Flaubert's works, including going back to *Sentimental Education* in the thirties, and his current

35. On this point see the discussion in Jameson, *Marxism and Form*, 279–81.

judgments of them, in entirely negative terms: "I have always had a kind of animosity toward Flaubert's characters. It is because he puts himself inside them, and since he is both a sadist and a masochist, he shows them to us as miserable and unsympathetic people. Emma is stupid and mean. . . ."[36] He does temper this just slightly by saying that he eventually came to feel if not sympathy than at least empathy toward Flaubert in his misery, but the attitude toward the man and his practice as a writer is not changed thereby; Flaubert remains an overwhelmingly negative example, investigated and presented in that light alone. His judgment of Emma Bovary is certainly dismissive and one-sided, acknowledging the manure pile in the passage from the novel which I cited earlier, but not acknowledging the integrity of her desire, the libidinal power and intensity of Emma in full bloom.

Sartre's position trivializes and thereby contains Flaubert's powerful social criticism, embodied, after all, in Emma's refusal to be satisfied by a life presented by Flaubert so as to embody boredom, sterility, smug self-satisfaction and pretentiousness with which one should *not* be satisfied. Emma is a great despiser, as in Nietzsche's fine phrase, and her discontent has its source in Utopian desire, though it is unacknowledged, mediated, distorted through its incarnation in the debased forms of the popular culture of her day. Emma had no model, no knowledge, no sense of any possibility whatsoever of a better social world and the political praxis which might be able to obtain it. Thus her Utopian desire could never be embodied in any overtly political forms, aspirations for political change. But for Sartre such forms were available, seemed absolutely urgent as moral imperatives for his own discursive practice. But the result seems to have been that that very urgency, with the guilt and doubts which necessarily accompanied it, blinded him to the rich complexity of modernist practice, caused him to see it from an ahistorical perspective, as a fixed and dangerous literary-historical category. He was thus able to see Utopian literary practice only in the future. He failed to see such strains submerged beneath the more negative, pessimistic tendencies in modernism. Thus in the *Flaubert* he devoted all his energies to showing quite correctly the devastating effects on Flaubert of the dominant and hegemonic discursive practices within and against which he had to work, his disgust with the political realities of his day, and his withdrawal into misanthropy and aesthetic formalism.

In his preoccupation with those negative, ultimately life-denying

36. Sartre, "On *The Idiot of the Family*," *Life/Situations*, 109.

aspects of the totalization he constructs of Flaubert and the world, Sartre fails to see the "romantic red" or the traces of the Utopian in the novels and the letters. His ahistorical literary history functions, despite his desires to the contrary, in such a way that Flaubert's connections to the future are denied. Sartre's own Utopian desires seem to have been both so intense and yet so fragile, so fraught with guilt and pessimistic irony and fear, that he could not let himself find their equivalents in Flaubert. Sartre's *Flaubert* is such an important book, right about so many things, that we must think in terms of his powerful arguments when we deal with Flaubert. But we must also place in dialectical opposition to such views Nietzsche's "arrows of longing," the aging misanthrope who could describe still himself as a romantic red.

PIERRE VERSTRAETEN

The Negative Theology of Sartre's *Flaubert*

The more appropriate title for this essay would have been "the wicked *belle* âme,"[1] but that might have been too obscure, in spite of the familiarity of the Hegelian form of the so-called "belle âme" or "beautiful soul," which occupies a significant chapter in the *Phenomenology of Spirit*. The point is that in Hegel the "belle âme" is unhappy: in Sartrean terminology, we may say that it is a form of consciousness characterized by the dynamic of the game called "winner loses." Whereas in Sartre's study of Flaubert, the "belle âme" undergoes a rather different fate—destabilized and split by its opposite, namely, *ugliness*, the will to evil. Ironically, however, for this very reason and on the strength of this very distinction, the Sartrean-Flaubertian "belle âme" turns out, on the contrary, to know a certain contentment and even happiness: in this instance, it is rather a case of "loser wins"!

But we must first describe the Hegelian antecedent. In the *Phenomenology*, the "belle âme" is one of four distinct configurations of Western individualism: unlike the other three, however, it is inverted. The other three basic forms of individualistic consciousness are world-oriented, and extraverted: they bear the names "the Man of desire," the "Law of the heart," and "Virtue," respectively, and involve individuals who imagine that they are the Whole. These moments can be dramatized respectively by Don Juan and his desire, Shiller's Karl Moor and his personal conception of justice (or if you prefer, Sartre's own Goetz, who imposes his equally idiosyncratic notion of what justice is), and finally Don Quixote, with his rather different conception. In all of these figures, we witness a pathetic action, whose results reveal the just, the

---

1. Two articles by Christina Howells in *M.L.R.*, July 1981 and in the *Journal of the British Society for Phenomenology*, vol. 12, no. 1, 1982 discuss Sartre's *own* relationship to negative theology. We are dealing here with Sartre's use of the concept.

good and the true in themselves by provoking the world's reaction and causing the "course-of-the-world" to triumph; in Hegel's view (I would myself prefer to rewrite this conflict in terms of the values of the ancien régime faced with the rise of the bourgeoisie).

At any rate, the fourth form is the opposite of these three, an inverted dialectic, a figure which refuses to throw itself into the world and into struggle, but rather chooses to transform its refusal to act into action itself: the "belle âme" will therefore offer a sublime—and thereby an impossible and an unhappy—alternative to the "course-of-the-world," which is in turn forced by the former's absence to reveal its true corruption. Hegel elsewhere dramatizes this alternative in terms of the opposition of science and philosophy: the contingent laws of a fallen or God-forsaken world, and the existence of Reason as it has withdrawn from this last and rendered it problematic by its own absence.

The first three configurations refer to attitudes and positions taken with respect to the ancien régime itself. The "belle âme" however presupposes that the Revolution, and its universal reconciliation, have already taken place. Hence the radical character of the withdrawal into oneself. This is disillusioned ambition, the philosopher's ambition par excellence, the ever yet pending horizon, which has suddenly transformed itself into a *pure factum*, into an essence, *Wesen ist was gewesen ist*, past. Worse still, not only is it a past and as such superseded *factum*, but a destroyed hope, ambition disqualified, the moral atheism of the world. Hence the soul seeking refuge in itself would win itself, hollowing itself specularly and speculatively in the mirrors of its beauty, but losing itself anew:

> Maint rêve vespéral brûlé par le Phénix
> Que ne recueille pas de cinéraire amphore. . . .
> Sur les crédences, au salon vide: nul ptyx,
> Aboli bibelot d'inanité sonore

> [Many a vesperal dream burnt by the Phoenix / Is not received by any cinerary amphora / Upon the credenzas, in the empty drawing room no ptyx / Abolished baubles of sonorous inanity.] (Mallarmé)

Hegel is also very fierce:

> It lacks the power to externalize itself, the power to make itself into a Thing, and to endure [mere] being. It lives in dread of besmirching the splendor of its inner being by action and an existence; and, in order to preserve the purity of its heart, it flees from contact with the actual world, and persists in its self-willed impotence to renounce itself which is reduced to the extreme of ultimate abstraction, and to give

itself an actual existence, or to transform its thought into being and put its trust in the absolute difference [between thought and being]. The hollow object which it has produced for itself now fills it, therefore, with a sense of emptiness. Its activity is a yearning which merely loses itself as consciousness, becomes an object devoid of substance, and, rising above this loss, and falling back on itself, finds itself only as a lost soul. In this transparent purity of its moments, an unhappy, so-called "beautiful soul," its light dies away within it, and it vanishes like a shapeless vapor that dissolves into thin air.[2]

Hence indubitably, the beautiful soul starts to lose itself as soon as it is won . . . unless one turns this self-cultivation into a perfectly viable destiny. Indeed one has to be quite convinced, like Hegel, of the dialectical necessity of the institution of marriage to consider that those—Kafka, Proust, Kirkegaard—who confine themselves to the "question of betrothal" and make of the continued deferral of their decision the very meaning of their existence, vanish as so much vapor on the surface of the "course-of-the-world." But it does not behoove dialectical orthodoxy to value the question of betrothal. Hence this is unambiguously a case of *winner-loses.*

On this play is grafted in a perverse derivation Flaubert's wicked *belle âme:* a supplementary catch in the negation of the world, with no privilege accorded to him who carries out the refusal. Indeed, the man, the thinker, the soul have gone through the dismantling of their spiritual autonomy. We are vain forms of matter, as Mallarmé was to write. Therefore, whether at the level of revolutionary failure or at the level of the discovery of the entropy of matter and more generally of all energy, the worst is bound to happen. No longer is any privilege accorded to the inner fortress of the soul; it too is washed away in the universal shipwreck, a soul as devoid of beauty as the rest of the world. The beautiful soul devoid of any illusion as to its beauty, intrinsically ugly, bad, void, doomed to nothingness as everything else founders in the very movement of the élan with which it breaks with the world. This is where Flaubert, from his childhood on, enters upon the stage, in a prophetic anticipation of 1848, the massacre of the "Journées de Juin" after the fall of the monarchy in February 1848. Sartre writes the following about this period:

> 1848: the fall of the monarchy deprives the bourgeoisie of its protective cover. Poetry thereby loses its two traditional themes: Man and God.

2. Hegel, *Phenomenology of Spirit,* trans. A. V. Miller (Oxford: Oxford University Press, 1977), 666.

God first of all: Europe had just heard a stunning piece of news, questioned by some today: "God is dead. Stop. Intestate." When the inheritance was declared open, panic ensued: what had the Departed actually left then? Coincidences; man was one of them; deprived of the preferential Status which Divine Will guaranteed him, he was looking in vain for what Mauriac calls "that part of the creature where God has imprinted his mark." Gone the Creation, whose shepherd he was. Nature—the despised Nature of 1793—reentered upon the stage. Aged, hardened, it no longer even manifested those vestiges of finality which had justified the hopes of the revolutionaries. After it had dissolved the great monarchic syntheses, the analytical spirit, the bourgeois weapon par excellence, had vanquished, imperceptibly, almost without its knowledge, the ultimate synthesis, the crowning piece of the structure, the Being which was its own cause, the Whole which produces and governs its parts. The universe went to pieces: Nature was nothing but an infinite dance of dust; beneath the unctuous chemistry of life, man sensed his hidden mineral nature.[3]

To put things in concrete terms, we should specify the convergence of this premonition of shipwreck or of universal disaster in Gustave's experience at three levels:

—the level of his biographical experience
—the level of his cultural inheritance as an apprentice writer in 1840.
—the level of his historical experience, and notably of the convergence of his prophecy that the world was impossible and of the crime of June 1848, destined to split the unity of the French population for many years to come.

At the biographical level, everything started badly from his very birth; a mother without the warmth of genuine love (she wanted a girl) but too adequate to her function to cause the pathos of revolt. His mother's inadequacy thus makes him aware of his useless contingency, his mere being-there, devoid of all affective polarization. Flaubert's being doomed to *passivity*, was exacerbated by the failure of his relationship of *vassality* to the Father, almighty Lord and medical worthy, who wants more than a submissive vassal, another himself. Flaubert, conditioned to passivity, cannot fulfill this expectation. Such is the drama of his inadequacy, communicated to him by his father and lived in his very flesh. This initiates a sequence of negative behavior, increas-

---

3. "L'Engagement de Mallarmé," *Obliques*, [Sartre issue], ed. Michel Sicard (Nyons: Bordérie, 1979), 169.

ing in resentment and hatred, soon in a will-to-wickedness. A solution will be provided by his sister and by the oblique paths leading him from a passion for the theater to one for writing—a way out invented by all geniuses when all alternatives are blocked, according to Sartre. Hence Flaubert's writing is filled with aggressivity, revenge, and destruction.

This is confirmed in its negative component by the twofold patrimony of the elder brothers (the romantics) and the fathers (the writers of the eighteenth century). For his is a contradictory patrimony. The eighteenth century is analytical and reduces man to a mass of molecules; the romantics are vanquished aristocrats extolling the sacrificial function of the nobility for the prince, under God's approving eye. Both are disastrous, but inversely: one from below, the other from above, with one and the same consequence, though seemingly intensified; what Sartre describes as 1.) the disappearance of God, intestate and 2.) the break-up of nature. Two contradictory deaths turning upon themselves, each of them dying to its own other: a meaningless molecular death, an all too meaningful spiritualist death for God. Sartre will call this condition absolute art, and define it as the non-being of being and the being of non-being; the destruction of being and the heavenly reconstruction of this destruction; the meaning of the molecular disaster, and the meaning of the shipwreck for a spiritual witness, unceasingly shifting from one meaning to the other: "yes I know we are vain forms of matter but sublime all the same for having invented God and our soul . . ."[4]

Thus *Madame Bovary* will realize this twofold component, psychological and cultural, by sublimating and ideologizing the historical catastrophe of June 1848, the lost hope of the Republican revolution of February 1848. A work of public demoralization, it crystallizes decisively as a scapegoat, human impossibility in the face of a godless sky, in other words a human hell digging itself in deeper as the Passion for the absolute intensifies; her indomitable love is totally sacrificial in the escalation which it successively accomplishes from Léon to Rodolphe and back to Léon.

Thus Flaubert is the prophet of the historical impossibility of the Second Empire, though he is at the same time carried away in the inanity of the storm. He is apparently caught in the game of *loser-loses,* and loses for real, and irreversibly. . . . Unless one believes that he is the only one to push to its ultimate consequences the impossibility of

4. Stéphane Mallarmé, "Lettre à Cazalis, mars 1866," *Propos sur la poésie,* ed. Henri Mondor (Monaco: Editions du Rocher, 1953), 66.

human destiny and thereby thinks himself enhanced in his heroism, saved by his reflective lucidity . . . "Vaine forme, mais combien sublime à ainsi s'élancer vers un rêve qu'elles savent n'être pas." ["Vain form of matter but sublime all the same for lunging into an impossible dream."]

One should for once fill in the blanks in the beginning of Mallarmé's sentence: 1.) we are vain forms of matter, 2.) though sublime indeed for having invented God and our soul, 3.) and how much more sublime for having given ourselves "le spectacle de la nature, ayant conscience d'être, et cependant s'élançant forcenément dans le rêve qu'elle sait n'être pas. . . ." ["the spectacle of nature, conscious of being, and yet desperately lunging into the impossible dream . . ."] This decisive third phase foreshadows the redemptive conversion, the change from loser-loses to loser-wins.

This is where one can witness the move from the unhappy-beautiful-soul to the beautiful-evil-soul. We had seen how evil this soul was, it must now remain beautiful in its very hideousness. Its operation cannot help unwittingly reveal or manifest a secret irridescence of malediction, the sun correlative of all shadow. For however somber its diagnosis may be, its vanity still involves in its futility the *fact* of having been able to conceive or imagine that in the eyes of which it imposes itself. There is no negative without a positive. Whereas in the case of the *unhappy* beautiful soul, withdrawal into the self was in itself the unveiling of the imaginary and benevolent stage of a world other than the one where the withdrawal was taking its Course. Here the situation becomes more tense since the inner stage itself is contaminated by the impossibility recognized by the outside world, the inner withdrawal having the paradoxical effect of increasing the dislocating effects of the outside world without advancing any alternative . . . unless it be that of divinity denied a possible meaning, decreed impossible up to now, in this inner stage. An unbearable contradiction—either the victim will obtain reformation, a change of heart, or will come to terms with this quandary by moving with enough speed from the negative to the positive pole, making the whirligig (*tourniquet*) the basis of his survival, a procedure which is all the more convincing since the positive moment of the negative pole, the Agency whose impossibility is observed beyond any hope still nurtured or in that very pursuit, is attested in and through the very nothingness into which it unceasingly founders, in a series of indefinitely abysmal uncouplings. God is forever there, each time where that somber diagnosis is confirmed, present *through* his absence, incessantly receding as his work of annihilation is accomplished, endlessly eroding in this annihilation and in its abyss the ever renascent illusion which will fall prey to the movement of disappointment.

Flaubert thereby invents the absent God, exclusively present through his absence, falsely present or present in his falsity only—the ever volatilized *immanence* of the hope for truth turning to untruth which never ceases to triumph on the ruins of this hope, hence, in its turn, to founder through its very triumph. So much certainty in leading to ruin can only testify to the very suffering involved in prophesying it, the irredentist schemes of the compacity of ideal plenitude alone being capable of revealing the ruination and thus of suffering from it.

In short, God is the winner in each of his apparent defeats, abetted each time, in its metaphysical vertigo, by logic, psychology and theology.

1.) Logically: *God is necessarily all the closer the more one moves away from him, unceasingly filling the abyss in which one thinks to dig the grave of his presence,* forestalling any further estrangement through an increased proximity, all the more present as his absence increases, ever similar to himself in the balance which he entertains with his negation, without privileging one meaning over the other, irremediably reciprocal, ever anticipating any blasphemy which would seek to offend the realm of his utterability, always in reaction to Him—no abjuration outside His Original utterance, in an increasingly circular exacerbation.

2.) Psychologically: *the searing of the soul, ever more incandescent as sin intensifies.*

3.) Theologically: God's radiance all the more infinite as the homage rendered to Him takes the paradoxical form of a deliberately assumed damnation, a headlong plunge into the finitude which He has allotted to us, the task, half started by Him, completed by those very people whom His goodness chose not to annihilate from the outset, an indignity claimed by its object, living up to its ascetic grandeur. God recognizes the elect, Good through Evil, without any suspicion that it is done for a reward, even if it were the celestial vision.

As Borges puts it:

> To attribute his crime to greed (as some have done, citing John 12: 6) is to resign oneself to the basest motive. Nils Runeberg proposes the opposite motive: a hyperbolic and even unlimited asceticism. The ascetic, for the greater glory of God, vilifies and mortifies his flesh; Judas did the same with his spirit. He renounced honor, morality, peace and the kingdom of heaven, just as others, less heroically, renounce pleasure. With terrible lucidity he premeditated his sins. In adultery there is usually tenderness and abnegation; in homicide, courage; in profanity and blasphemy, a certain satanic luster. Judas chose those sins

untouched by any virtue: violation of trust (John 12: 6) and betrayal. He acted with enormous humility, he believed himself unworthy of being good. Paul has written: "He that glorieth, let him glory in the Lord" (I Corinthians 1: 31); Judas sought Hell, because the happiness of the Lord was enough for him. He thought that happiness, like morality, is a divine attribute and should not be usurped by humans.[5]

Sartre was always interested in such perverse forms of the realization of the Absolute, in apparently damned authors, saved as soon as one looks more closely at them. Sartre forgives them infinitely, but also ironically—in that he is not God, and cannot believe in him as they do. There is a seemingly continuous and infinite ascent of defiance: Saint Theresa, Nietzsche, Gide, Jouhandeau, Genet.

In St. Theresa on the one hand, in Nietzsche and Gide on the other hand, there is this common ground, despite the radical opposition of their aims, that the movement of their asceticism is an ascending one; in Jouhandeau and in Genet it is a descent. The former rise above the forms of the good which they refuse: they eminently preserve them; the latter sink *below* the possessions of which they divest themselves and in fact lose them. The ascent of the former is ideal, it occurs in the spirit, so that their operation is reversible; the descent of the latter is real and is characterized by irreversibility. . . . We have already encountered the example, comical by dint of abstraction, which Genet gives of his descending ascesis: he betrays his best friend and sees to it that the reward is given him in that friend's presence.[6]

It was Flaubert who initiated all these theatrical ploys, proper to fanaticism, to impossible purity—*doing evil in order to be sure that one is not doing Good, with the suspicion that the ostentation with which one is doing it turns out to be a self-interested quest for its favorably impressing the Almighty*. . . . But he initiated them in a most radical way, since God never appears in this postulation which deprives itself of His vision through the very procedure by which it calls Him forth. He is the first to wait for Godot. But "this kind of expectation was rare in the first half of the nineteenth century; people were better trained (*encadrés*) . . ."

Had there been, between 1835 and 1840, a young priest in Rouen able to prove the Creator's existence by the eternal silence of created worlds, His ubiquity by His universal absence, His omnipresence by His radical

5. "Borelius inquires mockingly: Why didn't he renounce his renunciation? Or renounce the idea of renouncing his renunciation?" Borges, "Three Versions of Judas," *Labyrinths* (New York: New Directions, 1964), 97–98.

6. Sartre, *Saint Genet, Actor and Martyr*, trans. (New York: George Braziller, [French edition 1952], 1963), 207–10.

and consenting impotence, the inflexibility of His law by His muteness and the anarchy of human societies, His Goodness, His Love by our sufferings, His inexorable Justice by the mishaps of Virtue and the happiness of those who exhibit a will-to-wickedness, he would, radicalizing the bourgeois and Jansenist concept of the hidden realm, have told Gustave: "God is nowhere, neither in space, nor in time, nor in your heart: and that infinite void, everywhere, that feeling of cold, our eternal despondency, what do you think it could be other than He? You are peering beyond yourself to discover a sign, in yourself to discover a mandate; there is nothing, of course: the mandate and the sign are that absurd, vain quest which you will pursue against all evidence and against your father's reasons; no, you would not be looking for God if you had not found Him; and just for that reason, abandon all hope of ever seeing Him or touching Him: He is found, I tell you, therefore you shall search for Him to the bitter end, in ignorance, moaning all the while." In short, should that precursor have invented on his own and for use by the young schoolboy this religious dialectic of No, today everywhere put together and practised by specialists, he would have converted forever the son of the Voltairian philosopher. For that was what Gustave wanted, that and nothing else: that his religious impotence should be transformed into "God's gaping wound."[7]

There remains the enigma of such a contradiction for this young soul, why this unbearable and painful oscillation, and how can he give it any credence? God, given in his evasion only. Sartre of course uses the word "sophism" in connection with this negative theology. Since the argumentation of the latter theology can only work on condition that one is convinced from the outset, that one adheres to the conclusions at the very moment that one is working out the premises. In a word, he has to believe when he is pretending to persuade himself of the lack of any reason for belief.

The sophism is *necessary* for Flaubert since his is a believer's soul, vassalic and fervent, on a desperate quest for love—absent in the mother, lost in the father—and at the same time prohibited from all effective faith, vainly waiting for some answer, and ultimately doomed from the outset by the twofold familial deficiency: God always already withdrawn from his soul and withheld from his faith. His damnation gives rise to the damnation to which he in turn subjects the world and all souls deprived of Heaven: his reactional, compensatory or radicalizing will-to-wickedness is as always permeated by the absolute need of the love which has been withheld from him.

7. Sartre, *The Family Idiot*, trans. Carol Cosman (Chicago: Chicago University Press, 1981), 527.

However, is this position conceivable for him, can it be lived otherwise than in the expectation of an imminent explosion, and is it tenable in the clash of this polar oscillation? If God prevails through his evasion, does that mean that He wished it so? His intentions are unfathomable. Is there then any reason why one should suffer from it, since that is the lot of each and everyone? But the point is that Flaubert suffers from it, whereas naive souls accommodate themselves perfectly with this absence, which they don't notice, nor shrink from making it the basis of their faith. If he is the only one to suffer from it, wouldn't that be the sign of his election to damnation, hence of his remarkable singularity, as the only one among others to be so chosen? For the bearer of this negative sign of divinity, God is all the more present. Could Flaubert be waiting for Godot? "But he thinks with bitterness: Godot did not come because there was no point to his coming."[8] However, doesn't this infernal sin, this original guilt in its very election cause the greatest suffering, the despair imposed upon the heroism of its victim? "The greatest souls are those most severely punished."[9] Moreover, the damned particularity can only be condemned by Justice, hence in a guilt attributable to *its own* responsibility. Even if his election is the negative form of God's existence he should not be a monster impervious to all feeling, especially the painful feeling of his damnation. On the contrary he must be the source of his damnation in order to reap from it the greatest infernal merit, without however decreeing it with complete serenity. In fact, it will be enough for him to *believe* in his unbelief, to suffer from his inability to believe, and finally to assume his own despair as the ultimate sin of his damnation; his doubting God will be a defiance of his infinite Omnipresence. In sum, two systems of ideological and personal justification for the theological contradiction of the absent God coexist: "I am made that way," "I have made myself that way." But neither of the two is satisfactory; on the contrary each slides into the other when it has exhausted its own meaning. For, if I am damned, I must deserve it, and if I deserve it, it is still necessary for God to have tolerated my guilt, hence in both cases God must *be* and I am nothing in relation to Him or to his being. Either He has made me that way or He has allowed me to make myself that way. God is omnipresent according to both hypotheses. An infernal machine where the *why* of its construction is perfected by its *how*. *I am made that way*, hence God has willed me to be this decisively repulsive worm, itself repelled by its own horror,

8. *Family Idiot*, 515.
9. Ibid., 528.

hence experiencing himself as such, making himself that way in despair of all hope in God, hence the Prince of Evil, God's damned alter ego, infinite despair that God should resort to such extremes, to make me doubt Him, hence damning me, as an exception, hence return to the starting point: *I am made that way.* . . . . The sophism is present at each turn since the mechanism of his damnation only works in each of its stages because of the abyss to which it leads in both cases, inducing its reversal into the other: I am made that way, I have made myself that way, malefic being made by God and tolerated by Him, favored by Him to the point of by assuming this blasphemous extremism, God is indifferent and therefore evil. A circularity which in both cases postulates God as the secret operator of the two revolving interpretive faces of Flaubert—disgusting and disgusted worm, the Prince of Evil. He therefore saves himself through the diabolic divinity of the unceasing pendular movement; God is perforce present somewhere in this descent into Hell, but never assumed by Gustave, since that would be tantamount to acknowledging that election to Evil is a *Grace*, too much goodness for this willfully wicked man—he will accept it when after the "Fall" of Pont-l'Evêque he will know himself to be decisively and irreversibly subhuman. For the time being to acknowledge God in the infinity of his lived and assumed despair would be a way of being redeemed too cheaply, or, worse still, it would entail acknowledging that he is a subhuman being, deprived of all hope of expiation, in other words an irredeemable contingency. In a word, that would be an event in which his free responsibility is not involved as it will be in 1844 at Pont-l'Evêque. Therefore for the time being he is definitively "mediocre."[10]

But the circularity of the machine, with its twofold functioning, breaking down as it reconstructs itself in its inverted face, allows in this genesis of the impending "Fall," the unceasing aggravation of the worst, with inevitable total destruction. "This unhappy consciousness whose finitude is pierced through by a need for the infinite which can be nothing for him but an infinite need—(without a doubt the worst in all circonstances)—Gustave pictures it to himself as a lacuna whose edges recede indefinitely. . . . God did not wish for this opening to being which is the essence of the cursed little boy; on the contrary, irritated by this superhuman demand, he conceals himself to punish this soul for its greatness. No: Gustave has opened himself unaided: he has opened his

10. Ibid.

own heart as one cuts open one's wrists. Not through some violent action but through his haughty refusal of compromise he has made himself . . . the witness of the dreadful concealed God whose absence devours his liver.[11]

The formula of Kant's moral law "You must, therefore you cannot" could be applied by an inverted perversion to this beautiful *evil* soul.[12] *Inversion* since duty does not entail the freedom to accomplish it: the proof in Kant, already at work in him, that man goes beyond himself, can aspire to pure disinterestedness, can and therefore *must*, if he wants to question the nature of authentic behavior. On the contrary, Duty only manifests itself here at the outer limit of action only to forbid it, to sanction its impossibility, to reduce Flaubert to the larval inertia of the unfit, and to sollicit his going beyond himself only to plunge him more deeply into his gaping lack. But a perverse or diabolical inversion, since it is not the categorical imperative which is irreducibly unattainable, as in Kant; the principle of all Goodness, its essential inaccessibility in its magnificence, its light dispensing morality on all those who inscribe themselves in the hypostasis of its eternal emanation, any order validly replacing the Law, more inconvenience in being subjected to injustice than advantages in committing it, the best always the friend of the Good; no, but paradoxically the Duty-to-be-Lord-of-Evil, knight of Nothingness. The damned person is supposed to emulate through the sin of despair the *Devil* himself, an inverted God, an ambition which can never reach complete fruition, as inaccessible as the moral Law in the perfection of its infinity. For to be forsaken by God for his inadequacies implies that God must tolerate them, and therefore that Gustave is either programmed as a task which God deliberately imposes on Himself through him in order to strengthen Himself, or his infamies are insignificant in the face of the diamond of the universe. On that ground he fails in both cases to live up to his Duty-to-be-malefic, always more mediocre than grandiose, and still too spiteful to believe in Grace and in his redemption through his nothingness, his youthful hatred too dependent on its object, and never reaching it except in the *finitude* of what he would like to live as *infinite* lack. Hence he is not up to it, although that is his only intention. There still remains writing, *scripta manent*, in Sartre's words: "it is perfectly possible to write the discourse of despair . . . he makes himself an intermediary between the dreadful Infin-

11. Ibid., 563.
12. *Saint Genet*, 572.

ite and this paltry aging world. He is not quite infinite suffering but he unveils and serves it, he introduces it into our Nature, which it will explode we can be sure: we shall see indeed that he insists that the writer should be a demoralizer."[13]

Translated by the author, Philippe Hunt
and Philip Wood

13. Ibid., 554.

JEAN-PAUL SARTRE

Sartre's Notes for the Fourth Volume of *The Family Idiot*

We are happy to be able to publish below the opening pages of Sartre's notes* for a fourth volume to his study of Flaubert, *The Family Idiot*. We are most grateful to Mme Arlette Elkaïm-Sartre for editing the French original, and to both Mme Elkaïm-Sartre and Gallimard Editions for granting us permission to publish a portion of it here.

The following extract comprises the first ten pages of a typed transcription of Sartre's original manuscript which runs to some 130 pages. The manuscript would appear, on the basis of Simone de Beauvoir's *La Cérémonie des adieux*, to have been begun in the Fall of 1971 and to have been abandoned with the onset of Sartre's partial blindness in 1973.

As will readily be seen, the notes are far from constituting the kind of coherent rough draft which has been able to be salvaged from Sartre's other abandoned projects like the second volume of the *Critique* or the *Cahiers pour une morale*. Indeed, much of the manuscript—including the extract published below—is fragmentary and remains enigmatic in many respects even if the reader is on terms of close familiarity with the rest of the *Idiot*. Other sections of the manuscript sometimes consist in little more than long lists of passages in Flaubert's *Correspondence* to be referred to or analysed. Nonetheless, these notes have an interest: we find, for example, the traces of the initial work of "progressive-regressive analysis" of both *Madame Bovary* and Flaubert's childhood which must have preceded the definitive version of the first three volumes; and they give us some idea of the general shape of the projected fourth volume itself—a lengthy analysis of the first *Temptation of St Anthony* and the criticisms of the latter work by Du Camp and Bouilhet, detailed consideration of Flaubert's travels in the Middle East and the genesis and evolution of *Madame Bovary* itself.

Unfortunately, what would have been Sartre's most extended piece of literary analysis never got beyond a series of overlapping rough sketches and adumbrations of the kind we find in this passage. Certainly, the major issues which the fourth volume was intended to address—for example, the extent to which Flaubert's neurosis expressed his freedom (*Idiot,* 2136)—do not find their resolution in these notes.

A word of explanation on the translation itself: if our choice of the English equivalent does not always seem to be the obviously correct one, this is because we have interpreted the text on the basis of the first three volumes.

Philip Wood

Note on references throughout the text

Pl.: this refers to the Pléiade edition of Madame Bovary, ed. A. Thibaudet and R. Dumesnil (Paris: Gallimard, 1946), not the more recent 1951 edition.

Bopp: Léon Bopp, *Commentaire sur Madame Bovary* (Paris: Editions La Baconnière, 1951).

Brom.: Victor Brombert, *Flaubert par lui-même* (Paris: Seuil, 1971).

Leleu: *Madame Bovary,* Ebauches et fragments inédits recueillis d'après les manuscrits par Mlle Gabrielle Leleu (Paris: Conard, 1936), 2 volumes.

Pom.: *Madame Bovary,* Nouvelle Version, précédée des scénarios inédits, textes établis sur les manuscrits du roman avec une introduction et des notes par Jean Pommier et Gabrielle Leleu (Paris: José Corti, 1949).

Abbreviations used by Sartre have been normalized, and in some cases the full form has been reconstituted, using square brackets.

Corr.: Correspondance

Mme B.: Madame Bovary

F.: Flaubert

Var.: Variant reading

Th.: Thibaudet

Un principe de toute sa psychologie: Les atmosphères déterminent (ni faux ni vrai).

Le bal (besoin de richesse et d'élégance) la détermine à aller à Yonville. Pommier 52: un peu putain.

A Yonville: entrée de Bournisien: théâtrale.

Lire la Corr. sur *Saint Antoine* (peu de choses. En parle plus tard *au passé*).

Le temps: un intermédiaire entre passé, présent et avenir: le fréquentatif (imparfait) temps de l'éternel retour—éternité. S'oppose à l'événement cf. Yonville: il y a l'événement—la passion d'Emma et sa mort et puis le fréquentatif (qui demeure avec d'autres individus—les servantes—pour faire les mêmes gestes)

Le temps: l'action disparaît (cahier 12) reste l'ennui (le vrai présent)

Psychologiquement: la maturation. Emma se donne à Léon quand elle est "mûre".

Mme B, roman de l'échec et de la fatalité. Pas de causes (Bouilhet les supprime? Parce qu'elles sont fausses ou parce que le lecteur comprendra?) Des matruations. Surtout le *fond* des personnages inconnu à F. "ou peut-être . . . sans doute . . ."

Les 2 manières d'aimer: Don Juan. Reprises dans Mme Bovary: Rodolphe—Léon. Evidemment Charles a la première.

Hystérie de F. prêtée à Mme Bovary.

Le langage trahit les sentiments. Non de Charles qui ne parle pas ou dit des banalités (mais alors il est insuffisant à vivre) ni de Rodolphe (qui est tout négatif)

Emma et Mazza: d'abord les sens non développés puis ils se développent (surtout Léon) et deviennent contraignants, l'emportent, créent la mort.

Insincérité du langage (cahier XIII): ajouter le langage muet, sans paroles (ils se regardent dans les yeux) qui est sincère.

La définition de l'art: la pensée rendue par la forme (souv. dernière page) exprimée ici.

Pommier 170: On remit à causer. . . . Inspire la correction On se remit à (Pléi. 348) qui veut dire le contraire. Le rêve sur les mots. Autre exemple: si l'Eglise l'interdit, c'est qu'elle a ses raisons (Pom.) Pl.: c'est qu'elle a raison.

Style indirect: interrogation (de l'auteur) Pl. 356

Neo-réalisme mais du coup la nature raconte l'homme passif et lui montre son destin.

Fréquentatif: peut désigner une période relativement brève

Le cheval a peur des *chiens:* motif déterministe. Dans le texte définitif on ne sait pas *pourquoi* il a peur: les chiens tirent sur leur chaîne. Cette fois pressentiment: les choses indiquent le destin: Pom. 153; Pléi. 337

Pl. 338–339: La main d'Emma. Qui dit cela? L'auteur.

PL. 340: Y eût-il *songé* (analyse). Qui parle? *Sans doute* = probablement

Pl. 342: *cette défense de la voir* . . . et puis la veuve était maigre. Cf. 333 Pl.: "sirop et un peu plus d'amour"

Emma *vue* de dos (Charles—Léon—Rodolphe): le désir.

B[ouvard] et P[écuchet] la veuve Bordin *de dos*

la veuve était maigre, et note 1

l'événement (souvent un fréquentatif *possible:* un médecin de campagne demande la main de sa fille à un paysan)

Du Camp demande [à] F. [de] supprimer la noce. Erreur venant de ce qu'il ne comprend pas F. Cette noce malgré quelques parfaits est un fréquentatif. Cela ne veut pas dire: voilà comment est une noce de campagne. C'est un événement *déja passé* (résumé à la fin du chapitre III) qui représente une éternité parce qu'il est au niveau du souvenir (pour Emma) et constitue le soubassement de leur mariage, Charles a l'air *d'une vierge dépucelée* (féminin). Emma: impénétrable. Se soustrait aux plaisanteries d'usage. Les mets et tout juste:"on mangea". Indifférenciation des choses et des hommes. Néo-réalisme et *pratico-inerte*. *Qui* voit les carrioles emportées la nuit? Et pourquoi "les femmes" (PL. 351)? sans l'explication que n'importe quel témoin nocturne aurait dans l'esprit : les femmes ne sont pas ivres? La raison: la cause n'est pas *visible* (le patron endormi). En marche vers *l'impression* (subjectivisme) et construction d'un système pratico-inerte où le lecteur a en lui même l'explication du prétendu témoin.

352: comme la source . . . pourquoi *comme?*

Il se chauffait à la société d'Emma comme: 2 métaphores. Avec la première tout est dit.

Plan: F. veut écrire. Il choisit la forme romanesque. Pourquoi? Qu'est-ce qu'un roman comme genre bourgeois?

Mme B. est elle un *erziehung* roman? Oui si le suicide apparaît comme conclusion d'une vie.

Répond-il à la définition de LuKacs?

Parti pour Saint Antoine (théâtre et vision-tableau), passe au roman. En avait écrit un (*Ed[ucation] sent [imentale] I: erziehung* roman)

Erziehung roman: un seul héros, un seul point de vue. Dans Mme B., point de vue de Charles aussi important (biographie complète) et les autres aussi;

prosopopée 360 Pl.

Mme B. esprit *positif* Pl. 361 cf. Pom. 190

Pom.: dessin et musique

Pom. 197: passage à l'imparfait pour Charles

L'orage (Fl. en connaît un semblable. Ce qu'il signifie) Pom. 196

PL. 364: métaphore

PL. 366 *une* peur la prenait. Pourquoi pas *la* peur? Mais demandons nous au contraire pourquoi la culture occidentale considère qu'il y a *la* peur, toujours la même. Progrès vers l'impression. Nominalisme de F.

PL. 369 "la statue regarde immobile". La mort. La flamme (Pom. 205), des flammes (Pl. 368)

Les impressions: blocs ni subjectifs ni objectifs à traiter tantôt d'une façon tantôt d'une autre.

Anéantir le paragraphe 370–373

Parler de la femme qu'on aime à l'amant de celle-ci (Jules et l'acteur, Frédéric et Arnoux, Charles et Rodolphe)

Une seule comparaison: nature physicochimique. (PL. 376: Vaubyessard et l'orage)

Mme Bovary *est* la métaphore de St. Antoine. M. B. "guère tendre" 385–86 Pl

banquet de mariage: 354 et 387 Pl.

Sujet Bovary: totalisation et mort.

Bovary et Don Quichotte: même sujet. Romantisme et livres de chevalerie: usage négatif; empêchent de comprendre le monde.
Tout le problème: ce qui reste de valeur dans les uns et les autres. S'ils n'avait rien, la mort ne serait pas nécessaire.

Description d'Yonville 240–43 Pom. 388–91

a) D'abord description d'un bourg pourrissant. Jusque dans sa configuration: comme on s'en tient aux "herbages" la ville se pousse paresseusement vers la rivière. Des "débouchés" qu'on n'utilise guère. Pas de développement. Lestiboudois, et les pommes de terre. Les morts sont oubliés (Pom.) Main *les vivants* s'en nourrissent. Ce qui marque la généralisation c'est, aussitôt après le texte Lestiboudois, les mots "en effet" (rien, en effet, n'a changé à Yonville) beaucoup trop lourds pour être justifiés par l'épisode Lestiboudois.

b) Et puis la conclusion: rien n'a changé. Conclusion qui va au-delà de la fin réelle: il reçut la croix d'honneur. C'est la pérennité des choses et même des hommes vus en pratico inerte. Il est regrettable que F. ou B[ouilhet] n'ait pas osé conserver le passage sur les servantes. Crainte de trop dire: ces servantes ne sont plus les mêmes. Mais qu'importe, si elles font les mêmes choses? En tout cas l'idée est d'effacer les événements. Ceux-ci, mince petit désordre à la surface de l'être, disparaissent sans le changer profondément. L'être et le fréquentatif indiscernables: les servantes mais aussi la paille en petits morceaux (ce n'est pas la même mais cela gêne moins puisque c'est *des choses*) Reste, malgré tout, un mouvement très lent de pourriture (foetus). Au fond Yonville disparaîtra, Homais ira à Rouen.

Les événements qu'on va narrer. Qui narre? Qui voit cet ensemble? Un paragraphe en mouvement depuis "au bas de la côte . . ." etc.: réplique de théâtre de l'époque: on doit présenter les personnages dans un même décor. Lestiboudois, la patronne, Binet, Bournisien, Homais, Hivert, Léon, M. Lheureux etc. Parfaitement inutile. Seul Léon était utile. "Mais ce lambin d'Hivert . . ." etc.: réplique de théâtre. "Six heures sonnèrent, Binet entra": effet de théâtre.

S'était cru en plein conseil: PL. 396: hystérie.

La mer: F. se moque d'Emma qui dit les mêmes choses que lui (Corr.) cf. les hébétudes de Djalioh devant l'Océan. Puis Corr. 6 (?) les marins et la mer. PL. 405: Tout le monde prétend connaître à fond l'existence humaine: Homais (Pommier 252), Emma et Charles; comique peut être tragique (à Louise)

PL. 406 Choix du nom: La pensée de F. est celle de ses lettres.

Le langage et la pensée inexprimable: PL. 382–362–411–412. Vieille thèse.Le langage ne peut pas *tout* dire. Suggérer indirectement.

F. et la métaphore: Goncourt II

1er temps: toute pensée psych. se construit matériellement: avec des mots ou des images. Elle n-est même pas différente des images pôles, bouts de bois, cercles, etc.)

2ème temps: l'image comme telle n'étant pas traduisible (bouts de bois ou cercles), on lui trouve un équivalent avec des objets connus un archer lance une flèche etc.) But: *éclairer l'idée*. Fonction *pratique*.

3ème temps: l'écrivain se plaît à sa construction. Il la cherche *belle*. F. En ce cas elle peut n'avoir pas plus de signification que l'idée abstraite exprimée avant le "comme."

4ème temps: Elle a cependant un sens (matérialiste-idéaliste). Chez F. en général matérialiste. 417 Pl.: Lézarde. *Lac et lézarde*. Comment concevoir l'intérieur? A travers l'extérieur?

415 Pl. Comme s'il eût marché sur quelqu'un. Nouveau sens de la métaphore: pratico-inerte; la robe *est* quelqu'un: Madame Bovary elle-même. Il sent la chose comme telle. Pas tout à fait: son geste apparaît tel au témoin, mais peut avoir d'autres raisons (adoration, respect des vêtements d'Emma etc.) En fait il n'en est pas conscient et la métaphore est pour suggérer qu'au fond de lui c'est bien cela.

Métaph. Leleu I 373–376 Pom. 276 Pl. 413

Pl: isolée et plus lointaine. L'image n'est plus spatiale; elle est psychologique. Dans les ébauches, F. l'avait gardée spat[iale]. Emma servait de fond (soleil) et les autres passaient devant. Sans doute Bouilhet.   Les passages coupés (276–277 Pom. Pl 413) sont conservés dans la tête de F. donc à lire entre les lignes. En particulier les prépositions[1] (mais) marquent que qq. chose manque.

Métaphore Leleu 388 sqq.

La comparaison est donnée dans la phrase avant "comme": exhaler. Pourquoi s'exhaler? C'est la pensée généralisée. Si elle s'exhale il suffira d'indiquer de l'autre côté du "comme" *ce qui* s'exhale.

---

1. Erreur de plume: les conjonctions de coordination (N. d. E.)

La phrase-image
Rendre l'objet dans sa présence matérielle
    Style de *l'ennui* (cf. Proust)
    Style *uni* (mur). Les objects s'y reflètent (Salammbô) et
par là sont existants dans le roman.
    Fins de chapitre: fausses fins; le thème en est développé au chapitre
suivant
            Texte supprimé (Pom 326). F. se moque de l'apprécia-
tion du pharmacien (des médecins, peut-être d'Achille) sur sa vie nocturne. Notez: "La veille se change en rêve; le rêve en veille". Idée de la
conduite esthétique. Et que la veille est toujours onirique. Et F. multi-
plie l'onirisme chez Emma. Le jour où elle va chez le curé, les boeufs
puis les hommes sont des *fantômes*. Ne reste rien dans Pl. Trop de
fantômes: dans Pom. Premier mouvement; supprimé dans Pl.
        Au moment où on veut lui supprimer les romans, Emma les
        trouve fades
    Pom. 327–28: gouvernements et familles (F. lui même).
    Métaphore: ne comprend pas ce qu'il fait: *comme* renvoie aux
comparaisons culturelles qq fois: Pom 320: des fantômes de vierges qui
sont mortes d'amour. Var.: des morts qui s'accoudent pour causer sur le
bord de leurs tombeaux.
        Souv-enir] de Léon. Pom. 320: passé et présent mélangés
    Le souvenir d'amour *nourri* de tout (passé, avenir Pom. 321)
    Bonheur fantastique "dont elle plaçait la possibilité dans des
conditions disparues".
        Emma n'a jamais aimé Léon (F. se décrit n'aimant son voyage
qu'une fois chaque séjour fini). Mais une fois le prétendu amour disparu,
reste qu'il fait saillir, par la vague idée de ce qu'il aurait été, la laideur de
l'existence à Yonville (qui est *bien vraie*). Donc une absence fétichisée
(et par ce fétiche embelli[t] Léon, plus sensible) fait ressortir la laideur de
l'existence qui n'est pas telle pour Charles, Homais, Binet. Devient
méchante. Au moment du "sacrifice", était méchante, mais le jeu lui
plaisait, "aimant" les enfants etc.
    Pom. 322 *rire atroce* (Romantisme Mazza)
    Style indirect libre: 322, une femme qui s'était imposé de tels sacri-
fices. C'est Emma qui parle.
        Paresse devant la culture. (Pom. 322–23)
    323: La maladie de FL; avec le *Enfin* elle eut un crachement de sang
(Attaque) Faux stoïcisme d'Emma (F. à Ernest juste après la crise)
        Maladie d'Emma: 1) Hystérie: voit le danger avec Léon mais ne
            tient pas à coucher avec lui. Aime mieux

s'amuser de son image. Communique à Léon l'idée d'un amour platonique. Change: vit la vie qu'elle *doit* -que la situation exige) vivre. En fait, privations conduisent à la haine (de Charles) et à un état d'adultère *avant* la lettre. Elle conduit cependant Léon au départ.

2) Départ: Brusque arrêt d'une virbation. Passe à l'imaginaire total (Maria Schlesinger embellit mais la réalité est la haine du mari.) Il s'agit à présent que son état se voie (soit vu par son mari). Cela équivaut à la chute de 44. Cependant elle a un crachement de sang trop désiré en Pomm.: "enfin". Supprimé ensuite comme trop lisible. Entre temps—donc *avant* la crise, la nervosité dont parle F. pour lui *après* sa crise (mais qui devait pour lui naître avant, à Paris, sans doute) cf. 323

3) Charles s'inquiète. Vient la mère. Diagnostic du pharmacien: psychosomatique.

PL. 448: et avec des haussements d'épaule: "haussements" est significatif; la suite ne l'est pas: un mouvement quel qu'il soit peut tirer les mailles du tricot. Ainsi la signification s'achève en insignifiant, le pratico-inerte en inerte.

Inversement l'insignifiant "les grandes basques et. . . ." passe au signifiant "emplissent beaucoup l'espace. . . ."

"Vous heurtaient . . ." 449–50. Ici abstrait. Vous, c'est les lecteurs. Mais comme ils n'étaient pas là, ils ne se sentent pas concernés. Ce sont les lecteurs s'ils avaient été présents.

Quelle signification peut avoir dans la phrase-image le rythme ternaire? Plus de lourdeur matérielle: 450: "A l'écart, en dehors des lices, cent pas plus loin . . ." Il suffisait d'écrire: A l'écart, à cent pas des lices . . .

Le romancier doit être ironique (Lukács) Peut-être mais pas comme F. Car c'est là que sa personnalité se révèle combattant l'impersonnalisme.

Le thème des fenêtres dans Mme B. Pl. 441: la fenêtre en province etc. . . .

Mais surtout *fenêtre* chez F. à Croisset.

Thème du *miroir* 473 Pl.

Confond oeil et regard: 454: appliqué dessus son oeil: *ne veut rien dire*

Comices. Rodolphe est *insincère*. Tout le monde est insincère chez F. Sauf brefs mouvements sans parole (Elle s'abandonna etc.)

Pl. 458: elle *vous* arrivait

461: La comparaison de Rodolphe: deux fleuves Pl. 461; on la trouve dans les lettres d'Alfred et de F.

464: miroir magique.

468–69 Pl.: cela peut-être semblerait drôle / c'est la personne qui parle et vos chevaux peut-être sont fougueux / c'est F. qui utilise ce tour.

474: l'amour jaillissait: cette fois il y en a deux; celui qui a été longtemps contenu est pour Léon, celui qui jaillit est pour Rodolphe. F. n'en considère *qu'un*, le même. Ce qui signifie un amour qui n'est *ni* de Léon *ni* de Rodolphe, mais un amour mystique et sans *objet*. L'amour est subjectif, l'objet indifférent.

474: comme si les murs se fussent écartés d'eux-mêmes. Chez Genet, même chose: pour le crime tout est facile.

373 Pom.: Rodolphe: *fatilité*

Les cercles: il y en a tout le temps. Totalisation. Au plus près (Elle s'abandonne), au plus loin (le fiacre).

Métaphore = métamorphose Brom. 8

Fascination par l'adultère (*Novembre*)

Style indirect libre Brom. 4=58–59

Notes de voyage: *l'excès est preuve d'idéalité*

Le rire dans Mme Bovary.

Les comparaisons sont souvent livresques: le feu dans la steppe russe (livres sur la Campagne de Russie?) et les vierges qui s'accoudent sur leurs tombeaux (textes sur les danses de Mort. Et reprendre les textes de jeunesse sur vierges et mortes).

"Qu'elle mente sciemment, il se peut que non. On ne voit pas toujours clair en soi etc. . . .": Texte fondamental pour les "peut-être", "sans doute"; etc. . . .

Livresque: les enfances de Charles sur le modèle des enfances de Gargantua.

"plus immobile qu'un roc . . .": usage outré du "*plus*" qui vient alterner avec un roc: le Suisse ne peut être *plus* immobile qu'un roc

St. Antoine—Mme Bovary = les deux narrateurs de *Novembre*

Style indirect (cf. le Robert)

Pom. 407: Ce qu'ajoute F.; des impressions à la relecture: le tourbillon du monde et "tu ne vas pas mourir, je le sais." Donc réflexions sur le premier texte.

407 Pom.: "Bournisien brave homme", Homais *brave homme*. Mais dans le sens d'un plan de Loven: "M. le préfet", Homais devient féroce (l'Aveugle).

408 Pom.: bel example de style indirect

L'ironie de F. dégage l'insincérité de chacun (Pied Bot)

Charles pense à sa carrière. Et c'est, en vérité, sur sa femme que l'accident du pied bot agit. Intéressant: n'a pas de conséquence sur le métier. Et pourtant tout partait pour ruiner Charles (la grand'rue pleine de monde, le mépris de Canivet).

Mme Bovary (son caractère, ses sources. Bopp, p. 25 note 1, p. 14 note 1)

Mme Bovary: je suis trop petit pour moi.

L'instinct conduit au fanatisme qui est adoration d'idoles.

Le vrai malheur de Mme Bovary: son instinct est d'adorer l'idéal qui devient niaiserie quand elle l'imagine (raison: langage, lectures. Le langage c'est *on* et c'est elle. Les lectures c'est l'Autre)

F. "géniteur-négateur"

Héloïse: tuée par l'argent

Charles chez Rouault n'entend que le battement intérieur de sa tête

Emma à la fin n'entend que le battement de son coeur

Emma *positive* Pl. 361

les mots soulignés (Pl. 364): procédé de F. au départ. Recourra de plus en plus au style indirect libre.

Emma "incapable de comprendre ce qu'elle n'éprouvait pas comme de croire à tout ce qui ne se manifestait pas par des formes convenues" Pl. 365

Mme Bovary mère: Mme Flaubert?

la dame et le billet (Vaubyessard): présage de l'adultère.

Emma: jette aux pauvres, puis à l'Aveugle toutes ses pièces blanches (385 Pl) "quoiqu'elle ne fut guère tendre . . . ni facilement accessible à l'émotion d'autrui . . . callosités" Toujours *l'aumône-orgueil* chez F.

Comédienne (Pomm. 235)

Instinct naturel de dissimulation (?).

Le temps du fiacre. Temps réel et signifiant: *au-dedans*. Comporte:

1) le temps d'une action concertée. Tous les deux veulent baiser. Mais il y faut un certain temps.

2) temps de la fatalité: dégradation de la Bovary. Mais ce temps irrétrogradable est enveloppé dans un temps contingent, hasard, rétrograda-

ble (ils *re*passent) et sans signification, souligné Pl. 548 en bas de page "sans parti pris, ni direction, au hasard, elle vagabonda" qui lui-même vient de la "démoralisation" du cocher et de la supression du temps de l'action (la calèche va en général faire une chose précise). Et ce temps enveloppe l'autre. Par volonté de Léon. Et le temps contingent tend par lui-même à devenir du fréquentatif: la machine repasse aux mêmes endroits.

"confondre sa passion avec le milieu qui l'avive" (Pom. 491)

"la stupéfaction" (l'inverse) Pom. 493

Temps: 1) Elle n'arrive pas. Temps vide mais ne se sent pas trop parce que Léon est heureux.

2) Elle arrive mais veut cèder dans les formes: donc son temps à elle (quoique rigoureux et signifiant: elle doit lutter) est opposé au temps de Léon (action pure). Conclusion: Les deux temps (vus par Léon) se contrarient. Une résistance du temps.

La figuration du néant (Pl. 546) signification de *tout le temps;* prophétie.

Pl. 550: le temps du cabriolet: incident. Et celui d'Hivert (fréquentatif).

L'incident: Félicité présente et le temps du fréquentatif: le jour des confitures.

Pl. 554–555: le temps du parfait dénonce le temps de l'imparfait (ce peut être le contraire)

Ils entendirent le bruit sec (555): le temps romanesque. L'objet est nommé *après.*

Thème d'Emma-oiseau Bopp. 400

les adverbes ("avec") temporels et spatiaux

Thème du cheval et de la voiture.

des fenêtres

de la femme-oiseau.

Thème d'Emma-serpent (s'oppose à Emma-oiseau) Pl. 582–83

Thème du râle qui traîne (Rodolphe—devant le couvent—l'Aveugle—le bal masqué de Rouen)

Adieux de Rodolphe et adieux de Léon: chaque fois elle leur demande de faire un acte qu'elle fait elle-même (Rod.) ou qu'elle ferait ("Si c'était moi" . . . Léon) et chaque fois ils lâchent.

603 Pl. Un moment vrai et "grand" pour Mme Bovary. Cf. lettre à Louise: quand tu es seule etc. . . .

Rôle de Bouilhet Pl. 599, Bopp. 469

le battement des artères d'Emma (Pl. 611) et Pl. 616

feu d'artifice (Pl. 611): exp[ression] de F. pour décrire ses crises.
Néo-réalisme Pl. 611: les murs tremblaient, le plafond l'écrasait.

Le premier contact sexuel: par derrière, dos et croupe: Charles (Pl. 340), Rodolphe (442), Léon (Pl. 552).

Pl. 345: il entendait seulement le battement de sa tête

Th. 105: l'argent

Th. 114: Rodolphe et Flaubert pas jaloux.

Qu'elle mente sciemment, il se peut que non (Corr. III 23) "Il ne faut jamais craindre d'être exagéré" (Corr. Le génie exagère le réel (imag.) et par là atteint à l'idéal.

Les deux images de pourriture, Emma: "cette pourriture instantanée des choses où elle s'appuyait". Le rêve de Charles après la mort d'Emma.

Idée neuve (elle existe depuis longtemps mais c'est le sujet d'Emma): on ne peut pas sortir de l'endroit où l'on est, ni par l'action (fuite impossible: Rodolphe), ni par les objects du désir (inférieurs au désir lui-même). D'où l'idée de la couleur *normande*.

En écrivant à Léon, perçoit un autre homme. cf. F. écrivant à Eulalie

L'image comme *pensée* de Fl. Pourquoi?

L'élément magique: les ensembles; se groupent en présages. Cela n'est pas *nécessaire*. d'où vient que le futur influe à ce point sur le présent?

Presque toute la laideur du style chez F. réside dans les verbes. Par ex., Pl. 350: se dressait l'eau de vie, dans des carafes; Pl. 355: composaient la continuité de son bonheur.

Circularité: l'univers n'excédait pas le tour soyeux de son jupon.

Verbes laids: 362 Pl.: un détachement intérieur se faisait

365: s'égrenaient de pourriture

Pl. 383: le thème du serpent (homme qui veut des qualités féminines)

Mme Bovary: Manifeste du post-romantisme. Une âme conduite à la mort par le romantisme. Romantisme = faux imaginaire contesté par le réel. La solution: choix d'un *autre* imaginaire, n'est pas donné.

Le fréquentatif (ou itératif): deux possibilités. On donne l'impression de force: les choses ne se sont pas passées deux fois de la même manière. On donne aux scènes une présence beaucoup plus forte: elles étaient telles dans le passé (plusieurs fois) et sont telles pour l'avenir restreint qui enveloppe la scène. Du coup *deux présents:* celui qu'exprime le fréquentatif et celui qu'exprime le parfait qui a deux caractéristiques: c'est ce qui disparaît pendant que les fréquentatifs restent, celui qu'on ne voit qu'une fois, qui enveloppe sa mort dès qu'il a lieu (du point de vue de la mort). C'est aussi chez F. un fréquentatif qui n'a pas eu de chance, qui aurait pu devenir fréquentatif. Cf. 341 Pl. "Une fois par [un] temps de dégel . . ." Il suffisait d'écrire "Parfois . . ." un geste motivé par la situation et qui aurait pu se reproduire vingt fois. D'ailleurs en même temps qu'il est présent-parfait, il passe au fréquentatif. Deux verbes passés et le reste imparfait. En général imparfait introduit par un parfait. Première mort: 381: il prit un abonnement àla Ruche Médicale. Ensuite, après le temps de la volonté, celui de la volonté disjointe, ridiculisée par les choses, qui laisse sa trace sur le fréquentatif (lirait-il sinon?) mais devient grotesque: pourquoi dormir *sur un livre!* C'est lc tcmps du ressentiment.

* * *

A principle of his entire psychology: atmospheres have a decisive influence (neither true nor false).

The ball (need for wealth and elegance) determines her to go to Yonville. Pommier 52: something of a slut.

In Yonville: entrance of Bournisien: theatrical.

Read the Corr. about *Saint Antoine* (not much. Later speaks about it in the *past tense*).

Tense: an intermediary between past, present and future: frequentative (imperfect) tense of eternal return—eternity. Is opposed to the event cf. Yonville: there is the event—Emma's passion and her death and then the frequentative (which remains with other individuals—the maids—to perform the same gestures)

Time: action disappears (notebook 12) there remains boredom (the real present time)

Psychologically: ripening. Emma gives herself to Léon when she is "ripe."

Mme B., novel of failure and of fatality. No causes (Bouilhet does away with them? Because they are false or because the reader will understand?) Ripenings. In particular the *fundamental reality* of characters unknown to F. "ou peut-être . . . sans doute" ("or perhaps . . . no doubt . . .")

The two ways of loving: Don Juan. Taken up again in Mme B.: Rodolphe-Léon. Clearly Charles has the first one.

Hysteria of F. passed on to Mme Bovary.

Language cannot do justice to feelings. Not those of Charles who says nothing or only utters banalities (but then he is not up to life's demands) nor those of Rodolphe (who is through and through negative)

Emma and Mazza: first of all the senses undeveloped, then they develop (especially Léon) and become compelling, triumph, create death.

Insincerity of language (notebook 13): add mute language, without words (they look into each other's eyes) which is sincere.

The definition of art: thought rendered by form (frequ. last page) expressed here.

Pommier 170: On remit à causer (They deferred talking)* . . . suggests the correction On se remit à causer (They resumed talking) (Pl. 348) which means the opposite. The dream about words. Other example: if the Church prohibits it, it must have its reasons (Pom.) Pl. 19: it must be right.

Indirect discourse: questioning (of the author) Pl. 356

Neorealism but therefore nature narrates man as passive and shows him his destiny.

Frequentative: can designate a relatively brief period.

The horse is afraid of the *dogs:* deterministic motive. In the definitive text we do not know *why* it is afraid: the dogs tug at their chain. This time presentiment: things indicate destiny: Pom. 153; Pl. 337

Pl. 338–39: Emma's hand. Who says this? The author.

Pl. 340: Would he have *thought* of it (analysis). Who is speaking? *Sans doute* (no doubt) = probably

Pl. 342: *this prohibition against seeing her* . . . and then the widow was thin. Cf. 333 Pl.: "some syrup and a little more love"

Emma *seen* from behind (Charles-Léon-Rodolphe): desire. *B[ouvard] et P[écuchet]* widow Bordin *from behind*

the widow was thin, and note 1

the event (often a *possible* frequentative: a country doctor asks a peasant for his daughter's hand)

Du Camp asks F. to do away with the wedding feast. Mistake stemming from his not understanding F. This wedding feast, notwithstanding a few perfects, is a frequentative. This does not mean: this is what a country wedding feast is like. It is an *already past* event (summed up at the end of chapter 3) which represents an eternity because it is at the level of memory (for Emma) and constitutes the base of their marriage. Charles looks like *a deflowered virgin* (feminine). Emma: impenetrable. Keeps aloof from the customary jokes. The dishes and nothing more than: "on mangea" (they ate). Undifferentiation of things and men. Neorealism and *practico-inert. Who* sees the carts

---

* As far as we know "remettre à" is a solecism, but its meaning is tolerably clear in the context. (Translators' note)

taken away during the night? And why "les femmes" (the women) (Pl. 351)? without the explanation that any nocturnal witness whatsoever would have in mind: the women are not drunk? The reason: the cause is not *visible* (the sleeping innkeeper). On the way to *impression* (subjectivism) and construction of a practico-inert system where the reader has in himself the explanation of the spurious witness.

352: comme la source (as the source) why *comme?*

Il se chauffait à la société d'Emma comme (he was warming himself in the company of Emma as): two metaphors. Everything is already expressed in the first one.

Plan: F. wants to write. He chooses the novel form. Why? What is the novel as bourgeois genre?

Is Mme B. an *Erziehungsroman?* Yes if the suicide appears as the conclusion of a life.

Does it correspond to Lukács's definition?

Starting with Saint Antoine in mind (theatre and vision-tableau) moves on to the novel. Had written one (*Ed[ucation] Sent[imentale]* 1: *Erziehungsroman*)

Erziehungsroman: only one hero, only one point of view. In Mme B. Charles's point of view also important (complete biography) and the others too;

prosopopoeia 360 Pl.

Mme B. *positive* attitude Pl. 361 cf. Pom. 190

Pom. drawing and music

Pom. 187: shift to imperfect for Charles.

The storm (F. knows a similar one. What it means) Pom. 196

Pl. 364: metaphor

Pl. 366 *a certain fear seized her. Why not *fear?* But let us ask ourselves on the contrary why Western culture holds that there is *fear*, always the same one. Progress towards the impression. Nominalism of F.

Pl. 369 "la statue regarde immobile" (the statue looks on, unmoving) Death/The flame (Pom. 205), flames (Pl. 368)

The impressions: blocks, neither subjective nor objective, to be treated once in one way once in another.

Annihilate the paragraph 370–73

Talking about the woman one loves to her lover (Jules and the actor, Frédéric and Arnoux, Charles and Rodolphe)

One single comparison: physical-chemical nature.

(Pl. 376: Vaubyessard and the storm)

Mme Bovary *is* the metaphor of St. Anthony. Mme B. hardly kindhearted: 385–86 Pl.

wedding feast: 354 and 387 Pl.

Subject Bovary: totalization and death.

Bovary and Don Quixote: same subject. Romanticism and tales of chivalry: negative use; make it impossible to know the world.

The entire problem: the value which is left in both of them. If they had nothing, death would not be necessary.

Description of Yonville 240–43 Pom. 388–91

a) First, description of a decaying borough. Even including its configuration: as it is limited to "pastures" the town lazily crawls towards the river. "Openings" which are hardly ever used. No development. Lestiboudois and the potatoes. The dead have been forgotten (Pom.). But *the living* feed on them. What indicates the generalization is that, immediately after the Lestiboudois text, the words "en effet" (indeed) (nothing indeed has changed in Yonville) much too heavy to be justified by the Lestiboudois episode.

b) And then the conclusion: nothing has changed. A conclusion which goes beyond the real end: he received the croix d'honneur. It is the perenniality of things and even of men seen in terms of the practico-inert. It is a pity that F. or Bouilhet should not have dared to keep the passage about the maids. Fear of saying too much: these maids are no longer the same. But does it matter, if they do the same things? In any case the idea is to obliterate events. These events, ever such a small disorder on the surface of being, disappear without changing it in depth. Being and the frequentative indiscernible: the maids but also the straw in little bits (it is not the same but this is less bothersome since it is a matter of *things*). There remains, after all, a very slow movement of rotting (foetus). In fact Yonville will disappear, Homais will go to Rouen.

The events that will be narrated. Who narrates? Who sees all of this? One paragraph on the move from "au bas de la côte" (at the bottom of the slope) Theater construction of the period: the characters have to be presented in the same decor. Lestiboudois, the lady innkeeper, Binet, Bournisien, Homais; Hivert, Léon, Mr. Lheureux etc. Perfectly useless. Only Léon was useful. "Mais ce lambin d'Hivert . . ." (But that dawdler Hivert . . .) etc.: theatrical utterance. "Six heures sonnèrent, Binet entra" (On the stroke of six, Binet came in): theatrical effect.

Had thought he was in the middle of the council: Pl. 396: hysteria.

The sea: F. mocks Emma who says the same things as he (Corr.) cf. the stupors of Djalioh in the face of the Ocean. Then Corr. 6 (?) the seamen and the sea.

Pl. 405: Everyone claims to know human existence in depth: Homais (Pommier 252), Emma and Charles; comic can be tragic (to Louise)

Pl. 406 Choice of name: F's thinking is that of his letters.

Language and inexpressible thought: Pl. 382–62–411–412. Old thesis. Language cannot say *everything*. Suggesting indirectly.

F. and metaphor: Goncourt 2

1st stage: all psych. thought is constructed materially: with words or images. It is not even different from images (poles, pieces of wood, circles, etc.)

2 [nd] stage: the image in itself being untranslatable (pieces of wood or circles) an equivalent is found for it using well-known objects (a bowman sends an arrow etc.) Aim: *to clarify the idea. Practical* function.

3 [rd] stage: the writer enjoys his construction. He tries to make it *beautiful*. F. In this case it may not have more meaning than the abstract idea expressed before the "as."

4 [th] stage: It certainly has a meaning (materialist-idealist). In F. usually materialist. 417 Pl.: fissure.

Lake and fissure. How does one go about conceiving the interior? Through the exterior?

415 Pl. As though he had walked on someone. New meaning of the metaphor: practico-inert; the dress *is* someone: Madame Bovary herself. He feels the thing as such. Not quite: his gesture looks like that to the witness, but may have other reasons (adoration, respect for the clothes of Emma etc.) In fact he is not conscious of this and the metaphor tends to suggest that at the bottom of his mind this is it.

Metaph. Leleu 1 373–76 Pom. 276 Pl. 413

Pl. She is isolated and more distant. The image is no longer spatial: it is psychological. In the sketches, F. had kept it spatial. Emma served as background (sun) and the others came in front. No doubt Bouilhet.

The passages left out (276–77 Pom. Pl. 413) are conserved in F.'s head, hence to be read between the lines. In particular the prepositions* (but) indicate that something is missing.

Metaphor Leleu 388 ff.

The comparison is given in the sentence before "comme" (as): exhale. Why exhale? It is generalized thinking. If it exhales it will be enough to indicate on the other side of the "as" *what* exhales.

The *sentence-image*

---

* The word "prépositions" is a lapsus calami: the text should have "conjunctions de coordination" (coordinating conjunctions). (Editor's note, Arlette Elkaïm Sartre)

Render the object in its material presence

Style of *boredom* (cf. Proust)

Smooth style (wall). The objects are reflected on it (Salammbô) and are therefore existent in the novel.

Ends of chapters: false ends; their theme is developed in the following chapter.

Deleted text (Pom. 326). F. mocks the comments of the chemist (of doctors, perhaps of Achille) on his own night life. Note: "La veille se change en rêve; le rêve en veille" (Waking life changes into dream; dream into waking life). Idea of aesthetic behavior. And that waking life is anways oniric. And F. multiplies onirism in Emma. The day she goes to the vicar, the oxen then the men *are phantoms*. Nothing remains in Pl. Too many phantoms: in Pom. first movement; deleted in Pl.

At the moment the attempt is made to deprive her of novels Emma finds them insipid.

Pom. 327–28: governments and families (F. himself)

Metaphor: does not understand what he is doing: *as* sometimes refers to cultural comparisons. Pom. 320: phantoms of virgins who died for love. Var.: dead people who lean on their elbows to chat on the edges of their tombs.

Mem[ory] of Léon. Pom. 320: past and present mixed.

Memory of love *feeding* on everything (past, future Pom. 321)

Fantastic happiness "dont elle plaçait la possibilité dans des conditions disparues" (the possibility of which she placed in vanished conditions)

Emma never loved Léon (F. describes himself only liking his trip once each stay has ended). But once the pretended love has vanished, the fact remains that it stresses, through the vague idea of what it might have been, the ugliness of existence in Yonville (which is *quite true*). Hence a fetishized absence (and through this fetish Léon, more sensitive, is embellished) stresses the ugliness of existence that is not felt as such by Charles, Homais, Binet. She becomes nasty. At the moment of the "sacrifice," she was nasty, but she enjoyed the game, "loved" children etc.

Pom. 322 *atrocious laughter* (Mazza romaticism)

Free indirect discourse: 322, a woman who had imposed such sacrifices on herself. It is Emma who is speaking.

Laziness in the face of culture (Pom. 322–23)

323 F.'s illness; with the *Enfin* (At last) she spat blood (Attack). Sham stoicism of Emma (F. to Ernest immediately after the crisis).

Emma's illness 1) Hysteria: sees the danger with Léon but she is unwilling to sleep with him. Prefers to have fun with his image. Communicates to Léon the notion of a platonic love. Changes: lives the life she *has to* (which the situation demands her to) live. In fact, deprivations lead to hatred (of Charles) and to a state of adultery in advance. She however leads Léon to leave.

2) Departure: sudden cessation of a vibration. Shifts to utter imaginary (Maria Schlesinger embellishes but the reality is the hatred for the husband). It is necessary [to her] at this stage that her state should be visible (should be seen by her husband). That is equivalent to the fall of '44. However she has an all too desired spitting of blood in Pom.: "enfin" (at last). Thereafter deleted as too obvious. In the meantime, therefore *before* the crisis, the state of nerves which F. mentions in his own case *after* his crisis (but which was bound for him to start earlier, in Paris, probably) cf. 323

3) Charles starts to worry. The mother comes. Diagnosis of the chemist: psychosomatic.

Pl. 448: et avec des haussements d'épaule (and with shrugs): "haussements" is significant; what follows is not: any move whatsoever can stretch the stitches of her sweater. Thus signification ends in the non-signifying, the practico-inert in the inert.

Inversely the non-signifying "les grandes basques etc. . . . ." (the large tails) moves on to the signifying "emplissent beaucoup l'espace. . . ." (take up a lot of space)

"Vous heurtaient . . ." (Bumped into you) 449–50. Here abstract. *Vous* is the readers. But since they were not there, they do not feel involved. It is the readers if they had been present.

What signification can the ternary rhythm have in the sentence-image? More material weight: 450: "A l'écart, en dehors des lices, cent pas plus loin . . ." (At a distance, outside the arena, a hundred yards further on). It would have been enough to write: "A l'écarte, à cent pas des lices . . ."

The novelist must be ironical (Lukács). Perhaps but not as F. For that is where his personality appears in its fight against impersonalism.

The theme of the windows in Mme B. Pl. 441: the window in the provinces etc. . . . But above all *window* in F.'s house at Croisset.

Theme of the *mirror* 473 Pl.

Confuses eye and gaze: 454: appliqué dessus son oeil (directed his eye to it): *does not mean anything.*

Agricultural show. Rodolphe is *insincere*. Everybody is insincere in F. except for brief wordless movements (She let herself go etc.)

    Pl. 458: it reached one

        461: Rodolphe's comparison: two rivers Pl. 461; it is found in the letters of Alfred and F.

464: magic mirror

468–69 Pl.: this perhaps would seem strange / it is the person who is speaking and your horses are perhaps fiery / it is F. who is using that turn of phrase

474: love sprang up: this time there are two of them: the one which has been kept down for a long time is for Léon, the one which springs up is for Rodolphe. F. only considers *one of them*, the same. Which means a love which is *neither* for Léon *nor* for Rodolphe, but a mystic love, without an *object*. The love is subjective, the object indifferent. 474: as though the walls had parted of their own accord. In Genet, same thing: for crime everything is easy.

    373 Pom.: Rodolphe: *fatality*

    The circles: they are there all the time. Totalization. As near as possible (She lets herself go), as far as possible (the cab).

    Metaphor-metamorphosis Brom. 8

    Fascination for adultery (*Novembre*)

    Free Indirect Discourse Brom. 58–59

    Travel notes: *excess is a proof of ideality*

    Laughter in Mme Bovary

The comparisons are often bookish: a fire in the Russian steppe (books on the Russian Campaign?) and the virgins who lean with their elbows on their tombstones (texts on the dances of Death. And reread the early texts on virgins and dead young women).

"Qu'elle mente sciemment, il se peut que non. On ne voit pas toujours clair en soi etc. . . ." (That she is lying wittingly may not be the case. One doesn't always have a clear insight into oneself etc. . . .): fundamental text for the "perhaps," "no doubt," etc.

Bookish: the childhood [escapades] of Charles modelled on the chidhood [escapades] of Gargantua.

"plus immobile qu'un roc . . ." (more unmoving than a rock): excessive use of the *"plus"* which alternates with a rock: the Swiss cannot be *more* unmoving than a rock.

St. Antoine-Mme Bovary = the two narrators of *Novembre*
Indirect Discourse (cf. the Robert)

Pom. 407: What F. adds: impressions on rereading: the vortex of the world and "tu ne vas pas mourir, je le sais" (you're not going to die, I know it) Hence reflections about the initial text.

407 Pom.:"Bournisien brave homme" (Bournisien decent fellow), Homais *decent fellow.* But in the sense of a plan by Loven: "M. le Préfet" (His honor the Prefect), Homais becomes fierce (the Blind Man).

408 Pom.: Fine example of indirect discourse

F.'s irony brings out the insincerity of each and every one (Club-foot)

Charles is thinking of his career. And it is, in fact, on his wife that the accident of the club-foot works. Interesting: has no consequences on his job. And yet all was set to ruin Charles (the main street full of people, Canivet's scorn).

Mme Bovary (her character, the sources. Bopp p. 25 note 1, p. 14 note 1)

Mme Bovary: I am too small for myself.

Instinct leads to fanaticism which is the adoration of idols.

The true misfortune of Mme Bovary: her instinct is to adore the ideal, which becomes foolishness when she imagines it (reason: language, readings. Language is *one* and it is *she.* The readings are the Other)

F."genitor-negator"

Héloïse: killed by money

Charles at Rouault's farmhouse only hears the beating inside his head.

Emma at the end only hears the beating of her heart

Emma *positive* Pl. 361

the words underlined (Pl. 364): initial device of F. Will later resort more and more to free indirect discourse.

Emma "incapable de comprendre ce qu'elle n'éprouvait pas comme de croire à tout ce qui ne se manifestait pas par des formes convenues" (incapable of comprehending what she did not experience and equally of believing all that failed to manifest itself through generally accepted forms) Pl. 365

Old Mme Bovary: Mrs. Flaubert?

the lady and the note (Vaubyessard): portent of the adultery.

Emma: throws to the poor then to the Blind Man all her small change (385 Pl.) "Quoiqu'elle ne fût guère tendre . . . ni facilement accessible à l'émotion d'autrui . . . callosités" (Although she wasn't very kind-hearted . . . or easily aware of the feelings of other people . . . callosities) Always *charity as pride* in F.

Dissembler (Pom. 236)

Natural instinct for dissimulation (?)

The time of the cab. Real and signifying time: *inside*. Includes:

1) the time of a concerted action. Both want to fuck. But a certain time is needed.

2) time of fatality: degradation of "la Bovary." But this irreversible time is embedded in a contingent, random, reversible time (they go round and round) and devoid of signification, underlined in Pl. 548 at the bottom of the page "sans parti pris, ni direction, au hasard, elle vagabonda" (without bias, or direction, at random, it roamed) which itself comes from the "demoralization" of the cab-driver and from the suppression of the time of the action (the cab will in general do something specific). And this time envelops the other one. Through Léon's will. And the contingent time tends of its own accord to become a frequentative: the machine goes again through the same places.

"confondre sa passion avec le milieu qui l'avive" (confusing his passion with the environment which quickens it) (Pom. 491)

"stupefaction" (the converse) Pom. 493

Time: 1.) She isn't coming. Empty time but not so much felt as such because Léon is happy.

      2.) She comes but wants to yield according to established forms: hence her own time (though rigorous and meaningful: she has to fight) is opposed to Léon's time (pure action). Conclusion: the two times (seen by Léon) thwart each other. A resistance of time.

The figuration of nothingness (Pl. 546) meaning of all time: prophecy

Pl. 550: the time of the cab: incident. And that of Hivert (frequentative)

The incident: Felicity present and the time of the frequentative: the day of jam-making.

Pl. 554–55: the time of the perfect denounces the time of the imperfect (it may be the other way round)

They heard the sharp rap (555): novelistic time. The object is named *afterwards*.

Theme of Emma-bird Bopp 400
the adverbs ("avec") of time and space
Theme of the horse and the carriage
    of the windows
    of the bird-woman
Theme of Emma-snake (opposed to Emma-bird) Pl. 582–83
Theme of the death rattle which goes on and on (Rodolphe—in front of the convent—the Blind Man—the masked ball in Rouen)

Farewells of Rodolphe and of Léon: each time she asks them to perform an action which she herself performs (Rod.) or which she would perform ("If I were you" Léon) and each time they chicken out.

603 Pl. A genuine and "great" moment for Mme Bovary. Cf. letter to Louise: when you are alone etc. . . .

Role of Bouilhet Pl. 599, Bopp 469
the beating of Emma's arteries (Pl. 611) and Pl. 616
fireworks (Pl. 611): exp[ression] of F. to describe his crises.

Neorealism Pl. 611: the walls were trembling, the ceiling was crushing her

The first sexual contact: from behind, back and rump: Charles (Pl. 340), Rodolphe (442), Léon (Pl. 552).

Pl. 345: he could only hear the beating in his head
Th. 105: money
Th. 114: Rodolphe and F. not jealous.

That she is lying wittingly may not be the case (Corr. 3, 23) "Il ne faut jamais craindre d'être exagéré" (One should never be afraid of being excessive) (Corr. Genius exaggerates the real (imag.) and thereby attains to the ideal).

The two images of putrefaction. Emma: "cette pourriture instantanée des choses où elle s'appuyait" (this instantaneous putrefaction of the things on which she leant). Charles's dream after Emma's death.

New idea (it has been in existence for a long time but it is the subject of Emma): one cannot escape from the place where one is, neither through action (flight impossible: Rodolphe), nor through the objects of desire (inferior to desire itself). Hence the idea of *Norman* color.

Writing to Léon, perceives another man. Cf. F. writing to Eulalie.

The image as *thought* in F. Why?

The magical element: the ensembles; are grouped into omens. This is not *necessary*. How come that the future should have such an influence on the present?

Almost the entire ugliness of style in F. resides in the verbs. For example, Pl. 350: se dressait l'eau de vie, dans des carafes; Pl. 355 composaient la continuité de son bonheur.

Circularity: the universe did not go beyond the silky circumference of her petticoat.

Ugly verbs: 362 Pl.: un détachement intérieur se faisait

365: s'égrenaient de pourriture Pl. 383: the theme of the snake (man who desires feminine qualities)

Mme Bovary: manifesto of postromanticism. A soul driven to death by romanticism. Romanticism-false imaginary contested by the real. The solution: choice of *another* imaginary, is not given.

The frequentative (or iterative): two possibilities. One gives an impression of strength: things have not happened twice in the same manner. One gives to the scenes a far greater presence: they were such in the past (several times) and are such for the restricted future which envelops the scene. Thereby *two presents:* that which the frequentative expresses and that which the perfect expresses, and which has two characteristics: it is that which disappears while the frequentatives remain, that which one only sees once, which envelops its death as soon as it takes place (from the point of view of death). It is also in F. a frequentative which has had no luck, which could have become a frequentative. Cf. 341 Pl. "Une fois par[un] temps de dégel" (Once, as it was thawing). It would have been enough to have written "Parfois" (Sometimes) and to have changed the tense of the verbs: it would become a frequentative. *Nothing* happens here apart from a gesture motivated by the situation and which could have reoccurred twenty times. Moreover, at the same time that it is a present-perfect, it shifts into a frequentative. Two verbs in the past and the remainder in the imperfect. In general imperfect introduced by a perfect. First death: 381: il prit un abonnement à la Ruche Médicale (he took out a subscription to the *Ruche Médicale*). Then after the time of will, that of disjointed will, ridiculed by things, which leaves its trace on the frequentative (would he be reading otherwise?) but becomes preposterous: why dormir *sur un livre* (sleep *over a book*)? It is the tense of resentment.

Translated by Philippe Hunt and Philip Wood

Part V

PATRICK McCARTHY

Sartre, Nizan and the Dilemmas of Political Commitment

Paul Nizan haunted Sartre from the day he entered the classroom in Henri IV until the last years of Sartre's life. He and Nizan were comrades in arms both at Henri IV and at the Ecole Normale but then, says Sartre, "the party came between us."[1] A study of the Sartre-Nizan relationship teaches us, however, to sift through Sartre's statements about his life and thought and we may decide that Nizan's communism, which indeed separated him from his friend, also fascinated Sartre and that in general Sartre's retrospective view of his pre-1939 years can be misleading. The fascination Sartre felt was strengthened by Nizan's death in 1940, even if the Sartre of the Liberation and the Cold War still did not know what to make of his friend. Not until 1960 did he offer a convincing portrait of Nizan in the preface to *Aden Arabie*. Even then he returned to him in the *Nouvel Observateur* interviews of 1975 which are perhaps Sartre's most dispassionate review of his youth. The study of Nizan's role in Sartre's life is, then, a study of the various answers which Sartre found to the problem of political commitment.

Meanwhile Nizan had left five major books: two pamphlets, *Aden Arabie* (1931) and *Les Chiens de garde* (1932), and three novels, *Antoine Bloyé* (1933), *Le Cheval de Troie* (1935) and *La Conspiration* (1938). Although all spring from his decision to embrace Marxism and join the PCF (the French Communist Party), these are complex and varied works. Are they satisfactorily interpreted by Sartre? Probably not and indeed Nizan's admirers are severe in their judgments of Sartre's efforts. "Sartre n'a jamais vraiment compris Nizan . . . il s'est simplement rapproché de lui" ["Sartre never really understood Nizan . . . he merely

---

1. Jean Paul Sartre, *Avant-propos* à la réédition d'*Aden Arabie* (Paris: Maspéro, 1960), reprinted in *Situations* 4 (Paris: Gallimard, 1964), 146. References are to the latter volume; in the text the Avant-propos is hereafter referred to as "the Preface."

became closer to him."], writes one of them.[2] Even if one must modify this statement it is a good starting-point from which to analyse the presence of Nizan in Sartre's thought.

Certainly Sartre's preface is an attempt less to understand Nizan than to reconstruct a mythical figure, a Sartrian character who could be an ally in the political battles of the 1960s. The preface should be read in conjunction with *La Critique de la raison dialectique* and the essays on the Algerian War. Similarly Sartre's earlier and less successful attempts to grapple with Nizan in his 1938 article on *La Conspiration* and in *Qu'est-ce que la littérature?* (1948) as well as through the character of Vicarios-Schneider in *Les Chemins de la liberté* reflect his interest in phenomenology and his conflicting post-Liberation view of the PCF. But Sartre was not simply drawing closer to Nizan. To state only the most obvious difference between the two men—even at the moment when he was most favorable to the PC and wrote *Les Communistes et la paix*, Sartre never joined the party, whereas Nizan's decisions to join and then in 1939 to leave the PC were the crucial decisions of his adult life. Nizan was to Sartre brother, rival and opposite; he was a guide towards political commitment but Sartre followed him by different paths. Moreover Sartre's writings do elucidate certain aspects of Nizan's achievement. If he hesitates over *La Conspiration*, he casts a powerful beam of light on the pamphlets and *Antoine Bloyé*. And it was the preface which triggered the revival of interest in Nizan which took place in the 1960s.

This study is divided into three parts: a review of the Sartre-Nizan friendship; an analysis of what committed writing meant to Nizan which helps us understand the various possibilities his work offers Sartre; Sartre's attempts to interpret Nizan and use him as an ally.

Clearly no attempt can be made here to cover the entire friendship. It has been discussed from Nizan's viewpoint in two recent critical biographies and the task of reconstructing it as Sartre lived it must be left to Sartre's future biographers.[3] All that can be done here is to indicate how certain parallels and differences between Sartre's and Nizan's thought emerge from their relationship.

Although she did not enter the group until 1929, Simone de Beauvoir captures the tone that Sartre and his friends set: "Ils dégonflaient

2. Annie Cohen-Solal, *Paul Nizan, communiste impossible* (Paris: Grasset, 1980), 226. Translations mine.
3. Annie Cohen-Solal, op. cit., and Pascal Ory, *Nizan, destin d'un révolté* (Paris: éditions Ramsay, 1980). See also: William Redfern, *Paul Nizan* (Princeton, N.J.: Princeton University Press, 1972).

impitoyablement tous les idéalismes; il tournaient en dérision les belles âmes, les âmes nobles, toutes les âmes et les états d'âme, la vie inté-rieure . . . ils manifestaient que les hommes n'étaient pas des esprits mais des corps en proie au besoin et jetés dans une aventure brutale." ["They jabbed a pin in every inflated idealism, laughed high-minded souls to scorn—in fact, every kind of soulfulness, the 'inner life' . . . they set out to prove that men were not rarefied spirits but bodies of flesh and bone, racked by physical needs and crudely engaged in a brutal adventure that was life."][4] Debunking one's elders is too common a phenomenon to merit much attention in itself but Sartre and Nizan were making a systematic critique of the culture of the previous genera-tion. It may be significant that in 1960 Sartre begins his preface with an onslaught on Gide and Valéry because "ils faisaient tous les jours, publi-quement, la toilette de leurs âmes" ["every day they bedecked their twin souls in public."][5] Although well able to appreciate the *NRF (Nouvelle Revue Française)*, the young Sartre and Nizan rejected what may be its principal tenet—the integrity and independence of inner life. Simone de Beauvoir, who was initially more respectful, discovered that Sartre did not share her enthusiasm for that monumental record of private, individual existence, the *Correspondance Rivière-Fournier.*

Along with this went a great political cynicism, and a critique of idealist philosophy as exemplified then by Léon Brunschvicg who was to be excoriated in *Les Chiens de garde.* When Sartre and Nizan re-sumed their friendship in 1920 France was in the throes of postvictory patriotism and governed by the "Chambre bleu horizon." Shaped by reaction against it as well as by more personal factors, they rejected along with flag-waving chauvinism the entire social order. Although both Sartre and Simone de Beauvoir in their postwar reconstructions of this period minimize Sartre's political awareness there are signs that it might have been greater than they would retrospectively have us be-lieve. Simone de Beauvoir grudgingly admits that in 1929 Sartre "was interested in social and political questions; he sympathized with Nizan's position."[6] This is a matter to which we must return but one may simply note here that the radically negative quality of Sartre's and Nizan's thought had clear political implications. In the 1975 *Nouvel*

4. Simone de Beauvoir, *Mémoires d'une jeune fille rangée* (Paris: Gallimard, 1958), 335–36. *Memoirs of a Dutiful Daughter*, trans. James Kirkup (New York: Harper and Row, 1974), 336.
5. *Situations* 4, 130. *Situations*, trans. Benita Eisler (New York: George Braziller, 1965), 115.
6. De Beauvoir, *Mémoires*, 540; *Memoirs of a Dutiful Daughter*, 341.

Observateur (NO) interviews, Sartre points correctly to the episode of the museum portraits in *La Nausée* as an example of his prewar political awareness.

According to *Les Mots* Sartre's earliest, instinctive rejection of bourgeois society came from his sense that his grandfather was, like the people who had sat for their portraits, playing out a series of roles as humanist and patriarch. Bourgeois life was a blend of pretence and pretension which sought to mask man's alienation. Later Sartre would define alienation in a more directly political way but he first felt it as the falsity which lay behind those artfully constructed personalities. From this comes the Sartrian concept of awareness as a flight and his view that alienation could only be overcome if awareness entered into contact and conflict with the external world. Whereas Gide had sought to discover a real self and more sincere values beneath the masks, Sartre felt that man must look outwards. As Simone de Beauvoir puts it, Sartre "saisissait dans leur profusion les choses toutes vives" ["The freshness and dogged tenacity of his perceptions grasped the very essence of things"] and "accordait tout son poids à la réalité" ["he came down very heavily on the side of reality."][7]

Nizan discovered alienation differently and he depicts its socioeconomic mechanisms in *Antoine Bloyé*. Bloyé is a working-class youth who is separated from his fellows by his rise to a management position; capitalist society makes him rule over his comrades, which mutilates him. Clearly the young Sartre had no such insights and his sense of external reality and the problematic engagement that man might have with it led him to phenomenology. But, although phenomenology cannot *merely* be considered a steppingstone to Sartre's political commitment, it certainly *was* such a steppingstone since it allowed Sartre to affirm that man could only be himself "sur la route . . . chose parmi les choses, homme parmi les hommes" ["on the road . . . a thing among things, a man among men."][8] Moreover Sartre already felt an attraction towards working-class people, as he describes in the pages on the cinema in *Les Mots*, because they did not delude themselves with game playing but knew they were "men among men."

If one were to seek the psychological origins of Nizan's decision to join the PC in early 1928, they would be found in his acute sense of death and his consequent determination to put down roots. Most students at

---

7. Ibid., 339; 340, and *La Force de l'âge* (Paris: Gallimard, 1960), 35. *The Prime of Life*, trans. Peter Green (Cleveland and New York: The World Publishing Company, 1962), 30.

8. *Situations* 1 (Paris: Gallimard, 1947), 35.

the Ecole Normale talked about death but "Nizan était le plus obsédé: parfois en pleine veille, il se voyait cadavre; il se levait les yeux grouillants de vers . . . disparaissait; on le retrouvait le lendemain, saoul avec des inconnus." ["Nizan was the most obsessed of all. At times, when fully awake, he would see himself as a corpse; he would stand up, his eyes swarming with worms . . . and would disappear. The next day we would find him, drunk, with strangers."][9] But, once made, the decision changed the entire course of his thought. In 1928 the PC had only nine percent of the vote, its membership was down to thirty thousand and it was pursuing the class against class line imposed by Stalin. This did not deter Nizan who was attracted by the semi-illegality in which the party had to operate and which he depicts in La Conspiration. By 1932 he was a full-time party official and in 1934 he made the obligatory pilgrimage to the Soviet Union. During the Popular Front years he made himself useful as a journalist and by forming contacts with intellectuals like Gide, who might be useful to the party, or with Dominicans as part of the "main tendue" policy. Annie Cohen-Solal argues that Nizan was growing dissatisfied with the PC and certainly his writing does not follow the accepted canons of socialist realism. Such discontent is the background to the crisis of 1939 when the Nazi-Soviet pact and the Russian invasion to Poland drove Nizan out of the party.

In the preface Sartre sums up the difference between them: Nizan wanted to destroy the established order; "j'aimais qu'il existât et pouvoir lui jeter ces bombes: mes paroles." ["I wanted this order to exist in order to throw bombs at it—my words."][10] This is the all too neat antithesis which Simone de Beauvoir also offers—Sartre man of literature and Nizan man of politics. Not only does it ignore the complexity of Nizan's writing but it once again distorts Sartre's political awareness. Again and again he and Simone de Beauvoir dismiss their prewar stance as a trivial bohemianism. "Nous ignorions sur tous les plans le poids de la réalité," writes de Beauvoir. "Nous nous targuions d'une liberté radicale." ["At every level we failed to face the weight of reality, priding ourselves on what we called our 'radical freedom.'"][11] Sartre's detractors have said that his flair for self-criticism comes from a neurotic feeling of guilt but one might argue that it is chiefly a polemical weapon, and that by criticizing his past positions, Sartre is defending his present views. However, the unity between his pre- and postwar thought is

9. Sartre, Les Mots (Paris: Gallimard, 1964), 163. The Words, trans. Bernard Frechtman (New York: George Braziller, 1964), 196.

10. Situations 4, 147; 132.

11. La force de l'âge, 19; 18.

greater than he would have us believe; both by its negativity and its critique of subjectivism, his vision was in the act of becoming political. It is interesting to note that Nizan did not share the postwar Sartre's dismissal of *La Nausée*. In *Les Mots* Sartre emphasizes what he now considers the false resolution of Roquentin's anguish by means of words: "J'étais *moi*, l'élu, l'annaliste des enfers, photomicroscope de verre et d'acier penché sur mes propres sirops protoplasmiques." ["I was *I*, the elect, chronicler of Hell, a glass and steel photomicroscope peering at my own protoplasmic juices."][12] In 1938 Nizan argued that Roquentin's metaphysical alienation would drive his creator to resolve it by action.[13] More recently a critic has written that Sartre's prewar concept of freedom was "not simply the privatized individualism of the petty bourgeois nor the glamorous estheticism of the bohemian intellectual."[14]

So the simple notion that the party separated Sartre and Nizan must give way to a more nuanced view. In 1975 Sartre admitted that his year in Germany awakened him to the evils of Fascism and that he was already an antifascist. He attributes this to Nizan's example: "I adopted a position close to that of Nizan."[15] So Nizan was steering Sartre towards political commitment, even as he was also throwing up a barrier—"I felt that Marxism was challenging me because it was the thinking of a friend and it was cutting across our friendship."[16] Impressed by Nizan, Sartre received this double and contradictory influence. Moreover it tended to falsify his view of his friend. Whether he admired or resented Nizan's membership in the PC, Sartre considered him the perfect communist, briefed in the diplomatic secrets guarded so jealously by the International, and always in agreement with the party's policies. The unorthodoxies of Nizan's writing and his opinions eluded Sartre, which explains the hesitations of his article on *La Conspiration*.

Before turning to this article one must consider Nizan's work which is one of the best examples of committed writing in the France of the 1930s. His books are based on a fundamental decision which also involves a series of further choices. As Sartre puts it, "ses yeux furent marxistes; et ses oreilles; Et sa tête." ["His eyes were Marxist, and his

12. *Les Mots*, 210; 251–52.
13. Pascal Ory, op. cit., 189.
14. Mark Poster, *Existential Marxism in post-war France* (Princeton, N.J.: Princeton University Press, 1975), 78.
15. J.-P. Sartre, "Autoportrait à 70 ans," *Nouvel Observateur*, 23 juin, 30 juin, 7 juillet 1975, reprinted in *Situations* 10, 179. *Life Situations*, trans. Paul Auster and Lydia Davis (New York: Pantheon Books, 1977), 47.
16. Ibid., 192; 59.

ears, as well as his head."][17] But Nizan's books were anything but propaganda for the PC and, as his biographers have pointed out, the party complained that there was insufficient economic analysis of colonialism in *Aden Arabie* and that in *Antoine Bloyé* the critique of capitalism was not accompanied by an apology for the new Marxist culture.[18] Yet Nizan's work is Marxist in that political commitment gives structure to his anger and makes literary discourse possible. Then he experiments with several forms of discourse from the fury of the pamphlets to the nuanced irony of *La Conspiration*.

The cry of condemnation hurled at capitalist society is well suited to the pamphleteers who need such intolerance because it permits them to divide the world into good and evil. Marxism, says Carré, the communist leader of *La Conspiration*, is the least pluralist of all doctrines. Such wilful simplicity suits the genre of the pamphlet and enables Nizan to renew a tradition of pamphleteering that runs from the late nineteenth century on and includes both right-wingers like Drumont and, albeit less frequently, left-wingers like Vallès. From this tradition Nizan borrows his rhetoric, his *ad hominem* attacks and his deliberate contempt for subtlety. When he first read *Aden Arabie* Sartre considered it "un tourbillon de paroles légères" ["a whirlwind of airy words"][19] which prompts him later to yet more self-criticism. But if he had omitted the adjective, his observation would have been correct because Nizan's pamphlets are literary exercises inspired by the insight into the social order which Marxism has given him.

In *Les Chiens de garde* he does not refute what he calls the idealist philosophers; instead he accuses them; "Nous vivons dans un temps où les philosophes s'abstiennent. Ils vivent dans un état de scandaleux écart, une scandaleuse distance entre ce qu'énonce la Philosophie et ce qui arrive aux hommes." ["We are living in a time when the philosophers are abstaining. They are living in a scandalous state of absenteeism. There is a scandalous divergence, a scandalous gap between what Philosophy propounds and what happens to men."][20] If the tone of this passage, which is characteristic of *Les Chiens de garde*, reminds us of certain passages in Sartre, then this is a sign that there is in Sartre too a pamphleteer who emerges precisely in the preface. Nizan anticipated Sartre in the discourse of anger.

17. *Situations* 4, 173; 158.
18. Annie Cohen-Solal, op. cit., 127, 132.
19. *Situations* 4, 149; 134.
20. Paul Nizan, *Les Chiens de garde* (Paris: Rieder, 1932), 29. *Watchdogs*, trans. Paul Fittingoff (New York: Monthly Review Press, 1971), 28.

Each of his novels offers a different although equally Marxist voice. *Antoine Bloyé* has the trappings of nineteenth-century realism: a regular procession through time, lists of objects, description of the environment. But instead of the remote, clinically objective narrator, there is present in the book a critical consciousness which interprets Bloyé to the reader. In the preface Sartre writes that, although this novel is ostensibly about Nizan's father, Nizan himself is present. This is another way of saying that there is a Marxist narrator who links Bloyé's career to the growth of French capitalism. The analysis of the railway system—the epitome of nineteenth-century capitalism—has as counterpoint Bloyé's imprisonment by it "Antoine était pris comme un insecte dans cette toile vibrante des voies ferrées." ["Antoine was caught like an insect in this quivering web of railway lines."][21]

After this critique of the old order Nizan depicts the birth of the new culture in *Le Cheval de Troie*. Although partly written in the Soviet Union and in the aftermath of the 1934 Moscow Congress, which saw the triumph of socialist realism, and although seeming to answer *L'Humanité*'s rebuke by portraying a group of communists, *Le Cheval de Troie* does not depict the inevitable triumph of the revolution. Nizan uses the technique of the film shot to depict each of the communists in action and out of their actions there emerges a greater but partial understanding of history. The PC militants have no infallible party secretary to guide them and they are inventing the revolution as they go along. As one of Nizan's critics puts it, this is "an open-ended book";[22] it is Marxist in its depiction of men in rebellion against the capitalist order but it is unstalinist in its lack of dogmatism.

This is the link with Nizan's last novel, *La Conspiration*, where the Marxist awareness is most obviously present as irony. The narrator, a mature communist, looks back on the group of young bourgeois conspirators and in a sentence that was to become all too famous Nizan writes: "Rosenthal publia dans la *Guerre Civile* des pages qui n'avaient pas de chances sérieuses d'ébranler le capitalisme." ["In the *Guerre Civile*, Rosenthal published views which could not seriously shake the foundations of capitalism."][23] Yet, contrary to what Sartre affirms, the book is not entirely written by a narrator who smiles sarcastically as his characters struggle. *La Conspiration* shifts from one discourse to another—from the authoritative but brief pronouncements of Carré to the

21. Paul Nizan, *Antoine Bloyé* (Paris: Grasset, 1933), 123. *Antoine Bloyé*, trans. Edmund Stevens (New York: Monthly Review Press, 1973), 102.
22. William Redfern, op. cit., 42.
23. Paul Nizan, *La Conspiration* (Paris: Gallimard, 1938), 64.

flat despair of Régnier's diary. The sarcasm that marks the early depiction of Rosenthal gives way to sympathy and even complicity as he struggles against his family. *La Conspiration* is a polyphonic novel where Nizan uses the diverse possibilities which Marxism offers a writer.

Although *Le Cheval de Troie* seems the most Sartrian of these novels, Sartre's first attempt to grapple with Nizan was his article on *La Conspiration*. Chiefly interesting as a guide to Sartre's concept of the novel and as a preface to his article on Mauriac, this review does not show great understanding of Nizan and illustrates the differences rather than the parallels between the two friends. After making a half-hearted attempt to annex Nizan to phenomenology, Sartre criticizes the characters of *La Conspiration* and draws the conclusion: "Un communiste peut-il écrire un roman? Je n'en suis pas persuadé: il n'a pas le droit de se faire le complice de ses personnages." ["Can a communist write a novel? I am skeptical: he does not have the right to become his characters' accomplice."][24]

The conception of the *"complice"* will be clarified in the essay on Mauriac published three months later. According to Sartre, Mauriac indulges in a "va-et-vient" between himself and his heroine: now Thérèse speaks for herself, now Mauriac speaks through her with the insight of an omniscient narrator. This destroys her liberty and prevents the appeal to the reader's liberty which Sartre considers the crux of the author-reader relationship.

Although Sartre admits there can be Christian novelists and cites Dostoevsky as an example, he seems to think that communists are bound to interfere with the freedom of their creations. Because of their claim to understand the workings of history, they crush their characters and prevent them from engaging the reader. This criticism, which might possess a certain validity if directed at *Antoine Bloyé*, where the narrator does impose one view of Bloyé's experience, can only apply to *La Conspiration* if one accepts the notion that Nizan toys with his young conspirators from the heights of some communist Olympus. If one considers the shifts of point of view they may discover the *"complice"* concept which Sartre extols. But Sartre, disturbed by Nizan's Marxism, insists on defining Nizan as the perfect communist, indeed as a Stalinist communist.

When he returns to Nizan in *Qu'est-ce que la littérature?* (1948), his view of his friend has partially changed because his own concept of

24. J.-P. Sartre, *"La Conspiration* par Paul Nizan" in *Situations* 1, 29.

liberty has changed. The dialogue between author and reader is now situated within history; the committed writer will encourage the reader to treat the other members of society as an end and not, as the capitalist ethos dictates, as a means of production; the reader will be stirred to exercise his freedom by political and social action. The political element in Sartre's thought, which was potential and hesitant before 1939, is now crystallized and he draws closer to Nizan. *Le Cheval de Troie* and *La Conspiration* are cited as examples of works which liberate their readers, and Nizan is implictly contrasted with nineteenth-century novelists who denounced existing society without provoking the reader to imagine new forms of freedom.

Yet the problem of Nizan's communism returns by a different route. To the image of Nizan the perfect communist is added the image of Nizan the ex-communist. Moreover Sartre is himself embroiled in a dialogue and conflict with the PC which will last at least until the late 1950s. His relationship with the party confuses his view of Nizan and, paradoxically, Nizan is too much of a communist to please the 1948 Sartre and too much of an ex-communist to please the 1952 Sartre.

In *Qu'est-ce que la littérature?* Sartre did not consider the PC an ally in the battle for committed writing. Reacting against the party's Stalinism he was hoping to carve out an area of influence on the left. Since they well understood his intentions, the Communists considered him a rival and their press was frequently vituperative in its attacks on him. But Sartre forged ahead, using *Les Temps modernes* as his main intellectual weapon and the short-lived Rassemblement Démocratique Révolutionnaire as an alternative form of political organization. One must set *Qu'est-ce que la littérature,* in this context since Sartre here defends his view of the author-reader relationship against the Stalinist view of literature, holding that approval or disapproval is bestowed by the party with its infallible insight into history. Using and renewing Nizan's phrase, Sartre insists that "nous n'irons pas rejoindre les chiens de garde du PC" ["we will not join the watchdogs of the Communist Party."][25] But, while he affirms that Nizan launched an appeal to freedom in his novels, he continues to argue that the reader's response is distorted by the PC which intervenes with its theological judgments on Nizan's orthodoxy.

The obvious solution was for Sartre to separate Nizan from the party so that he could consider his thought as an autonomous entity. Sartre did undertake a campaign to defend Nizan whom Communist leaders from Thorez to Aragon were denouncing as a police spy. In 1947

25. *Situations* 2 (Paris: Gallimard, 1948), 287.

Sartre helped to organize a protest, signed by twenty-six writers including Camus and Aron, pointing out that Nizan had simply left the party
and calling on the PC to produce proofs that he was a spy.[26] The party
did not oblige and Sartre did not press the matter. In the preface he
blames himself for not doing more to rescue Nizan's work. He was held
back, he maintains, by his growing sympathy for the PC: "nous les
aimions bien dans le fond, ces injustes soldats de la justice" ["We really
liked them at heart, these unjust soldiers of justice."][27]

This dilemma explains why the shadow of Nizan flits rather un-
satisfactorily throughout *Les Chemins de la liberté*. William Redfern
argues that Nizan helped to inspire the characters of the model communist Brunet and of Schneider-Vicarios, the journalist who has been expelled from the party.[28] In one version of the ending Sartre depicted
Brunet setting out to rehabilitate the dead Schneider but then decided to
cut out this episode.

Sartre's reticence over Nizan is explained by his growing feeling
that the PC was an ally rather than a rival. In this new context Nizan
became primarily an ex-communist and Sartre's reluctance to vindicate
Nizan's work is yet another version of the "il ne faut pas désespérer
Billancourt" ["Billancourt must not be driven to despair"] argument.
Having been a victim of the Nazi-Soviet pact Nizan became a victim of
the Cold War. Sartre decided that anticommunist rhetoric was merely
another piece of game-playing by the French bourgeoisie which was
determined to hold on to its power. After the RDR split and faltered as
U.S.-Russian relations grew steadily worse, Sartre came to perceive the
PC as the only force able to combat the reconstruction of France along
capitalist lines. This led him in 1952 to write *Les Communistes et la
paix*, where he argues that the PC is the legitimate party of the workers
because it alone is capable of giving shape to their revolt, which would
otherwise remain inchoate or fragmented. This implies that the PC can
indeed interpret history correctly and hence that its judgements foster
rather than obstruct man's freedom. So it was difficult to make a case for
Nizan, the ex-communist. Sartre's neglect of his old friend coincided
with his angry rejection of his more recent friend, Camus; both were
sacrificed to the struggle against General Ridgway.

By the time he wrote the preface in 1960 Sartre had separated himself from the PC and hence was able retrospectively to divorce Nizan
from the party. The preface must be placed in a new context: alongside

26. Ory, op. cit., 250 ff.
27. *Situations* 4, 132; 117.
28. Redfern, 207 ff. See also Ory, 234, 263.

La Critique de la raison dialectique, Sartre's support for the FLN and his growing interest in Third World revolution. Nizan is the model whom Sartre offers to the youth of 1960: a heretical Marxist rather than a perfect or an ex-communist. Not that Sartre has suddenly become an orthodox historian; rather than considering Nizan's work as an autonomous entity, he wishes to stress certain aspects of it which are useful to him in his new political battles.

The invasion of Hungary and the PC's shifty attitude to the Kruschev revelations had destroyed the always troubled dialogue between Sartre and the Communists. Although they seemed his natural allies in the protest against the Algerian War, Sartre felt that they were dragging their feet. In particular they refused to accept FLN violence and to sanction the deliberately illegal activities of the network set up by Sartre's collaborator, Francis Jeanson, to help the FLN in France.

This convinced Sartre both that the PC was no longer a revolutionary party and that a new, more audacious revolutionary movement must be created. This belief, which contrasted with the general political situation in Western Europe where left-wing parties, whether communist or noncommunist, were moving towards more reformist positions, is affirmed by Simone de Beauvoir: "Nous espérions radicaliser une gauche déplorablement respectueuse." ["We hoped to restore some radical feeling to a Left that had become deplorably 'respectful.' "][29] And, since Europe offered little inspiration, Sartre looked to the national liberation movements of the Third World.

A year after writing the preface, he published his introduction to Frantz Fanon's *Les Damnés de la terre* where he reaffirms his support for the revolutionary violence of the FLN. To this period too belongs the essay on Patrice Lumumba which concentrates on Lumumba's failure to found a genuine revolutionary movement, a failure that explains, according to Sartre, why his opponents were able to get rid of him. But the experience which is most closely linked with the preface is a trip to Cuba which Sartre made in 1960. Indeed he worked on the preface while he was in Havana and presumably in between his meetings with Castro and Che Guevara. Cuba delighted Sartre because, to quote Simone de Beauvoir, "pour la première fois de notre vie, nous étions témoins d'un bonheur qui avait été conquis par la violence." ["For the first time in our lives, we were witnessing happiness that had been attained by violence."][30] The enthusiasm of Cuban youth was especially important

29. Simone de Beauvoir, *La Force des choses* (Paris: Gallimard, 1963), 531. *The Force of Circomstance,* trans. Richard Howard (New York: G. P. Putnam's Sons, 1965), 506.
     30. Ibid., 515; 491.

and it leaves traces in the Nizan essay. Simone de Beauvoir writes that
the preface grows from "la confrontation de sa [Sartre's] propre jeunesse
avec celle des Cubains d'aujourd'hui." ["(Sartre's) confrontation of his
own youth with the youth of Cuba today."][31] The result of this confrontation is Sartre's attempt to resurrect Nizan as an elder brother of the
young Cubans and hence a model for young Frenchmen.

The theoretical framework for the new revolutionary movement is
set out in La Critique which Sartre has called "un ouvrage écrit contre
les communistes, tout en étant marxiste" ["a work written against the
Communists, although it remained Marxist."][32] Gone is the theme of
Les Communistes et la paix where the PC was the legitimate organization of the working class. In and after Critique Sartre analyses other,
looser kinds of organizations, less dogmatically linked with the working class but better able to transmit without distorting or exploiting its
need to rebel. Although these reflections do not find space in the preface, Nizan is considered as an individual whose years in the PC were
only one part of his total activity, and whose revolt springs from his own
alienation rather than from the oppression of his class.

Sartre's interpretation of Nizan is of course arbitrary. His attempt
to analyse Nizan's life through his novels has drawn a cry of pain from at
least one of Nizan's critics.[33] Nor does he tackle all of Nizan's books,
concentrating instead on the pamphlets and Antoine Bloyé. This is less
a literary study than a political portrait, while the preface as a whole is
best read as a political pamphlet.

Sartre catches the tone of Aden Arabie and directs its fury against a
different target: "Croit-on qu'elle puisse attirer les fils, la Gauche, ce
grand cadavre à la renverse où les vers se sont mis? Elle pue cette cha-
rogne." ["Could the sons then be attracted by the Left, that corpse, lying
on its back and full of worms? This cadaver stinks."][34] Attacking the
post-Liberation period, Sartre considers that he and his friends were too
self-satisfied and thus, whether communist or noncommunist, they
missed the opportunity to transform French society. This has left them
unworthy to address the generation of 1960, but from the wreckage of
his generation Sartre salvages the figure of Nizan: "un jeune monstre,
un beau jeune monstre comme eux [1960 youth] qui partage leur terreur
de mourir et leur haine de vivre dans le monde que nous avons fait" ["a
young monster, a handsome young monster like them, who shares their

31. Ibid., 523; 498.
32. Situations 10, 150.
33. Redfern, 73.
34. Situations 4, 138; 123.

terror of dying and their hatred of living in the world which we have created for them."][35]

Sartre stresses Nizan's intransigence which is contrasted with Liberation flabbiness and compared—by implication—with the audacity of Castro's guerrillas. The new generation of French youth can be created only by a negative reaction against the failures of what will eight years later be called the old left. As yet there is no need for revolutionary strategies or organizations; the first impetus must be a violent refusal of the social order and the human condition. Describing the Nizan of 1939 Sartre writes: "il ne restait que la révolte, la vieille révolte anarchique et désespérée: puisque tout trahissait les hommes, il préserverait ce peu d'humanité qui reste en disant non à tout" ["only revolt remained, the old anarchistic and desperate revolt. Since everything betrayed men, he would preserve the little humanity which remained by saying no to everything."][36]

As well as depicting the radical negativity of Nizan, the author of *Aden Arabie,* Sartre describes the mechanism of alienation analysed in *Antoine Bloyé.* Noting that economic exploitation is only one part of Bloyé's suffering, Sartre stresses his private loneliness: "les ressorts de sa vie, les mobiles de son action ne sont pas en lui." ["But the sources of his life, the inner spring of his actions are not found within him."][37] Reacting against the PC's emphasis on purely economic exploitation and on its simplistic definition of class, Sartre uses Bloyé and his creator as examples of the universal alienation created by the capitalist order. One definition of the existentialist Marxism prescribed in *Critique* is that it is "a way of seeing the individual in the act of living his alienation,"[38] and the Nizan of the preface is the supreme example of such a man.

So William Redfern is somewhat unfair when he rebukes Sartre for turning Nizan into a "neurotic rebel."[39] Sartre's Nizan is the forerunner of the New Left militant: disrespectful of the PC, suspicious of all authority, at least as much concerned with metaphysics as with economics, and drawn from the bourgeoisie as frequently as from the working class. As Sartre hoped "sa préface toucha particulièrement les filles et les garçons de vingt ans." ["his own preface was particularly affecting

35. Ibid., 140; 125.
36. Ibid., 186; 171.
37. Ibid., 160; 145.
38. Mark Poster, op. cit., 285.
39. Redfern, 213.

to girls and boys of twenty or so."][40] Maspéro sold twenty-four thousand copies of *Aden Arabie* and, although the complex question of Sartre's influence on the protagonists of May '68 must be left to sociologists of intellectual life, the preface, offering a vivid, readable illustration of *Critique*, must have exerted considerable influence in student circles.

Now Sartre and Nizan were working together, for *Les Chiens de garde* and *Antoine Bloyé* were also republished and Nizan acquired a substantial number of left-wing readers. The attack on official philosophy in *Les Chiens de garde*, now considered "le discours de l'extrême-gauche" ["the discourse of the extreme left"],[41] seemed to foreshadow the tumult in the Sorbonne. Conversely both Sartre and Nizan may have had less influence in the mid-70s by which time the New Left movements were largely spent. This provoked a mood of gloom in Sartre which is present in the last volume of the *Situations*, and which prompts him to look back on his youth in a more disenchanted way than he does in the preface. He returns to Nizan as well, retouching the portrait he has painted, as if he is still not quite sure that he has captured the elusive figure of his friend.

40. *La Force des choses*, 523; 498.
41. Cohen-Solal, op. cit., 125.

DOUGLAS KIRSNER

Sartre and the Collective Neurosis of Our Time

FRANZ: "I am every man and all mankind. I am the century, like anyone.

—Les Séquestrés d'Altona

Sartre was always interested in the relation between an individual and his or her time. The early Sartre seemed to focus on the manner in which we deny the freedom which constitutes us, while the later Sartre emphasises the limits to this freedom, which result from our familial and social contexts. In fact, Sartre devoted more pages to understanding the individual in context than to any other matter. How much can we know about a person who is free and yet situated? Sartre's study of Genet shows what Genet made of what was made of him. His study of Flaubert asks both what Flaubert can tell us about his time and what the time can tell us about Flaubert:

> For a man is never an individual; it would be more fitting to call him a *universal singular*. Summed up and for this reason universalized by his epoch, he in turn resumes it by reproducing himself in it as a singularity. Universal by the singular universality of human history, singular by the universalizing singularity in his projects, he requires simultaneous examination from both ends.[1]

In this article I want to look at Sartre in the same way in which Sartre treated Genet and Flaubert. Sartre himself wanted to be "as transparent to posterity . . . as Flaubert is to [him]."[2] I want to investigate empathically Sartre's "lived experience," as the way his culture lived him as well as the way he lived his culture, in order to achieve the same end as Sartre achieved with Flaubert. How did Sartre live our contemporary culture? How did he reflect and express central problems of our time as a "universal singular"? Sartre's own view of our age is depicted in *The Critique of Dialectical Reason*. It is a pessimistic work which focusses on our radical alienation from ourselves and our world. The groups into which we are born terrorize us and dominate the very cate-

1. Jean-Paul Sartre, *The Family Idiot*, vol. 1, trans. H. E. Barnes (Chicago: University of Chicago Press, 1981), ix.
2. Sartre, *Life Situations*, 123.

gories with which we think. Our Western world of late capitalism is ruled by a counterfinality in which loser wins. Advanced technological rationality may be seen to enshrine the final outcome of the fetishism of commodities—human beings are constituted as objects of administration. We blindly produce a world that controls us. Where technology has become the prevailing ideology, human relations often become relations between things. Freedom and choice are fundamentally illusions for there is no ground on which freedom and choice can become realized. In *Search for a method* Sartre shows how we can use a method of cross-reference to explain the relation of the individual to society and, in *The Family Idiot,* Sartre goes further in developing a way of characterizing our time. He understands Flaubert's neurosis as

> a neurosis *required* by what I call the objective spirit . . . In the first two volumes I seem to be showing Flaubert as inventing the idea of art for art's sake because of his personal conflicts in reality, he invented it because the history of the objective spirit led someone who wanted to write in the period 1835 to 1840 to take the neurotic position of postromanticism, that is to say, the position of art for art's sake[3]

The "objective neurosis" of Flaubert's time then provided the setting and the impetus for Flaubert's subjectively conditioned creativity. Sartre's work is specific—he understands Flaubert through documents and texts and also as reflecting and expressing his own time. Sartre uses the method of empathy, which he could not use in writing about himself, in understanding the writer's lived experience.

How are we to define the "objective spirit" of our age in an effort to understand Sartre in his time and ours? I will attempt to cross-reference Sartre's own statements and writings with a view of our time in which the psychological is firmly rooted in the sociological. Sartre has often criticized psychoanalysis for its stereotyped use of categories as labels, as though psychoanalytic categories were final explanations. Sartre's work is antipsychological insofar as psychology is seen as stripping responsibility from us and placing it somewhere else in the past, i.e. insofar as it is reductionist. Yet Sartre himself uses psychological categories in a nonreductionist way in his works on Genet and Flaubert: it is difficult to discuss the singularity of an individual which includes experience of childhood without it. Sartre's ambivalence about psychoanalysis does not prevent his using a similar approach in his later works, although it is neither stereotyped nor reductionist. I will approach Sartre himself as a universal singular of our time in terms of the rela-

3. Ibid., 118–19.

tionship between the objective or collective neurosis and the subjective neurosis that Sartre discusses in Flaubert.

Sartre has provided documentation in abundance to allow us to know him and his world. Novels such as *Nausea* and *The Age of Reason* give us a picture of some of Sartre's central fantasies, while *The Words* reveals much of his past and inner world. There are many interviews which include material of great frankness (e.g. the interviews following de Beauvoir's *La Cérémonie des adieux*).[4] His *Carnets de la drôle de guerre*[5] provide insight into his wishes for greatness and fantasies about the future. His literary criticism and biographies such as *Saint Genet* tell us as much about Sartre as about their subjects. His political tracts and dramatic pieces (e.g. *Les Séquestrés d'Altona*) often deal with issues of relationships "in situation" as well as with action and its consequences. Sartre wrote much about writing itself and never separated the writer from his work. *The Words*, his autobiography, is even divided into "Reading" and "Writing." In fact there is an enormous variety of material which spans the range of his ideas, reactions, childhood, politics, love life, and fantasies. Sartre is a Sartrean biographer's dream! However, my interest is not in his biography but in understanding the mainsprings of his world, a task which requires a particular kind of reading of Sartre.

Let me begin this investigation into Sartre's world by looking at the extraordinary interviews with Sartre conducted by Simone de Beauvoir and published after his death in *La Cérémonie des adieux*.

In these interviews Sartre speaks of many aspects of his personal life including his attitude towards surrender (*l'abandon*), his body, his sexual relations, women, food, nature, literature, philosophy, money, his own writing, and his past. These interviews are illuminating about Sartre the person and his approach to life. Since Sartre's personality and outlook so permeate and suffuse all his work, they provide much illumination about the foundations of his world. They well illustrate his need to be in conscious control of any situation.

Sartre saw his body as "an action essentially." He perceived his bodily feeling (cenesthesia) as outside his consciousness and disliked it very much—he refused to surrender to his body. He often took amphetamines which obliterated cenesthesia. Illness was the only time Sartre could consider surrender. He always rejected and detested passivity—he could not lie on the sand or read in an armchair or in bed. He always

4. Simone de Beauvoir, *La Cérémonie des adieux* (Paris: Gallimard, 1981).
5. J.-P. Sartre, *Les Carnets de la drôle de guerre* (Paris: Gallimard, 1983).

maintained an aggressive attitude towards his body and identified with the fantasy of Pardillon, a hero of cape and sword, who would constantly destroy columns of enemies.[6]

In sexual activities Sartre would never succumb to "losing consciousness in orgasm, nor in any love act."[7] He did not like sexual intercourse itself—"just a little pleasure in the end, but mediocre enough." He made love because it appeased obligations—not because he wanted to do so. "I would rather have been in bed, nude with a nude woman, to caress, to embrace her, but not go as far as the sexual act."[8] He was not interested in sex except for his caressing a woman. "In other words I was rather a masturbator of women than one who had intercourse." For Sartre "the essential and affective relation implied that I embrace, that I caress, that I explore with my lips. But the sexual act—it exists also. And I did it, often even—but with a certain indifference."[9]

Sartre had always hated the idea of succumbing to contingency. For Sartre "man or woman is an active being. And consequently the pull is always towards the future, whereas surrender is in the present or pulls toward the past. This contradiction made me prefer activity, which is to say, the future, to the past."[10] Sartre recalled that a psychologist had showed him a picture of a boat which was traveling quickly in the water. Sartre associated this boat's tearing away from the water with contingency; "the boat was hard, constructed, solid, in contrast to the water."[11]

This is linked with Sartre's aversion to nature and to fecundity which manifests itself best in his attitude toward food. He preferred cooked to natural food because it was created by a human being. He preferred to eat a tart or cake to fruit. With cakes, "the way they look, are made, even the taste has been willed and rethought by man. Whereas fruit has a taste by chance; it is on a tree, it is on the ground in the grass. That is not for me; it does not come from me. It is I who decided to make it food. A cake, on the contrary, has a regular shape, like a chocolate or coffee *éclair* for example; it is made by bakers, in ovens, etc. It is thus a completely human object. . . . It's necessary for food to be given by work made by men. Bread is like that. I have always thought that bread had a relation with men."[12] Sartre had a strong aversion to shellfish, oysters

6. S. de Beauvoir, *La Cérémonie des adieux*, 397.
7. Ibid., 401. Unless otherwise indicated, all the translations are mine.
8. Ibid., 400.
9. Ibid., 385.
10. Ibid., 402.
11. Ibid., 402.
12. Ibid., 423.

and crustaceans. He saw them as emanating from a totally different universe.[13]

These are only a few selections from these interviews, which are replete with such musings. What is clear above all is the refusal of surrender and the absolute emphasis on activity that Sartre applied in all areas. His interest in freedom, in the "for-itself," not only related to the big issues of our time but, as we have seen, was exemplified in his sexual preferences and in the food he ate. The emphasis on freedom and activity and the refusal of passivity bespeaks a deep dread of dependency and relationship. Sartre's is a narcissistic world in which the only thing we can trust is what we have created ourselves. It is not safe to relax, to receive, to succumb, to lose oneself for even a moment, to enjoy anything that is simply there in nature. Yet despite Sartre's hatred of passivity, his sexual fantasies are often infantile and refer to activities more akin to those of a mother and child. Sartre probably projected the passive aspects of himself on to the woman he desired to caress and at the same time denied that he had any passive longings himself. The viscous or slimy, representing an engulfing mother, is attractive as well as repulsive. The solid boat that tries to tear itself away from the engulfing sea is at the same time a part of it. The boat in Sartre's fantasy fights merging with the sea. Similarly, if Sartre let himself go sexually, he could be swamped and fused with the woman. The actual coitus is most threatening because of the greater threat of loss of self.

Sartre's attitudes in these interviews can be seen to suffuse his life and work as a whole. Sartre is always concerned with such issues as identity, trust, intrusiveness, loss of self, futility, dependence and envy—whether it is possible to be a self at all and relate to other people. From a psychoanalytic perspective these concerns involve the "schizoid" problem. Our world today has been described as "schizoid" and "narcissistic."[14] Pre-Oedipal issues receive much attention. Freud's hysterical patients seem to have given way to narcissistic or schizoid ones who feel an abiding sense of futility, a greyish remoteness from the world (life passes them by), a fear of involvement with anyone at all, a sense of indifference about themselves and others, a lack of trust in the care and love of others as even a possibility. They are not able to invest themselves in others, as others, but instead relate everything back to themselves. They find it difficult to give or receive, basically feeling that they have been betrayed. Life is often seen as a game and a tragic

13. Ibid., 422.
14. See Rollo May, *Love and Will* (London: Souvenir Press, 1970), Christopher Lasch, *The Culture of Narcissism* (New York: Norton, 1978).

vision has now given way to an ironic and cynical perspective. Nothing is assumed and the very idea of whether to relate at all to another person replaces the question of whether a particular relationship is good or bad—not "what sort of person am I?" but "AM I?" Life seems to have no experiential meaning.

According to Harry Guntrip, a leading analytic thinker of the British school of object-relations, many people today suffer from schizoid problems which concern identity, "people who have deep-seated doubts about the reality and validity of their very 'Self,' who are ultimately found to be suffering various degrees of depersonalisation, unreality, the dread feeling of 'not belonging,' of being fundamentally isolated and out of touch with their world." They do not feel other people at all as being capable of being related to as they are trapped inside their own fantasy world. These people "feel cut off, apart, different, unable to become involved with real relationships,"[15]

> The schizoid sense of futility, disillusionment and underlying anxiety (is apparent) in existentialism. These thinkers, from Kierkegaard to Heidegger and Sartre, find human existence to be rooted in anxiety and insecurity, a fundamental dread that ultimately we have no certainties and the only thing we can affirm is "nothingness," "unreality," a final sense of triviality and meaninglessness. This surely is schizoid despair and loss of contact with the verities of emotional reality, rationalised into a philosophy. Yet existentialist thinkers, unlike the logical positivists, are calling us to face and deal with these real problems of the human situation. It is a sign of our age.[16]

I want to argue that Sartre's problematic fits this view. The most important issues in Sartre's life and work express and reflect these issues and tell us much about Sartre and our age. Often the creative writer distills much of the mood of an era, and is especially sensitive about the flavor and problems of human relations. This is not to say that Sartre's views are to be dismissed as "metaphysical pathology" (as Garaudy once called *Being and Nothingness*.)[17] On the contrary we must read them as enlightening us about ourselves and our experience today. For the world Sartre describes is no alien one and his work has been very popular and influential. As many theories in the history of ideas express

15. H. Guntrip, *Psychoanalytic Theory, Therapy and the Self* (London: Hogarth Press, 1971), 148.
16. H. Guntrip, *Schizoid Phenomena, Object-Relations and the Self* (London: Hogarth Press, 1978), 481.
17. Roger Garaudy, *Literature of the Graveyard* (New York: International Publishers, 1948), 8.

an age and are thus historically situated, so Sartre's ideas need to be historicized. This does not detract from the very real insights he made but rather tells us about the way he lived out history.

Herbert Marcuse has argued that Sartre's ontological categories are in fact the historical categories of late capitalism.[18] While this may be true, it does not go far enough. As Sartre says, we are not lumps of clay; and what is important is not what people make of us, "but what we ourselves make of what they have made of us."[19] We are obviously conditioned by our historical context but are also "transhistorical" beings, that is, the fact that we are born small and dependent in need of suckling is true of all cultures and of all times. We live our historical conditioning in individual ways which emanate from our own childhood relations, as Sartre reminds us in *Search for a Method*. For example, the end point of the logic of technocratic rationality in an age where people are treated as commodities may be an emptying out of the self from childhood on. This can result in the child being treated as a medical or technical object rather than as a person in his own right. Society is filtered through the family context and manifests itself in different ways at different stages of development. Where issues of identity are uppermost during the first year, the baby will react to society through the medium of the mother and will react in relation to issues relevant to that stage of development. The final result of capitalist society's effects on the individual through the family may be a disease of production or consumption in which the commodity, infused with human value, is experienced as having more value than the human beings who produce or consume it, as Joel Kovel argues.[20] If Sartre's life and work are taken as a whole, a thread emerges which also links his world with our time— Sartre's schizoid and narcissistic world can be viewed as an instance of our neurosis. Let us look at this world in more detail. Sartre's worldview is essentially pessimistic. The world is an unfriendly viscosity bereft of meaning. Confronted with a godless world, human beings who are themselves defined as absence have an abiding sense of futility. We are not defined by what we are and will, but by what we do. There is no inner core of being. Our actions are not even within our control—loser so often wins.

Sartre's world is radically split. The "for-itself" will never be united

18. H. Marcuse, "Sartre's Existentialism" in his *Studies in Critical Philosophy* (London: New Left Books, 1972).

19. Sartre, *Saint Genet: Actor and Martyr*, trans. B. Frechtman (London: W. H. Allen, 1964), 584.

20. See J. Kovel, *The Age of Desire* (New York: Pantheon Books, 1982).

with the "in-itself". We are "the desire to be God" but in this we are a "useless passion." Human relations are intrinsically "locked in conflict" and sadomasochistic pleasures are poor substitutes for love and friendship—all relationships are between exploiters and exploited. As the individual is an empty nonentity, life becomes a grim and constant struggle to preserve a minimal personal integrity against hostile others or else a self-deceiving loss of identity in another person, ideology or organization. We long to escape the freedom to which we are condemned. But in this we are doomed to frustration and despair.

In the world Sartre describes there is a fundamental failure of basic trust in both self and environment to provide the basis or the development of what Laing terms "primary ontological security."[21] We are abandoned by a God who does not care and life becomes a losing battle with despair. Condemned to a freedom we do not want, we are basically deprived of the fullness of being. The good Lord does not exist but acts as a silent partner in Sartrean ontology. In fact the dialogue with the silent bespeaks a manichaeism without God—deprived of God, the world is evil and liberation is not possible.

Except perhaps in the battle of Sisyphus. For joy consists in our consciousness of not being overwhelmed and controlled by the circumstances to which we are condemned. The ability to say "no" which constituted a final refusal was, for Sartre, the ultimate foundation of choice. There was never the Promethean vision of an open future. The ability to turn the tables on one's torturers means an *incontrovertible conviction of meaning*. But even here as in *The Wall* we cannot be certain of the consequences of our not giving in to the demands of our masters. Sartre's optimism is that we "do not suffer from nothing"[22] and Sisyphean freedom is a last-ditch stand against an otherwise invasive world. Certainly it is the freedom in chains that Sartre proclaims and sometimes rails against, but defiance can be seen as appropriate for a world where this is the only real freedom left; the very emphasis on our ontological freedom is an index of how far social freedom has ceased to exist.

Even where there are dreams of freedom, there is no exit anywhere. The theme of sequestration provides a vital underlying theme in Sartre's work.[23] Many scenes in Sartre's literary works are set in rooms almost hermetically sealed off from the outer world. The room of the madman Pierre in *La Chambre*, the second empire drawing room of

21. R. D. Laing, *The Divided Self* (Harmondsworth: Penguin Books, 1965).
22. Sartre, *Saint Genet*, 544.
23. M. D. Boros, *Un séquestré: l'Homme sartrien* (Paris: Nizet, 1968), 13.

Huis Clos, the room in *Morts sans sépulture* where the resistance fighters await torture and death, Hoederer's room in *Les Mains sales* and that of Franz in *Les Séquestrés d'Altona*, provide some examples.

These symbolize the human situation as one of imprisonment. We are enveloped by forces beyond our control and condemned to possessing a freedom we cannot use authentically. Our inner void which demands fulfillment can never be filled. Our relations with others are intrinsically frustrating and, as if this were not enough, death destroys all the significance we thought we could attain. For Sartre, "Life does not only take place in a prison, it is itself a prison."[24]

Sartre's interest in sequestration finds its origin in his own childhood experience of being an only child without peers who was shut up in a house where his only friends were his grandfather's books. Sartre's mother was treated as a child in the household which was ruled by Sartre's domineering grandfather. Sartre had no respect for her and came to regard her as an older sister in need of his protection.[25] He was treated as a doll, a cute exhibition piece, an object—even a little prince. But never was he treated as a worthwhile person in his own right with real and valued feelings of his own. The young Sartre's internal reality was systematically invalidated: his being became his being-for-others. Sartre felt himself to be in the hands of adults. Feeling empty, he was an impostor playing the part he understood was expected of him by adults. The world of reason, books and ideas was substituted for the emotionally real, meaningful and confirming experience he lacked. As he experienced only his false self, he felt as malleable as clay, like a jelly fish inside, and was disgusted with what he saw as the "trivial unreality" as the world.[26] Sartre sees childhood as a "solitary" reality in which what and how the child internalizes is beyond his control. It is scarcely suprising that his work denigrates the reality of feeling in favor of an intellectual rationality which sees the human being as a void, a lack, a nothingness.

Sartre always saw himself as marginal—as never really being in anything. He missed the games with other children in early childhood, and later only watched others' games. The proletariat was only on his horizon at the Ecole Normale and it was really only the war that brought him a sense of solidarity and membership in society. But even then,

24. S. Doubrovsky, "Sartre and Camus: A Study in Incarceration," *Yale French Studies* 25, 1960, 87.
25. Sartre, *The Words*, trans. I. Clephane (Harmondsworth: Penguin Books, 1967), 13–14.
26. Ibid., 143.

Sartre felt envious of those who did the actual fighting; as a writer he was still on the sidelines. After the war he continued to feel marginal, since he wasn't a worker but a "useless mouth" so far as the communist party was concerned. Sartre's portrait of the party man, Brunet, certainly depicts a man deceiving himself, yet the opposite position, that of Mathieu, is also untenable.[27] Sartre says in the interviews following *La Cérémonie des adieux*: "Mathieu, Antoinne Roquentin had lives other than mine, but neighbouring lives, expressing what, in my own eyes, was most profound in my own life."[28]

Brunet's solidity was given by his identification with the party. Mathieu, the indecisive, intellectualized, evasive, bourgeois, impotent, self-searching philosophy teacher is counterposed to the solid, powerful, resolute, real proletarian man of action, Brunet. Duped by nature we are, like Mathieu, nothing at all, or else we impersonate what we are, like Brunet. Brunet, who seems like a whole man, is really a caricature, for his raison d'être is based on self-deception, on the delusional identification of being a soldier of the Party. Thus, Mathieu is ambivalent towards Brunet. He would love nothing more than to be able to make the leap of bad faith to become like Brunet. Yet he cannot act without sufficient reason—conviction must follow reason and not vice versa.

For Mathieu there is a complete split between reason and feeling. A life based on reason alone is as much a lie as one based exclusively on feeling. Demanding absolute certainty in his actions, Mathieu sees himself as an embodied refusal whose identity would be at stake in a world in which he would have to say "Yes." He defines himself *against*—like Sisyphus he knows what he is by what he is not. His nothingness forms the boundary between himself and others and prevents his merging with them. Brunet, on the other hand, does not experience his nothingness as he has merged with the Party. But Brunet's strength and identity are based on a collusively accepted myth.

Mathieu can either renounce his freedom by joining the Party or he can maintain his precarious identity by keeping his distance from the menacing world that threatens to engulf him. Mathieu has a constant grip on himself; feelings will never rule him. He will not let himself go for fear of losing himself. Feeling that there is nothing inside him is preferable to losing his boundaries altogether. To keep away from his feelings he represses them. His attachment to reason is rationalization. Mathieu and Brunet can be seen as two parts of the same person, a split

27. Sartre, *The Age of Reason*, trans. W. E. Sutton (Harmondsworth: Penguin Books, 1961).
28. *La Cérémonie des adieux*, 537.

personality that can never come together. The vitality is in Brunet, yet Mathieu can never reason himself into embracing it. Intellect and emotion are radically split.

Feeling himself to be a shell, Mathieu never explores any core feelings, only his defenses against them. His lack of commitment is not a happy one since there is nothing he desires more, yet at the same time fears more. He can do neither with nor without relationships. If he forgets himself for a moment, flies and cockroaches appear. If he commits himself to an action, he loses control of its consequences. Yet by not doing anything, he is pushed around by personal or impersonal forces.

Mathieu has only a pseudoindependence, invoking the outer world to give his life meaning. This characterizes the schizoid dilemma in which the self feels so empty that it relies suicidally on relationships with precisely those others who might swallow it up. Mathieu reaches a schizoid compromise in which he is "half-in and half-out" of relationship.[29] He is sympathetic to the Party but will not join, has a lover but will not commit himself, attacks bourgeois living but remains bourgeois. His compromise means diminished desires but also diminished rewards. Feeling is erased in his general state of continuous withdrawnness. He is never really unhappy, but his life is full of chronic frustration. He is cut adrift in his own futile world, floating aimlessly, ruminating, waiting. In the aloofness and fastidiousness he so enjoys, Mathieu can remain cold, detached, even icy. Mathieu has committed a form of psychic suicide; devoid of feeling, how can he feel any point to life? Living becomes an intellectual exercise. In a life full only of missed opportunities Mathieu waits for the lightning flash which could fuse reason and emotion in a self-certain conviction; this is precisely what his radically split ego cannot achieve. Mathieu sees himself as a rotter, a washout who needs to be thoroughly cleansed. Purification comes only in his putative suicide in which he takes revenge on his past failures through firing on the approaching Germans. Mathieu knows this absurd and futile act will put the German timetable back only fifteen minutes and has warned a comrade against doing just that. Killing his first German is his first definite action—it is his own German. Commitment is for Mathieu linked with self-destruction. But Mathieu's first definite live action means that he has not only projected his bad parts on to the Germans, but also that he has put his vitality into them. This is suicidal as there is nothing left in him emotionally after his act. This demon-

29. Guntrip, *Schizoid Phenomena*, 58 ff.

strates the final loss of self on the one hand subjectively and on the other a magical feeling of omnipotence which in fact is the likelihood of actual self-annihilation. Commitment for Mathieu is life and death at the same time. Doing what he most wants means self-annihilation. Moreover, Mathieu projectively identified parts of himself with the Germans as he had with the Party. The other often serves as a repository for menacing projections in the Sartrean world.

For Sartre action means losing oneself in it. There is no autonomous self behind an action or role. The waiter sees himself and is seen primarily as a Waiter. His role defines him—he cannot be in *his* actions without being his actions,[30] The self as shell remains by not being engulfed, for neither symbiosis nor aloneness is a viable alternative. Symbiosis means a total dependence on a constricting and frustrating mother who will contract to supply all needs only at the price of the child's soul. It involves the ultimate in projective identification—everything is in the other with whom one is psychologically merged. Aloneness is being cast out helpless without relationship into the unfriendly and untrustworthy menacing wilderness. This represents the paranoid position described by the psychoanalyst Melanie Klein in which all the badness is outside and normal introjections have failed. Real relationships as opposed simply to projections of oneself on to others, are not possible. Sartre presents an ego in a primitive stage of infantile dependence, in a state of projective identification with the parent.[31]

Sartre's analysis of "being-for-others" in *Being and Nothingness* confirms this. All human relationships are of a mutually devouring kind—one's being is swallowed up by or absorbed by another and vice versa.

> While I attempt to free myself from the hold of the Other, the Other is trying to free himself from mine: while I seek to enslave the Other, the Other seeks to enslave me. . . . Conflict is the original meaning of being-for-others.[32]

All relationships involve either sadism or masochism; one attempts to "appropriate" the "freedom" of the Other or surrenders one's own to him. But "the Other is on principle inapprehensible; he flees me

---

30. Sartre, *Being and Nothingness*, Part III, trans. H. E. Barnes (New York: Washington Square Press, 1966), H. Guntrip, *Personality Structure and Human Interaction* (New York: International Universities Press, 1961), 391–92.

31. Melanie Klein, "Notes on some Schizoid Mechanisms" in her *Envy and Gratitude and Other Works* (London: Hogarth Press, 1975).

32. Sartre, *Being and Nothingness*, 474–75.

when I seek him and possesses me when I flee him." Thus a satisfying sado-masochistic equilibrium is impossible; relationships are doomed to frustration. One wishes to "absorb" and "assimilate" the Other to achieve recognition, one is in perpetual danger and has no security. Again we find the paranoid position described by Melanie Klein where relationship is equivalent to persecution.

Apart from indifference—which is no relationship at all or withdrawal from relationship—hate is the only alternative relation to love. For Sartre hate involves my wishing the Other dead so that I will not be an object for him. The close relation of this hate to love is paralleled by Guntrip's view of hatred:

> It is love grown angry because of rejection. We can only really hate a person if we want their love. Hate is an expression of frustrated love needs, an attempt to destroy the bad rejecting side of a person in the hope of leaving their good responsive side available, a struggle to alter them.[33]

According to Sartre the self, as a nothingness, is so empty, so inherently deprived of satisfactory fulfilment that he feels he needs to be certain of the Other—which he cannot be by the nature of the Other's separateness and subjectivity. This leads to a sadistic drive to incorporate or absorb the Other with the concomitant fear of destroying the very person he desires. One wants to have the Other as subject or person, not as an object or instrument. But one cannot have one's cake and eat it. One seeks to control and secure the freedom of the Other, but it is precisely the unconstrained freedom of the Other, upon which the self cannot depend, that is required for secure recognition.

Sartre's conceptions of being-for-others in the outer world are generated by the emotions of the inner world. The relationships that Sartre describes reflect the internal bad objects of a barely developed inner world. The Other upon whom the self cannot rely is the breast that may be snatched away at any time. As Guntrip remarks, "The schizoid is very sensitive and quickly feels unwanted, because he is always feeling deserted in his inner world." Guntrip's description of the schizoid who cancels his object-relations because they are too frustrating, frightening and dangerous applies to many of Sartre's situations.

> Retreat into indifference is the true opposite of the love which is felt to be too dangerous to express. Want no one, make no demands, abolish all external relationships, and be aloof, cold and without any feeling, do

33. Guntrip, *Schizoid Phenomena*, 26.

not be moved by anything. The withdrawn libido is turned inwards, introverted. The patient goes into his shell and is busy only with internal objects towards whom he feels the same devouring attitude. Outwardly and in consciousness everything seems futile and meaningless . . . The depressive fears loss of his object. The schizoid, in addition, fears loss of his ego, of himself.[34]

Huis Clos is a dramatization of Sartre's analysis of being-for-others in *Being and Nothingness*. The three occupants constantly thwart and frustrate ech other in the hermetically closed "*Second Empire*" drawing-room which is their Hell. Garcin concludes that "Hell is other people" since each person acts as torturer of the other two. However at one stage the door to their prison opens to Garcin's insistent knocking, but no one, including Garcin, leaves. They are "*inséparables.*" Garcin claims that his reason for not leaving and for his not pushing Inez, who hates him, out of the room is his need for her "confirmation." However, if Hell really is other people, why does no one leave?

Huis Clos may be regarded as an image of the inner bad object world which is a "closed system" that is a "static internal situation." This closed system is what Sartre's concern with sequestration, with imprisonment, is basically about. This inner world of bad objects revealed by Melanie Klein is understood by Fairbairn to constitute "the most formidable resistance in psychoanalytical treatment".[35] This inner world is often dreamed of as a torture house, a prison, or a concentration camp in which the self is a prisoner.[36] This system is "run on hate," and the self is the victim of a large amount of persecution. Of course the prison in which the person finds himself has been erected by himself. But it is a prison which is very difficult to breach, and this indicates just how strongly the person holds on to his persecutory system of internal object-relations. Many people do not want to leave their prisons—it is felt to be far more dangerous outside.[37]

The persecutory internal object-relationship is that of the internalized bad parents whom it is impossible to do without, since the person would then be all alone without any relationship at all. It is better to be hated than ignored—far better to be something than nothing. The closed system is part of a struggle to keep going, to have some degree of independence. Further, the internal closed system of persecu-

34. Ibid., 27.
35. W. R. D. Fairbairn, "On the Nature and Aims of Psychoanalytical Treatment," *International Journal of Psychoanalysis* 39, 1958, 38.
36. Guntrip, *Schizoid Phenomena*, 198 ff.
37. Guntrip, *Personality Structure*, 422.

tion "confers a sense of power, if only over the self."[38] Identification with powerful objects, even where these are self-destructive, gives some security. Guntrip writes:

> The entire world of internal bad objects is a colossal defence against loss of the ego by depersonalisation. The one issue that is much worse than the choice between good and bad objects is the choice between any sort of objects and no objects at all. Persecution is preferable to depersonalisation.[39]

This is why the inmates in *Huis Clos* dare not leave their prison. Garcin, for example, has a hate relationship with Inez, which is preferable to being alone in absolute isolation. Further, since Estelle is of no account to Garcin, it is imperative that Inez stay to provide a meaningful, if hostile, relationship. The worst ultimate terror is to be a "psyche in a vacuum."[40] The irresolvable relationships of *Huis Clos* are staunch defenses against personal annihilation. Hell is not other people—it is being utterly alone.

This is very clear in one of Sartre's first stories, *Erostratus*.[41] The ancient Greek of that name achieved notoriety by burning down the temple of Diana at Ephesus. Nobody remembers the builder of the temple, but its destroyer became immortal. In Satre's story Hilbert carries out Breton's pure surrealist act; he takes a rifle and shoots randomly at people in the street. Instantly this nobody becomes recognised as somebody. It is better to be a "bad somebody" than a "weak nonentity."[42]

Futility is a basic theme in *Nausea* which chronicles a period of the existence of Roquentin. Roquentin is overwhelmed by the viscous, elusive, nongraspable character of being itself. He experiences himself as a dull and jellylike sensation, and is a constant observer of his own lack of involvement in an essentially meaningless world. Self-conscious, Roquentin keeps constant watch over himself for fear that he may disappear. He has no place in the world and feels no sense of continuity. Alone in a crowd, a stranger everywhere, he is essentially cut off from any sense of reality. Life is a constant struggle to preserve a precarious individuation as any sort of ego at all. All resources are marshaled to maintain this separation. The nothingness Roquentin experiences as himself is a defense against engulfment or impingement by an over-

38. Guntrip, *Schizoid Phenomena*, 205.
39. Guntrip, *Personality Structure*, 431–32.
40. Guntrip, *Schizoid Phenomena*, 238.
41. Sartre, "Erostratus" in his collection, *Intimacy*, trans. L. Alexander (London: Pantheon, 1960).
42. Guntrip, *Schizoid Phenomena*, 137.

whelming reality.[43] The ego is withdrawn into the deepest recesses of the self, out of reach of being hurt, while at the same time a wall is erected around itself keeping reality at a distance. Thus, alienated, it would be impossible to feel anything but futile. For security is a function of good object-relations. A feeling of inner value and integrity can only emerge from a warm, reliable human relationship that is personal on both sides and through which growth toward autonomy in relationships of mature dependence may occur. The beginnings of autonomy should emerge in the first six months of life. Roquentin's world has not eached even this level of development. He is stuck in a state of confusion between himself and the world, in a feeling of engulfment.

From a psychoanalytic perspective Roquentin's repulsion from existence may constitute a refusal of the mother's breast and milk which is viewed as nauseating. The mother is seen as bad and rejecting because she has not sufficiently fulfilled the earlier demands of the infant. If the mother is good enough, she will satisfy enough of the child's needs and the child will not turn from the other in rage. At this early stage of development the baby will have just begun the long journey towards separation and individuation. To do this he or she must be able to internalize good aspects of the mother and not be paralysed by a feeling that nothing good or reliable exists outside him or herself.

Since it is a threat for Roquentin, the world is to be kept as distant as possible. Objects have a power over him. There is a rage at the world for not providing fulfillment, a rage which is defended against to an extent by a cynical and cold detachment. Roquentin's world is totally narcissistic; he has turned in on himself as the only source of solace and cannot afford relationships. Anything beyond physical gratification of his body which he has emotionally split off from himself would lead to engulfment. Roquentin's pathological pseudoindependence reflects the fact that he is not able to be with anyone else.

Even objects repel him—"it's unbearable; I am afraid of entering into contact with them, just as if they were living animals." Roquentin remembered holding a pebble which occasioned a feeling of "sweet disgust" which passed from the pebble on to his hands bringing about "a sort of nausea of the hands." Objects provide a terrible threat then because Roquentin has projected his own inner world onto the entire outer world. Even the sun through its "impoverishing light" of "cold rays" projects "a pitiless judgment on all creatures." This light creates an unspeakable disgust in Roquentin.

43. Sartre, *Nausea*, trans. R. Baldick (Harmondsworth: Penguin Books, 1965), 185, 191, 22, 28, 31–32, 35, 148–49, 175, 252.

His only real pleasure and obsession is looking at himself in a mirror. He sees himself as below the vegetable level—his face disgusts him, especially his eyes. His face and body are actually split off from his body except for "a dull organic sensation." Roquentin would obviously like to be rid of his body. Though he has a narcissistic fascination with it, he does not feel it as his own.

But nausea overcomes him. It takes over his insides as well as being outside—so much so that he feels "it is I who am inside it." He later sees existence raping him from behind, it is so menacing. For Roquentin many people do not know they exist; they do not experience the great boundary between themselves and the outer world, nor the frightening engulfment, giddiness, nausea he feels when his withdrawn state is threatened.

Awareness of existence, which normal people hide from themselves because they are not detached, brings with it knowledge of contingency, superfluity, and gratuitousness and at the same time provokes nausea, because awareness of existence brings a union with objects which threaten annihilation and disintegration of the self. Better to be repelled, withdrawn and isolated than to be engulfed by the persecution of his own projected bad maternal objects.

Roquentin's only way out is to express his disgust and disdain for the world through writing a story which "would be beautiful and hard as steel and make people ashamed of their existence." The hardness of steel would be separate and definite and contrast with the sweet and soft, oozing merging of existence and nausea, of the persecutory anxiety which threatens disintegration of the self.

Nausea well illustrates Sartre's exhaustive alternatives of aloneness and fusion—either Roquentin will keep himself isolated or he will be merged with existence itself. For Sartre all relationships involve theft, the real self for Sartre is alone. From this narcissistic perspective all relationships are between exploiter and exploited. Needing another person is seen to involve humiliation, which exists in the demands, rage and envy of others as well as the inability to express gratitude and a hatred of dependency.[44] While many of Sartre's characters would ideally like to be alone, they cannot be. Therefore life is an unending struggle to preserve a precarious individuation.

Sartrean characters lack what Sartre terms a "mandate to live" from parents who would treat them empathetically. For Sartre this is a

---

44. See Otto Kernberg, *Object Relations Theory and Clinical Psychoanalysis* (New York: International Universities Press, 1976), 145.

failure of love. The mandated child "is the conscious arrow that is awakened in mid-flight and discovers simultaneously to the distant archer, the target and the intoxication of flight." On the other hand "when the valorization of the infant through love is accomplished badly or not at all, maternal inadequacy defines experience as non-sense." At a later point the mandated child can question the meaning of life, but the child will be at a severe disadvantage if his philosophical questionings are the result of early deprivation of empathy.[45] Yet empathy is precisely what Sartre and most of his characters lack.

The American psychoanalyst, Heinz Kohut, has written a good deal about how vital empathy is to the proper development of the child to maturity. Kohut sees empathy as a natural human endowment and he goes so far as using it in defining the field of depth psychology itself. Psychoanalysis for Kohut, "deals with the obstacles that stand in the way of empathic comprehension."[46] The mother needs to mirror the development of the infant and to be in tune with his needs. If the child is not mirrored empathically, i.e. does not feel "understood," the child will develop pathologically and narcissistically. Perhaps the importance of mirrors in Sartre's work (e.g. *Nausea* and *Huis Clos*) lies in the fact that most of these ontologically insecure characters have always been deprived of empathic mirroring so that they live in constant need of it.

In his *Carnets de la drôle de guerre* Sartre wondered why he was different from the characters he had created—Roquentin and Mathieu. "The essential difference between Antoine Roquentin and me is that I wrote the story of Antoine Roquentin."[47]

Sartre claims that in constructing his characters he removed from them important aspects of himself: "My manic passion for writing, my pride, my faith in my destiny, my metaphysical optimism, and by this fact I brought about a fatal defilement in them. . . . These heroes are incapable of living. *They* are me decapitated.[48]

So while identifying Roquentin and Mathieu with himself, Sartre also differentiates himself from them. They are, as it were, frozen sections of Sartre. But it is instructive to look at what Sartre finds lacking in Roquentin and Mathieu. Sartre's claim to a "metaphysical optimism" does not come through in his work which I have discussed above. There

45. Sartre, *The Family Idiot*, 1, 133 ff.

46. Heinz Kohut, *The Restoration of the Self* (New York: International Universities Press, 1977), 144.

47. Sartre, *Les Carnets de la drôle de guerre*, 410.

48. Ibid., 410.

is no ground in his philosophy for an optimistic option to emerge. Sartre's pride and faith in his destiny is an interesting explanation which relates closely to his manic passion for writing since Sartre saw his destiny primarily as that of a writer. Sartre wanted to have the life of a great writer[49] and even thought of himself as "the young Sartre, as one speaks of the young Berlioz or the young Goethe."[50] Sartre had viewed literature not just as his vocation but as his salvation.

His "manic passion to write" can be understood in these terms. As with Genet whose ten years of writing amounted to a "psychoanalytical cure,"[51] writing may well have been a therapy for Sartre himself. Sartre's constant flow of words may be his way of giving himself the milk of paradise denied by the nauseating reality described in this writing. Sartre's world of artistic fantasy was generated as a child in his grandfather's library and had sufficient autonomy to allow Sartre to depict the schizoid content of his literature; the investment in writing itself provided a counterweight to the despair of the landscape that he painted. Writing can keep the forces of the night at bay,[52] and in Sartre's case it has a compulsive quality.

But the world described in this writing as that of Roquentin and Mathieu is nonetheless that of Sartre. This is confirmed in his philosophical works which provide the same picture of our world. The visions and experiences of Roquentin and Mathieu are those of *Being and Nothingness*. All of Sartre's material, whether it is literary, philosophical, critical, biographical, autobiographical, or political, bears the same shape and the same issues arise in all of them. This is confirmed by what Simone de Beauvoir has communicated about Sartre and his work from her *Prime of Life* to *La Cérémonie des adieux*. Sartre wished to be understood as a child of our time—a time for which he wrote expressing internal and external reality and the possibilities of change as he saw them. I have attempted to render Sartre's world intelligible as a whole in terms of a guiding threat which expresses his schizoid and narcissistic perspective.[53]

Sartre wanted to rescue subjectivity in a dehumanized world, and to find the possibility of good reciprocal relationships in a better society; yet the deeper he probed the less real these possibilities seemed. The

49. Ibid., 96.
50. Ibid., 97.
51. Sartre, *Saint Genet*, 544.
52. Sartre, "To Show, To Demonstrate," Yale French Studies 30, 1960, 30.
53. For more detailed discussion of some of the themes in this article, see D. Kirsner, *The Schizoid World of Jean-Paul Sartre and R. D. Laing* (New Jersey: Humanities Press, 1977).

early Sartrean self can at least refuse to be controlled, yet we find a still bleaker view developing as Sartre senses the increasing power of the social world to control even the perception of the alternatives available to us. For Sartre the world is a vast prison in which the prisoners wittingly or unwittingly collaborate in the perpetuation of their servitude.

In his personal and philosophical refusal of surrender, Sartre wants consciously directed activity to dominate the body and nature. Sartre is echoing the view of the body and the world that has enshrined the project of Western civilisation for many centuries. This is the logic of domination which views the world as there to be subdued and controlled and uses an instrumental, managerial form of rationality that regards oneself, others and the environment as objects to be quantified and manipulated. Near nuclear catastrophe and ecological disaster are part of the runaway madness of a system that uses a logic whose "paradoxical" consequence is thoughtless technologization and "development." Why should we accuse Sartrean philosophy of being schizoid when the logic of the world at large pushes us so far in that direction?

Sartre is truly a "universal singular" of our time in that he describes in his work, and represents in his approaches and perspectives, some of the foremost problems of our era. Sartre's refusal of surrender to the body, the Other, and nature is itself an instance of the logic which has led to our collective insanity today. It represents the total abandonment of basic trust in ourselves and our world to provide for our vital needs. Yet has Sartre gone too far?

The world Sartre portrays is one in which our worst fears are seen to be finally true, but this situation need not be understood as ontologically inherent in history. Whatever else he has contributed, Sartre has expressed the vagaries and paradoxes of life in the modern world.

ALEXANDRE LEUPIN

A New Sartre

C'est notre tour, maintenant, de ne plus connaître le goût qu'avait ce que Sartre a écrit. Et de prendre goût à ce goût qu'on ne connaîtra jamais.[1]

—*Politique de la prose*

Truism: books exist only through the readings they are capable of producing. This is again proven in Denis Hollier's essay, *Politique de la prose, Sartre et l'an quarante*, which marks out in the work of a writer that we think we know well enough to consider him outmoded, a completely new text which does not fail to surprise everyone, including Sartre scholars themselves.

SITUATIONS

We know that Sartre does not permit any writer to except himself from history, to refuse the constraints of his "objective" situation in the class struggle. "[L'écrivain] est 'dans le coup,' quoiqu'il fasse, marqué, compromis, jusque dans sa plus lointaine retraite." ["(The writer) is involved, no matter what he does, marked, compromised, as far as his most distant retreat."][2] One could, of course, legitimately apply this rule to Sartre himself, taking as a pretext what he says about it. In *Qu'est-ce que la littérature* the description of the social situation which, in France, defines the producer of discourse is not irrelevant. The first characteristic, centralism:

La centralisation nous a tous regroupés à Paris; avec un peu de chance, un Américain pressé peut nous joindre tous en vingt-quatre heures. . . .
En vingt-quatre heures, un cycliste entraîné peut faire circuler d'Aragon à Mauriac, de Vercors à Cocteau, en touchant Breton à Montmartre, Queneau à Neuilly et Billy à Fontainebleau . . . un de ces

1. "It is now our turn no longer to know the taste that Sartre's writing had. And to taste this taste which we will never know." Denis Hollier, *Politique de la prose, Sartre et l'an quarante* (Paris: Gallimard, 1982), 138. Further references to this work will be given in the text.
2. Jean-Paul Sartre, *Situations 2* (Paris: Gallimard, 1948), 12. Further references will be indicated in the text. [Translations, when available, are from *What is Literature*, trans. Bernard Frechtman (New York: Philosophical Library, 1949). Translations without a reference are mine.—Translator's note]

manifestes, une de ces pétitions ou protestations pour ou contre le retour de Trieste à Tito . . . [*Situations 2*, 205–06]

Centralization has grouped us all in Paris. With a bit of luck, a busy American might join us all in twenty-four hours . . . in twenty-four hours, a trained cyclist might circulate—from Aragon to Mauriac, from Vercors to Cocteau, stopping off to see Breton in Montmartre, Queneau in Neuilly, and Billy in Fontainebleau . . . one of those manifestoes, one of those petitions or protests to Tito for or against the return of Trieste . . . [(*Literature*, 165]

Secondly, a position of class, accepted or not: "Nous sommes les écrivains les plus bourgeois du monde." ["We are the most bourgeois writers in the world" (*Situations 2*, 204; *Literature*, 163).] And finally, the impassable relationship with a literary tradition:

Bien avant de commencer notre premier roman, nous avions l'usage de la littérature, il nous paraissait naturel que les livres poussent dans une société policée, comme les arbres dans un jardin. [*Situations 2*, 204]

We were used to literature long before beginning our first novel. To us it seemed natural for books to grow in a civilized society, like trees in a garden. [*Literature*, 164]

From here on, Sartre's discourse is enunciated in a *"nous"* ("we") form which is both a dialectical repetition of its conditions of enunciation as well as the overtaking of these conditions in the name of a choice which opposes these parameters to a Marxist consciousness, to a generation, to a group of writers in which he recognizes himself. This peculiarity of the French situation (which geographically, temporally and politically localizes the members of the intelligentsia in Paris) appears more clearly in its historical contingency in the light of the counterexample that Sartre regularly chooses in order to point out its specificity: the example of the United States, which cocked its ear in the image of the American taking a literary tour of the Parisian world.

In fact, for Sartre, the United States is essentially a space which cannot find its center. Thus, in *Situations 3*, he deplores (rightly or wrongly) New York's lack of *quartiers* in the European sense of the word. He is surprised not to find *Les Deux Magots*, *Le Flore* or *La Closerie des Lilas* in Manhattan; the American city is an absence of space which does not permit any landmarks (sociological, historical, geographical) to fix themselves. In the same manner, the intellectual topography is characterized by a void which a vague morality seeks to fill, a fabrication of different mass media. The United States is thus a "démocratie capitaliste avec dictature diffuse de l'opinion publique" ["capitalist democracy with a loose dictatorship of public opinion" (*Situations 2*, 304; *Literature*, 284).] The writer is then lost in a geography which is so vast that it no longer exists and which in return does not permit him to lay claim to any sort of identity:

> Il n'a pas de solidarité avec les autres écrivains, souvent il est séparé d'eux par la largeur ou la longueur d'un continent. Rien n'est plus éloigné de lui que l'idée de collège ou de cléricature; on le fête un temps, puis on le perd, on l'oublie, il reparaît avec un nouveau livre pour faire un nouveau plongeon. [*Situations 2*, 203]

> He has no solidarity with other writers; he is often separated from them by the length or breadth of the continent; nothing is more remote from him than the idea of college or clerkship; for a while he is fêted and then is lost and forgotten; he reappears with a new book to take a new plunge. [*Literature*, 162]

Consequently, the "objective" conditions of a French type debate do not exist:

> Bien sûr, il y a tant de journaux, tant de contacts internationaux que les Américains finissent par entendre parler des théories littéraires et sociales qu'on professe en Europe, mais ces doctrines s'épuisent dans leur ascension . . . on sait que les intellectuels aux Etats-Unis assemblent les idées européennes en bouquet, les respirent un moment puis les rejettent parce que les bouquets se fânent plus vite là-bas que sous les autres climats. [*Situations 2*, 268]

> To be sure, there are so many newspapers, so many international contacts, that Americans finally get to hear about the literary or social theories that are circulating in Europe, but these doctrines are exhausted in their ascent. . . . We know that intellectuals in the United States gather European ideas into a bouquet, inhale them for a moment, and then toss them away because the bouquets wither more quickly there than in other climates. [*Literature*, 243–44]

Thus the geographical and social situation and the absence of cultural tradition make the American writer a floating signifier, difficult to define in class terms. Sartre praises this characteristic for its individual genius, but he also implicitly criticizes it (cf. the example of Faulkner in *Politique de la prose*), for he does not read anything positive in the fact of being free from centralism, of having to *invent* a tradition rather than reproducing or fighting against one. It appears that non-spatiality and non-historicity seem emminently suspicious to him.

At the same time, the fact that a writer can profit from his exile, or from his situation *between* two nations gives his books a dubious coloration. Hence, as Hollier remarks, Nabokov, Beckett and Ionesco will be condemned one after the other in the name of criteria which have little to do with internationalism, but which are a product of a regional discourse surprising in Sartre.

Hollier does not approach the whole of Sartrian textuality from this point of view. For in *Politique de la prose* there is an "I" ("*je*"), a crossing between the author and the narrator which discreetly yet insistently claims its place and which incessantly puts itself *en situation:* "Une bonne métaphore vaut le déplacement. Jusqu'où n'irait-on pour faire une citation? Mais la loi de l'insinuation implique qu'on ne les trouve que là où on se trouve, s'il faut parler d'où on parle" (*Politique,* 226). ["A good metaphor is worth the displacement. How far wouldn't we go to create a quotation? But the law of insinuation implies that we only find them where we are, if we must speak from whence we speak."] The question of place is not at all anecdotal; in a paradoxical manner faithful to Sartre it prepares the sudden appearance of a new style of reading, outdating the absence of the subject (the absence of writing and of style) which has too often been the trademark of the theory produced in the last twenty years.

Unlike the Sartrian writer, this "I" does not live in Paris as do the others: he learns of Sartre's death in Berkeley, California on April 15, 1980 at 7:00 P.M. Pacific time (*Politique,* 73). Although he had a French education, he only visits France intermittently, to give a lecture at Cerisy, for example (*Politique,* 146). Hollier does not avoid the relationship of biography and writing (criticism). His situation, which is not a situation, not really, permits him to invent a style of reading which is produced neither from the insularity of the United States where the amalgam of particularities takes the form of an indecipherable puzzle, nor from the cobweblike centralism which defines French intellectual life. The "exile" is not then the occasion of a nostalgic complaint, but sets the conditions for a new reading whose atopy is explicitly claimed:

> Une certaine atopie du scripteur (le fait qu'il n'arrive pas à être là où il paraît), bien qu'elle déçoive les espoirs que Sartre avait cru sérieux de placer dans le concept de situation, ne me paraît en rien impliquer quoi que ce soit de répréhensible. [*Politique,* 166]

> Although it disappoints the serious hopes that Sartre had placed in the concept of situation, a kind of atopy of the writer (the fact that he does not succeed in being where he appears to be), does not seem to me to imply anything reprehensible whatsoever.

Hollier thus reinscribes at the heart of his interpretation a principle which Sartre, aiming for an assumption of presence in writing, always refused: "Un texte n'a jamais lieu que de se détacher de son lieu d'émission" (*Politique*, 115). ["A text has no other raison d'être than its ability to detach itself from its place of emission."]

PRESENCE

La fonction de l'écrivain est d'appeler un chat un chat. Si les mots sont malades c'est à nous de les guérir. Au lieu de cela, beaucoup vivent de cette maladie. La littérature moderne, en beaucoup de cas, est un cancer des mots. [*Situation 2*, 304]

The function of the writer is to call a spade a spade. If words are sick, it is up to us to cure them. Instead of that, many writers live off this sickness. In many cases modern literature is a cancer of words. [*Literature*, 284]

Sartre thus denies a place to entire areas of "modernity." Seeing in language a pure instrument of communication and a transparence which is the trace of the thing (we know that the two motifs are profoundly interdependent) he coherently condemns all conceptions—literary or linguistic—which make language a system with its own laws different from the laws of reality, a whole shaped more by reflexivity and evocation than by communication. "Le langage, pour Sartre, ne fait pas un pli: il parle, mais cela va sans dire" (*Politique*, 100). ["Language, for Sartre, does not have any privilege: it speaks, but that goes without saying."] For Hollier, this refusal has two major consequences: first, the affirmation of the priority of meaning over the sign:

L'expérience du sens est, par conséquent, antérieure et indépendante de la pratique des signes: tout spécialement des signes linguistiques. La linguistique ne sera pas la science pilote que le structuralisme voulait. Le signifiant, c'est moi, dit Sartre en toute simplicité. [*Politique*, 99]

The experience of meaning is consequently anterior and independent of the practice of signs: especially linguistic signs. Linguistics is not the pilot science that Structuralism wanted. The signifier is me, says Sartre in all simplicity.

Secondly, and as a corollary, the exteriority of language in relation to the thing:

Tout le programme littéraire sartrien est ainsi solidaire d'une restauration du primat de la perception et de la réaffirmation de la transcendance de l'objet. [*Politique*, 100]

The whole Sartrian literary program is thus bound up with a restoration of the primacy of perception and with the reaffirmation of the transcendence of the object.

From that point onward, literature must aim at something other than itself: "L'engagement veut mettre un terme à l'auto-référentialité" (*Politique,* 105). ["Commitment tries to put an end to autoreferentiality."] The ideal of a style and its methods is sketched in Sartre's work in the refusal of the reflexivity of language and literature: it is a question of the journalistic report and of mass media (cf. *Situations 2,* 290; *Literature,* 268 and Hollier's commentary, *Politique,* 131). Written in the present about the present (or about the future, or about the past as a historical determinant of the two preceding terms), the report is also addressed to presence. Through this the public's reading, its reception, is supposed to escape "mythic communion" as well as "masturbation" in order to enter into the "companionship" ("*compagnonnage,*" *Situations 2,* 296; *Literature,* 274) of a community which is thus inscribed in the reappropriation of its presence:

> La capacité de saisir intuitivement et instantanément les significations, l'habileté à regrouper celles-ci pour offrir des ensembles synthétiques immédiatement déchiffrables sont des qualités les plus nécessaires au reporter. [*Situations 2,* 30]

> The ability to grasp significations intuitively and instantly, the skill to rearrange them in order to offer synthetic, immediately decipherable groups, are the most necessary qualities for a reporter.

Such is Sartre's utopia of language: that of a transparent, utilitarian verb which carries a reality or a project which is anterior to itself and of which it is only the form. It is interesting that he does not apply it only to his philosophical reflections or to his political interventions, but also to his novels. It is in this particular area that we discover a series of incoherences between the precept and its application.

In order to make clear what is at stake and what it implies, Denis Hollier here refers discretely but tenaciously to criteria of reading inspired by Blanchot and Derrida. This could seem surprising, or even offensive: what is more opposed to the neuter, to *différance* and to writing than Sartrian presence? Is the tool appropriate for the task?

In fact, the validity of the model could not be challenged here. First of all, unlike the hard and fast "deconstructionists" or "Blanchotiens," *Politique de la prose* does not set up its reference as a sacred axiom; everything is presented with nuance and finesse without, however, abandoning a basic rigor. Secondly, Sartre's text is not adapted to an irrelevant reading grid. The interpretation is effective not because it uses a theory, whatever it may be, as an argument, but because the Sartrian corpus (almost) alone itself furnishes indications of the validity of the gloss.

An extremely meticulous rereading of *La Nausée* furnishes the essential part of the demonstration. Hollier emphasizes the disparity of the literary project (*La Nausée* as a diary, private "report") and its practice, which condemns the time of the composition to a lack of absolute depth and consistency. This could seem futile; in any case, as Hollier notes, more than a million readers have not been in the least offended by these contradictions. But without entering into the details of the demonstration we must point out what is at stake: the troubling fact that Sartrian writing, aiming for existence and presence (such is at least the proclaimed project), systematically forgets to put itself on stage and into question, be it under the cover of the fiction of Roquentin in the process of composing. "Le récit ne prend pas de place" (*Politique*, 129). ["The narrative does not take any place."] From here, writing unceasingly evacuates its Real and brings about the return of that which Sartre decided to fight: the idealism of the beautiful soul (*belle âme*). The writing of *La Nausée* does not measure up in practice; it neglects to represent itself or represents itself with a neglect of which Hollier, with great tact, gives convincing examples, and it takes on an imaginary dimension, from which Sartre would have liked to save it, which frees it from the present instead of fixing it there. "L'écriture est sauve du désastre qu'elle retrace" (*Politique*, 179). ["Writing is safe from the disaster it recounts."]

Having intended to avoid autoreferentiality, *La Nausée* appears as a gratuitous act, much more than those of Proust or Gide whose ahistorical narcissism Sartre constantly denounced. Language here takes revenge for having been held back from its dimension: "A coller au présent de trop près, les mots prennent sa place" (*Politique*, 132). ["In sticking too closely to the present, words take its place."]

It is not that the reflexive dimension of the text is totally absent, but it pays the price of not being well thought out and concerted. It is not given a way to define itself, it appears as disengaged from history, apolitical:

> Ces passages au présent sont, en effet, des inducteurs de la plus grande étrangeté: il suffit que le texte passe au présent pour qu'on ne sache plus d'où il vient, à partir d'où il est émis. Dès que le texte se rapproche de sa source, il vient de nulle part. Son énonciation s'encrypte, se disloque.

L'origine se perd au présent qui est tout sauf le temps de sa présence à soi: la moins réaliste des instances intemporelles, la plus irréférentielle. [*Politique,* 134]

In fact, these passages in the present tense are inductors of the greatest strangeness: the text need only pass into the present tense for us to no longer know where it comes from, from where it it emitted. As soon as the text approaches its source, it comes from nowhere. Its enunciation becomes cryptic, dislocated. The origin loses itself in the present which is everything except the time of its own presence to itself, the least realistic of the atemporal instances, the most irreferential.

Very well, one may say, isn't this a relatively banal statement which comes from the very nature of writing? Certainly, but we see how it is directly opposed to the Sartrean project which, since it doesn't recognize the necessity, sees itself robbed of the political methods of bending it.

Hollier's reading thus delimits the impossible point where the text detaches itself from the immediate, from presence and from history, which are, however its proclaimed postulates. This point is precisely that of a transparent fiction of writing.

We are thus prompted to reread the Sartrean corpus from beginning to end as a denial of the nature of language (of its own language) and of the traps of writing. Not that the relationship between ethics, politics and literature then becomes an obsolete question, without interest, without impact, without pertinence. But as the reading of *Politique de la prose* demonstrates, it could only be advantageous for this problematic to compromise itself in the question of the neuter and of fiction; its effectiveness would be reinforced. In trying to avoid this detour, to precipitate the text—in the chemical sense of the term—in a fusion with the immediate, Sartre manages not to confront it with its real; a gesture of avoidance which is heavy with political consequences.

In this respect the "failure" ("*échec*") of Sartre (who as a literary critic is always ready to denounce the failings of writers—those of Baudelaire, Faulkner, Flaubert) carries an exemplary lesson. If we must necessarily discuss the question of the historical inscription of the writing practice, we must approach it cautiously, with indispensable nuance. Like Blanchot, for example, who draws an ethics of writing inscribed between the *ought* and the *failure* ("entre le *falloir* et le *faillir*") from the alienation of literature in relation to the historical present and from the problematic nature of this present itself. It is in this that Hollier's reading is not at all in the stingy nature of a savage attack; it points out the part of reflection in Sartre's work which, more than ever, is *present* (*"actuelle"*).[3]

THE MOTHER

Sartre deliberately cut his life in two: before 1940 and after. The war and his emprisonment in Germany play the role of a brutal awakening for him; he leaves behind the dream he had followed for forty years and commits himself to the reality of a companionship which henceforth fuses his trajectory to the common destiny:

> En 1940 Sartre comprend que s'il est bon de s'endormir pour parler à sa mère, pour se réveiller réellement il est préférable de s'adresser aux hommes. La guerre met fin à la narratologie clinique du récit hypno-gogique. [Politique, 260]

> In 1940 Sartre understands that if it is good to go to sleep in order to speak to one's mother, in order to really wake up it is better to address oneself to men. The war puts an end to the clinical narrotology of the hypnagogic story.

Hollier demonstrates the structure of this dream and this awakening, calling psychoanalysis into play. But again, this is not an application of a theoretical model to a corpus that it dominates and finally misses (*rater*). For "le psychoanalysme n'est souvent qu'une couverture pé-dante pour la plus vétuste grivoiserie universitaire en mal de se refaire une jeunesse" (*Politique*, 188). ["Psychoanalysis is often only a pedantic cover for the most timeworn academic sauciness trying to recapture its youth."] He prefers "insinuation" to the "penetration" which bends the text to its preestablished concepts, an approach which others have crit-icized, but which Hollier makes his own. What is it? Insinuation slips into the interior of its "object," it draws its arguments not from a crit-ical apparatus but from the text itself. It intends to draw out the motifs of the text's desire:

> Quand à l'insinuation, elle ne me déplaît pas. Tout le monde n'a pas droit à la pénétration. D'ailleurs, ça ne m'engage pas. Je n'ai pas à me mouiller. Je cite et ce n'est pas de moi. Je m'arrange pour que ce soit toujours lui qui l'ait dit. Dis-je. Ce qui ne me déplaît pas. [Politique, 188]

3. On the question of presence, see the pertinent remarks of J.-F. Lyotard in "Un Succès de Sartre," *Critique*, no. 430, mars 1983.

As for insinuation, I don't dislike it. Everyone doesn't have a right to penetration. Besides, this doesn't commit me. I don't have to get my feet wet. I make sure that it is always him who said it. I say. Which I don't dislike.

This does not mean that reading is innocent of the new that it produces in the citational practice of its "object." The subject of the interpretation *"s'arrange,"* it "says" what the interpreted text has already written. It works a putting into perspective, an active reading which is not simply a repetition of the Sartrean enunciation. *Politique de la prose* refuses to cut between the interpreted object and the interpreting subject, between the rigor of knowledge (Blanchot, psychoanalysis, Marxism) and the part of truth that this rigor brings to the reading subject. A third term, that of language and its fictional powers, is brought in to emphasize the difference between subject and object. Another equalizer in which the Sartrean text, like that of its critic, will have to recognize that which goes beyond them and confounds them.

As we know, *Les Mots* should be read as the systematic denunciation of a bourgeois childhood spent dreaming. In this sleep, Anne-Marie, the mother, occupies a privileged position: "Je lui disais tout: plus que tout."[4] A beatific union sealed by "un imaginaire de la langue" ["an imaginary order of language"] in which everything can be said, in which the mother's body and the child's do not have to be separated and all this favored by the premature death of the father.

From here on, the rupture with the bourgeoisie coincides with the abandonment of the maternal world: "Sartre comprend sa vocation, un jour il sera ce qui manque à sa mère" (*Politique*, 254). ["Sartre understands his vocation, one day he will be that which his mother lacks."] To leave his class of origin is thus to enter the world of men; the political, philosophical, literary decision is tied to a division which derives from a phantasm and perhaps informs it. At stake here is not a question of reducing the significance of the Sartrean *engagement* to a conflict revolving around the name of the father (*nom du père*) through the device of a reassuring and neutralizing psychoanalysis which would doom the doctrine to the wastebaskets of history. Hollier asks unavoidable questions which any politics of literature should confront in order to find there the terms of its validity, and without which it will find itself outdated as soon as it is enunciated.

4. Jean-Paul Sartre, *Les Mots* (Paris: Gallimard, 1964), 181. ["I told her everything. More than everything." *The Words*, trans. Bernard Frechtman (New York: George Braziller, 1964), 217.]

We must then ask how we can awake from words in order to finally grasp the thing. Is the awakening of 1940 really an awakening or is it merely the continuation of the dream in other forms?[5]

The response is double. One could demonstrate first of all, that the awakening is not unique, it is always already antidipated by another awakening. The break (*coupure*) is thus repeatable, it diffuses itself and loses the characteristics of an event. Thus, the father's death is inscribed in *Les Mots* as a rupture with sleep: "A la mort de mon père, Anne-Marie et moi, nous nous réveillâmes d'un cauchemar commun." ["Upon the death of my father, Anne Marie and I awoke from a common nightmare" (*Les Mots*, 9; *The Words*, 16).] At the same time, the rupture of 1940 was preceded by another awakening which broke the unity of the child and the mother when Anne-Marie remarried in 1917. The end of sleep thus has the appearance of a repeatable series, of a variation in a series without beginning or end: "Comme d'habitude, la rupture est condamnée d'avance à la répétition parce qu'elle ne s'aperçoit pas qu'elle répète ce avec quoi elle croit rompre" (*Politique*, 274). ["As usual, the rupture is already condemned to repetition because it does not notice that it repeats that which it believed it was breaking away from."]

Secondly, *Les Mots* can be considered an unfinished text. Not because it is not a complete biography (here autobiography has nothing to do with the totality), but because it calls for another work—that which was constituted after the awakening, which permitted the condemnation of the dream of childhood. *Les Mots* is only possible in an intertextual context from which the demystification of its imaginary would find its grounding.

Hollier finds no difficulty in demonstrating that just as the awakening is not really an awakening, the dream prolongs itself after the rupture of 1940 in the very work which is intended to denounce it. For Sartre "croyait rêver, mais il ne s'était simplement pas rendu compte qu'il ne s'endormait pas; il s'imaginait imaginer, rêvait rêver" (*Politi-*

5. "Même dans le réveil absolu, il y a encore une part de rêve qui est justement le rêve de réveil. On ne se réveille jamais: les désirs entretiennent les rêves. La mort est un rêve, entre autres rêves qui perpétuent la vie, celui de séjourner dans le mythique. C'est du côté du réveil que se situe la mort. La vie est quelque chose de tout à fait impossible qui peut rêver de réveil absolu." Jacques Lacan, "Improvisation: désir de mort, rêve et réveil," remarks collected by Catherine Millot and published in *L'Ane*, no. 3, automne 1981. [Even in absolute awakening, there is still a part of dream which is precisely the dream of awakening. We never wake up: desires keep dreams alive. Death is a dream among other dreams which perpetuate life, that of the stay in the mythic. Death is found on the side of awakening. Life is something completely impossible which can dream of absolute awakening.]

que, 26). ["(Sartre) thought he was dreaming, but he simply hadn't realized that he hadn't gone to sleep; he imagined that he was imagining, dreamed he was dreaming."]

In consequence, the awakening does come from the prolongation of the dream. *Les Mots* commits the useless murder of the child who since the beginning was preserved from this murder by the anticipation of death: "Malgré l'acharnement qu'il y met, Sartre n'arrive pas à le tuer: l'enfant imaginaire était mort depuis toujours. *Les Mots* sont un suicide" (*Politique,* 300). ["In spite of his determination, Sartre does not succeed in killing it: the imaginary child was always dead. *The Words* is a suicide."] We should also understand it in the sense that death, as Blanchot proposes, is always present in literature. Thus the work from after 1940, although it is intended to fit into the political community of living adults, into the presence of males, acts as the linguistic crypt of this always dead child who silently returns in it. Far from being written *against* this inevitable disappearance, the crypt is created *after* the forgetting of this suicide. By this it is condemned to repeat it, to return forever—beyond the child—to the Mother whom, however, it tries to pro-scribe (*pro-scrire*).

CONCLUSIONS

We have just seen that *Les Mots* could only be an unfinished text, a passage to an impossible act—impossible because it has always already taken place. But it is not the only such work in the Sartrean corpus. As Hollier shows in *La Nausée, Les Chemins de la liberté, L'Etre et le Néant, Cirtique de la raison dialectique* and *L'Idiot de la famille* (*Politique,* 20, 52, 80, 81), Sartre's books obey a law of incompleteness which means that, although they are more and more voluminous, they never reach an end. I will not here enter into the details of the demonstration which are, as elsewhere, nuanced and well informed—irrefutable.

What is to be said of this writing which is more and more interminable? In my opinion this infinite "to be continued" is symptomatic of Sartre's "failure" ("*échec*"). Writing can never complete itself; it does not manage to sum up nor, of course, to reflect itself in a totalizing manner. The work then manifests, in its unfinished state, the true nature of the methods that it denies; neither inside nor outside the thing, it cannot, in essence, finish with it. Here Sartre joins, whatever the circumstances, a literary history to which he would have liked to be the exception and which Barthes defines in these terms: "Le réel n'est pas représentable, et c'est parce que les hommes veulent sans cesse le représenter qu'il y a une histoire de la littérature."[6] Far be it from me to recuperate Sartre with a too familiar problematic in which he would lose the disturbing strangeness that Hollier's reading confers upon him. If his (hidden) drama remains exemplary, retains its virulence, it is because the conflict between presence and writing, politics and fiction, remains perpetually open. For the hemophiliac *récit* never succeeds in suturing its wound, which is the opening of the real, and it continues (denying it, accepting it) to write itself in bloody letters, without ever completely coagulating.

Translated by Peggy McCracken

6. Roland Barthes, *Leçon* (Paris: Seuil, 1978), 21. ["The real is not representable, and it is because men ceaselessly try to represent it by words that there is a history of literature." "Inaugural Lecture, Collège de France," trans. Richard Howard, in Susan Sontag, ed., *A Barthes Reader* (New York: Hill and Wang, 1982), 465.]

Contributors

RONALD ARONSON is Professor of Humanities in the University Studies/Weekend College Programme at Wayne State. He is the author of the study, *Jean-Paul Sartre: Philosophy in the World* (1980) and *The Dialectics of Disaster: A Preface to Hope* (1983). He is preparing a study, *Sartre's Second Critique*, which is forthcoming from the University of Chicago Press. He has received fellowships from the National Endowment for the Humanities and the American Council of Learned Societies.

GEORGE H. BAUER is Chairman of the Department of French and Italian at the University of Southern California. He is the author of *Sartre and the Artist* (1969) and has just published in collaboration with Michel Rybalka and Michel Contat *Les Oeuvres romanesques de Jean-Paul Sartre* (1982). He has published numerous articles on Sartre, Camus, Barthes, Duchamp, Apollinaire, Renaud Camus, and Robbe-Grillet. He is on the editorial board of *Enclitic*, *New York Literary Forum*, and *Visible Language* for which he recently edited a number on *French Currents of the Letter*. He is currently writing a book on Marcel Duchamp (Vois-elle Con-sonne) and two books on Robbe-Grillet.

VICTOR BROMBERT is the Henry Putnam University Professor of Romance and Comparative Literatures and Director of the Christian Gauss Seminars in Criticism, at Princeton University. Among his books are *The Intellectual Hero*, *The Novels of Flaubert*, and *The Romantic Prison*, which won the Harry Levin Prize for Comparative Literature. His latest book is *Victor Hugo and the Visionary Novel*, Harvard University Press.

HOWARD DAVIES is a Senior Lecturer in French at the Polytechnic of North London and has previously published articles on *La Nausée* in the *Australian Journal of French Studies* and on *Le Diable et le bon dieu* in the *Cahiers d'Etudes Sartriennes*. He has just completed a doctoral thesis at University College London on the subject of the realisation of Sartre's *anthropologie synthétique* by his monthly review Les Temps Modernes.

DAVID S. GROSS is Associate Professor at the University of Oklahoma. His most recent work includes articles on William Blake and Gramsci, William Morris, and E. L. Doktorov.

PHILIPPE HUNT is "assistant" at the Free University of Brussels and is currently enrolled in the Department of Comparative Literature at Yale University.

FREDRIC JAMESON is Professor of French and the History of Consciousness at the University of California at Santa Cruz. He is the author of many books, the latest of which are *The Political Unconscious* (1981) and *Sartre: the Origins of a Style*, published by the Columbia University Press (1984). He is co-editor of "Social Text."

DOUGLAS KIRSNER is Professor of Philosophy and History of Ideas at Deakin University, Victoria, Australia. He is author of *The Schizoid World of Jean-Paul Sartre and R. D. Laing* (1977) and is completing a book on an anthropology of the American psychoanalytic culture to be published by the New York University Press.

ALEXANDRE LEUPIN is Associate Professor of French at Louisiana State University. He is the author of *Le Graal et la littérature*, as well as of numerous articles on medieval and modern French literature.

PATRICK MCCARTHY is currently Associate Professor of French at Haverford College. He is the author of *Céline* (1975), *Camus* (1982), and articles on the N.R.F.

PEGGY MCCRACKEN is a graduate student in the French Department at Yale University.

JULIETTE SIMONT is writing a doctoral dissertation at the F.N.R.S. (Fond National de la recherche scientifique) in Brussels.

THOMAS TREZISE is writing a doctoral dissertation at Yale on Samuel Beckett's trilogy and currently teaches French at Dartmouth College.

PIERRE VERSTRAETEN teaches philosophy at the Université Libre de Bruxelles. He has published many articles on Sartre and a book on the Sartrean theatre, *Violence et pouvoir*.

PHILIP WOOD was teaching English Literature at Coimbra University, Portugal, at the time of writing this article. He is now a graduate student in the French Department at Yale University.

The following issues are still available through the Yale French Studies Office, 315 William L. Harkness Hall, Yale University, New Haven, Conn. 06520.

19/20 Contemporary Art $3.50
  23 Humor $3.50
  32 Paris in Literature $3.50
  33 Shakespeare $3.50
  35 Sade $3.50
  38 The Classical Line $3.50
  39 Literature and
      Revolution $5.00
  40 Literature and Society:
      18th Century $3.50
  41 Game, Play, Literature $5.00
  42 Zola $5.00

  43 The Child's Part $5.00
  44 Paul Valéry $5.00
  45 Language as Action $5.00
  46 From Stage to Street $3.50
  47 Image & Symbol in the
      Renaissance $3.50
  49 Science, Language, & the
      Perspective Mind $3.50
  50 Intoxication and
      Literature $3.50
  53 African Literature $3.50
  54 Mallarmé $5.00

  57 Locus: Space, Landscape,
      Decor $6.00
  58 In Memory of Jacques
      Ehrmann $6.00
  59 Rethinking History $6.00
  60 Cinema/Sound $6.00
  61 Toward a Theory of
      Description $6.00
  62 Feminist Readings:
      French Texts/
      American Contexts $6.00

Add for postage & handling

Single issue, United States $1.00
Each additional issue $ .50

Single issue, foreign countries $1.50
Each additional issue $ .75

- -

YALE FRENCH STUDIES   315 William L. Harkness Hall, Yale University, New Haven, Connecticut 06520

A check made payable to YFS is enclosed. Please send me the following issue(s):

Issue no.   Title   Price

_____   _____   _____
_____   _____   _____
_____   _____   _____

                                                 Postage & handling   _____
                                                       Total   _____

Name _____

Number/Street _____

City _____   State _____ Zip _____

The following issues are now available through Kraus Reprint Company, Route 100, Millwood, N.Y. 10546.

1 Critical Bibliography of	11 Eros, Variations . . .	25 Albert Camus
Existentialism	12 God & the Writer	26 The Myth of Napoleon
2 Modern Poets	13 Romanticism Revisited	27 Women Writers
3 Criticism & Creation	14 Motley: Today's French Theater	28 Rousseau
4 Literature & Ideas	15 Social & Political France	29 The New Dramatists
5 The Modern Theatre	16 Foray through Existentialism	30 Sartre
6 France and World Literature	17 The Art of the Cinema	31 Surrealism
7 André Gide	18 Passion & the Intellect, or	34 Proust
8 What's Novel in the Novel	Malraux	48 French Freud
9 Symbolism	21 Poetry Since the Liberation	51 Approaches to Medieval
10 French-American Literature	22 French Education	Romance
Relationships	24 Midnight Novelists	

36/37 Structuralism has been reprinted by Doubleday as an Anchor Book.
55/56 Literature and Psychoanalysis has been reprinted by Johns Hopkins University Press, and can be ordered through Customer Service, Johns Hopkins University Press, Baltimore, MD 21218.

The following issues are available through Yale University Press, Customer Service Department, 92A Yale Station, New Haven, CT 06520.

63 The Pedagogical Imperative:
   Teaching as a Literary Genre
   (1982) $11.95
64 Montaigne: Essays in Reading
   (1983) $11.95
65 The Language of Difference:
   Writing in QUEBEC(ois)
   (1983) $11.95
66 The Anxiety of Anticipation
   (1984) $11.95

67 Concepts of Closure
   (1984) $11.95
68 Sartre after Sartre
   (1985) $11.95
69 Forthcoming Issue on Paul De Man (1985)
70 Forthcoming Issue (1986)
71 Forthcoming Issue (1986)

Special subscription rates are available on a calendar year basis (2 issues per year):

Individual subscriptions $20.00
Institutional subscriptions $23.90

- -

ORDER FORM   **Yale University Press,** 92A Yale Station, New Haven, CT 06520
Please enter my subscription for the calendar year
☐ 1984   ☐ 1985   ☐ 1986
I would like to purchase the following individual issues:

_____

_____

For individual issues, please add postage and handling:
Single issue, United States $1.00   Single issue, foreign countries $1.50
Each additional issue $ .50   Each additional issue $ .75
Connecticut residents please add sales tax of 7½%.

Payment of $_____ is enclosed (including sales tax if applicable).

Mastercard no. _____

4-digit bank no. _____ Expiration date _____

VISA no. _____ Expiration date _____

Signature _____

SHIP TO: _____

_____

_____

- -

See the next page for ordering issues 1 – 62. **Yale French Studies** is also available through Xerox University Microfilms, 300 North Zeeb Road, Ann Arbor, MI 48106.

Of Special Interest

Children's Literature, 13

*Annual of the Modern Language Association
Division on Children's Literature and the Children's Literature Association*

edited by Francelia Butler and Margaret R. Higonnet

Founded in 1972, and published by the Yale University Press since 1980, *Children's Literature* has established a reputation for serious analysis and interpretation covering all aspects of literature for children and adolescents and representing a wide variety of approaches.

Included in this issue are the following articles: "Tintin and the Family Romance" by Jean Marie Apostolides, "Michel Tournier's Texts for Children" by Joseph McMahon, "Pierrot, or The Secrets of the Night" by Michel Tournier, and "Writer Devoured by Children" by Michel Tournier. $9.95

When the Grass Was Taller

Autobiography and the Experience of Childhood
Richard N. Coe

This is an engrossing study of a literary form that has developed only in the last 150 years: the autobiography of childhood and adolescence. Using as a comparative base a fascinating array of major and minor texts from European, American, Australian, and African literature, Coe defines an independent genre with its own history, laws, and conventions.

"An awesome, encyclopedic survey: rich in detail, thick with theory, strong on practically every account. . . . A probing, instructive study built on herculean scholarship." —*Kirkus Reviews* $25.00

Yale University Press
92A Yale Station   New Haven, CT 06520